In this book Graeme Gill traces the disintegration of the Communist Party of the Soviet Union from 1985 until the dissolution of the USSR in December 1991. Based principally on the contemporary Soviet press, this is the first book to follow the debates in the party over the implications of Gorbachev's reforms and how the party should respond to them. It is an in-depth analysis of the institutional dynamics of a party under pressure.

When it came under challenge and it could no longer use the weapon of suppression, the party was unable to mount a serious defence of its position and role. Confronted from the top by Gorbachev's call to reform itself and by his changes to the political arena, and from the bottom by new political forces taking advantage of that arena, the party's unity collapsed and with it any sense of purpose or possibility of survival.

D0493228

# THE COLLAPSE OF A SINGLE-PARTY SYSTEM

**Cambridge, Russian, Soviet and Post-Soviet Studies: 94**

*Editorial Board*

*Cambridge Russian, Soviet and Post-Soviet Studies,* under the auspices of Cambridge University Press and the British Association for Slavonic and East European Studies (BASEES), promotes the publication of works presenting substantial and original research on the economics, politics, sociology and modern history of Russia, the Soviet Union and Eastern Europe.

# Cambridge Russian, Soviet and Post-Soviet Studies

*Series list continues on page 256*

# The collapse of a single-party system

## The disintegration of the CPSU

GRAEME GILL

*Department of Government*
*The University of Sydney*

**CAMBRIDGE**
UNIVERSITY PRESS

Published by the Press Syndicate of the University of Cambridge
The Pitt Building, Trumpington Street, Cambridge CB2 1RP
40 West 20th Street, New York, NY 10011–4211, USA
10 Stamford Road, Oakleigh, Melbourne 3166, Australia

First published 1994

Printed in Great Britain at the University Press, Cambridge

A catalogue record for this book is available from the British Library

Library of Congress cataloguing in publication data
Gill, Graeme J.
The collapse of a single-party system: the disintegration of the
Communist Party of the Soviet Union / Grame Gill.
    p.    cm. – (Cambridge Russian, Soviet and post-Soviet studies: 94)
Includes bibliographical references.
ISBN 0 521 46537 0
1. Kommunisticheskaia partiia Sovetskogo Soiuza – History.
2. Soviet Union – Politics and government – 1985–1991. I. Title.
II. Series.
JN6598.K7G5235 1995
324.247'075'09048–dc20    94–5634 CIP

ISBN 0 521 46537 0 hardback
ISBN 0 521 46943 0 paperback

In memory of
Avril

# Contents

# Preface

This book is a study of organisational adaptability, or rather the inability of an organisation to adapt to a changing environment. It is a study of the Communist Party of the Soviet Union, of its changing institutional structures and the course of debate which unrolled within its ranks as it sought as an organisation to come to grips with the serious challenges to its position and power that arose after 1985. Its focus is therefore the party itself, its internal mechanisms, procedures, arguments and debates. It does not provide a comprehensive history of the Gorbachev period. Neither does it give an analysis of developments within the Soviet Union at large nor a kremlinological analysis of leadership politics; these are mentioned only in order to explain the fate of the party. No attempt is made to chart the course of the party's fortunes in the individual republics. The focus is the CPSU, and developments in the republics will be noted only in terms of their effect upon the all-union party.

A number of people have helped in the production of this book. Rod Pitty and Kathy Dempsey both did an excellent job of collecting materials. Great assistance was given by librarians in the Lenin Library, Moscow, the Social Sciences Library at Moscow State University, the Library of Congress in Washington, the Australian National Library, and Fisher Library of the University of Sydney. I would also like to acknowledge the assistance provided by the Australian Research Council in producing this book and the Australian National University for allowing me to participate in their exchange scheme with Moscow State University. And finally, Heather, without whose support and encouragement it would all have come to nothing.

# 1     An administrative party system

The comparative study of political parties has always had difficulty with the Communist Party of the Soviet Union and those other ruling communist parties modelled upon it. This is because our approach to political parties has been overwhelmingly shaped by the liberal democratic experience within which the discipline of political science developed. As a result, the concepts used to understand parties are well adapted to those parties which operate in such systems, but have less immediate relevance to those bodies which call themselves parties and which operate in non-liberal-democratic systems. The notion of the one-party system was the framework political scientists used to try to come to grips with the vast array of non-liberal democratic parties, but this alone was unsatisfactory; it could not encompass the vast range of differences between those parties ruling in the communist world and single-party regimes throughout much of the third world.

The chief area of difference between the ruling communist parties and those of the non-communist third world usually is seen in terms of the degree of control which the party seeks and is able to exercise. The tight control exercised by the communist party is contrasted with the looser degree of control enjoyed in the non-communist world, a dimension often seen in terms of the much more limited scope for opposition which existed under communist rule. The distinction between narrow and broad single parties, with the latter being much more relaxed about factions and internal dis-agreement than the former, is another aspect of this dimension of control.

Another means of approaching this question, and one which is useful for differentiating between ruling communist parties and other single parties, is to distinguish between parties that only rule and those which also play a dominant part in administration. The essence of the

1

Westminster system is to distinguish clearly between these two functions, with the party victorious at the polls gaining the right to rule but leaving administration in the hands of a neutral bureaucracy. In the American presidential system this clear division is modified by the right of presidential appointment to leading bureaucratic posts, but the weakness of the parties ensures that in no sense can it be said that the party dominates the administrative process. In many of the third world non-communist systems, the single ruling party will usually also be involved in the administrative structure, but principally through the participation of party members in that administrative structure rather than through organisational penetration of that structure. It is this organisational penetration of the entire administrative structure from base to apex that has characterised ruling communist parties. It is also the origin of the view of these systems as party-states.[1]

The original intention of the founder of the Soviet state was that the party should play only a limited role in administration. As early as 1919 the sovereign organ of the party declared that the functions of party and soviet were not to be confused and that the party was to implement its decisions through the soviets; it was 'to direct the activities of the soviets, but not replace them.'[2] However, this injunction, and many like it in subsequent years, had no practical effect upon the way in which the party functioned. Virtually from the outset, the party was functionally a part of the administrative framework of the state, with party organs being organised in all arms of the bureaucratic apparatus and party members subject to party discipline occupying responsible posts at all levels of that apparatus. There were a number of reasons for the intertwining of party and administrative structures. One was the sense of isolation and the fears held by party leaders about the vulnerability of their position and their rule. Concerned about the possible effect of opposition from within the petty bourgeois peasantry and deeply worried by what they believed to be extensive covert opposition from within the ranks of the administrative structure they inherited, party leaders sought to try to ensure the loyalty of the administrative machine by penetrating it with loyal party cells. Such penetration of the administrative structure was meant to ensure that party policy was followed and the administrative structure was kept loyal to the party's banner.

Party penetration of the administrative structure also reflected the weakness of the party as an institution. Upon coming to power, the Bolsheviks were confronted with ruling an enormous country which had a seriously under-developed transport and communications infrastructure, and a party which was small, organisationally primitive, and lacking an effective internal regulative regime.[3] Even had peace reigned within Russia in the years immediately following the October revolution, the party would not have been able effectively to spread its tentacles throughout the society; it lacked the organisational and financial resources necessary to achieve such a result. The best way it had of spreading its influence and control was by using the existing legislative and administrative structures of the state. Within a short space of time, party organisations were established in the soviets at all levels and in the state bureaucracy. It thereby began to use the state's administrative machine to achieve party aims because, despite the clear deficiencies that existed in that machine, it was in existence and functioned tolerably well, and could therefore serve as the vehicle for the party's quest for control. The model was set up by Sverdlov who, until his death in 1919, used his dominant position in the soviet hierarchy as Chairman of the All-Russian Central Executive Committee to mobilise the soviet network for the achievement of party goals. In this way, the party was able from the beginning to use the resources of the state's legislative and administrative structures to compensate for the deficiencies in its own structure. It is at this time that the state's funding of the party began, a process which clearly tied the party into the administrative process.[4]

Once this process was begun, the force of inertia and the course of Soviet history consolidated the party's place in the administrative structure. The high levels of institutional ambiguity in the early years of Soviet power, with many major issues fought out in party fora rather than state organs, reflect both the desire of leading political figures to play a part in the resolution of these issues despite their non-membership of state bodies, and the conviction by many that in any case the party was the most appropriate forum for resolution of these issues. The effect of these sorts of considerations was strengthened by the course of elite conflict within the party, and in particular Stalin's ability to confine that conflict principally to the party sphere. The continuing concerns about the reliability of the state apparatus, and particularly the infection effect of the petty bourgeois society, reinforced this reliance on the party and its consequent dominance of the administrative apparatus. Even when Stalin's personal dominance had reduced the party to the status of minor actor in the political arena, its intrusive place in the administrative structure remained unshaken.

## The party's role

In practice there were four aspects to the party's role in the politico-administrative system: decision-making, verification, implementation and staffing. The party's decision-making role was exercised at all levels of the party, from national organisations to the productive enterprise. It consisted of party bodies discussing and resolving all of the most important questions that arose affecting the area with which each particular party body was concerned: the Politburo at the national level discussed issues concerning the USSR as a whole, while the local enterprise organisation discussed issues concerning that enterprise. Such decisions were not made in isolation from the society within which the party existed: different sectors of society usually had informal representation in the party organs discussing these questions, and those organs had to interact with other bodies which claimed some competence in this area. National organs interacted with the leading organs of the state, while at the enterprise level the party committee interacted with factory management, trade union committee and the local government. These interactions were often crucial in shaping the outcome of issues being discussed, but they do not change the situation that, at base, the most important issues tended to be resolved within party fora; those that were not were decided by party members acting under party discipline in the organs of the state. The party as a coherent entity was clearly of fundamental importance in the decision-making process.

The second aspect of party activity was the verification of implementation. This too stemmed in part from party leaders' distrust of the reliability and loyalty of those officials in the administrative structure whose task it was to implement the decisions made by the leadership. Party organisations at all levels were therefore instructed, as one of their continuing concerns, to ensure that those decisions were carried out. The major means whereby this was to be achieved was through the activity of party members who were subject to party discipline in the implementing organs. In this sense, verification was not something external to the administrative process. It was to be conducted by people who were part of the administrative structure but who were acting under the spur of party discipline. The importance of the verification process in principle should not be under-estimated. In a society with an inert public and lacking a free press, the capacity of the central decision-makers to remain abreast of what was happening throughout the society was limited. What was needed was an administrative means of obtaining the upward flow of information, and the party's formal responsibility for verification was part of this. The fact that in practice this task was not always fulfilled satisfactorily detracts from neither the importance of the task nor the responsibilities the party carried for this task in the administrative structure.

The third aspect of the party's role in the administrative structure was that of implementation. Initially the party was meant to give the broad direction to policy and verify that that policy was implemented, but not become involved in the actual implementation itself. But this distinction could not be maintained. Reflecting the chaotic times of the early years of Soviet power, institutional ambiguities and the expansive views of their own roles possessed by many party leaders, it became natural for party bodies to become directly involved in the implementation of decisions. The frequent complaints from the centre about the way in which party bodies were substituting themselves for other organs, while reflecting the formal position, obscured the informal reality; party organs and their leaders were held directly responsible for the successful implementation of policy, and under such circumstances it is little cause for wonder that at many levels those leaders sought to take their own future into their hands by organising the implementation of the adopted decisions. The considerable overlap between party organisations and the respective state legislative and administrative bodies merely served to encourage this process.

The fourth aspect of the party's role in the administrative structure was staffing. Through the system of nomenklatura the party had the capacity to fill by appointment all responsible positions in state and other structures. This means that the identity of all leading personnel (both administrative and legislative) in the state sphere was decided in party fora. All leading state officers, as well as many people filling ordinary positions, were also party members and subject to party discipline. The control thus exercised over staffing decisions was a primary mechanism for the projection of party control throughout all levels of the state structure, and was the principal means through which the party exercised its other functions noted above.

The party was thus organically involved in all aspects of the politico-administrative process: decision-making, verification of implementation, actual implementation and staffing. The party played these roles at all levels of the structure, from the national to the local, and was clearly a central component of the administrative system. In this sense, the party was very different from parties in the liberal democratic systems. It also meant that party members in responsible positions had to face a variety of pressures different to those faced by responsible party officials elsewhere.

### The position of party officials

Like party officials in all systems and all parties, those occupying responsible positions in the CPSU were concerned with managing the internal processes of the party, with carrying out the regular house-keeping functions necessary to keep the institutional structure functioning. This included the organisation and conduct of regular meetings of party bodies, attendance to staffing matters in the party organisation on their own and lower levels, the conduct of central policy relating to party matters, particularly with regard to party membership, responding to demands for information and advice from above, and maintaining satisfactory records in the party organisation. The central authorities, principally through the CC Secretariat, for much of the period between the revolution and the rise of Gorbachev pursued an interventionist policy with regard to lower level party affairs. This had important effects on the position of lower level party leaders noted below. But it also meant that the centre frequently adopted policies designed to bring about what it saw to be an improvement in party affairs: personnel screenings, instructions regarding recording and reporting procedures, and criticism of the poor state of intra-party democracy were all common campaigns launched by the centre which affected internal party life and to which lower level leaders had to respond. The management of party affairs was therefore more complicated than it was in many other systems because of the intrusive nature of the central party leadership.

But party leaders had more to do than ensure that the party operated effectively in its internal procedures. They also had to carry out the manifold other tasks that followed from the party's role sketched above. This included oversight of the conduct of ideological education and propaganda, participation in the government of the relevant administrative area or areas, assistance to the production effort in all of the productive units of the region, and verification of the implementation of higher decisions. All of these tasks could consume immense amounts of time, particularly when the party first secretary had to negotiate with other powerful figures and groups in order to carry out the functions they were accorded. The demands of the job, if carried out satisfactorily, were immense. Party leaders were responsible not just for the effective functioning of the party apparatus under their control, but also for the peace and good government of their region, the successful economic performance of the production units under their oversight, high levels of morale of the people, and generally the smooth performance of all aspects of life in the regions for which they were responsible. This was a daunting list of responsibilities, and throughout much of the pre-Gorbachev period, the penalty for perceived failure was high: loss of position and, at times, under Stalin even loss of life could greet perceived failure in the assigned duties.

With these heavy responsibilities went an ambiguity in the position occupied by these people. One way in which this ambiguity has been conceptualised has been through the supposed red-expert dichotomy. This assumes that there are two basic types of orientation towards issues, one emerging out of ideological considerations and ensuring that the issue is resolved in accord with ideological principles, and the other reflecting concerns about technical rationality and administrative problem-solving which means that issues are resolved purely according to their merits with no intrusion of extraneous ideological factors. Some sought to argue that the former approach was characteristic of party functionaries and the latter of state officials. However both of these characterisations are extreme, and it is more realistic to see both approaches present in the way in which Soviet officials handled issues. Nevertheless the dichotomy does point to the diversity of pressures bearing down upon many party officials at all levels of the structure.

Seen in organisational terms, the red-expert dichotomy points to the way in which leading officials in the state structure found themselves under a form of dual pressure. On the one hand they were expected to react to the demands of their party superiors, abiding by party discipline and devoting their efforts to the successful implementation of party commands and policy. But on the other hand they were also expected to act as responsible public officials, treating all alike in the conscientious and efficient performance of their tasks. In practice there need be no necessary conflict between these two sorts of demands, and most of the time individuals did not have to choose starkly between alternative ways of acting. But in principle there could be conflict here between the demands made by the two organisational structures. Many individuals may have felt more at home in and greater loyalty to one of these organisations than the other. For many who made their careers through advancement up the ladder of state offices, party membership will have been little more than a necessary qualification for higher office. For them, the performance of party duties will have been a chore to be minimised, a necessary prerequisite to keeping a good job. For others, occupation of a state office represented fulfilment of a party direction. Their jobs in the state apparatus were seen less in career terms than as the completion of party assignments. Many of these people spent much of their working life in the party apparatus, with only short spells in the state bureaucracy.

The effect of the existence of potentially different sources of demands from above complicated the position of middle- and lower-ranking officials: when demands or instructions were not completely compatible, to which should they respond? This does not assume a distinction between an ideologically based institution and one based on considerations of technical rationality, but merely the presence of two structures whose perceptions were not always identical. The potential uncertainty generated by this situation was exacerbated for many by the nature of the demands coming from above, particularly from party leaders in the pre-war period. At this time, party leaders were very demanding in what they expected from their subordinates. They sought to change Russia, and in the struggle to achieve this they expected nothing short of total commitment on the part of those below them. But their expectations of success were also high. Total commitment alone was unsatisfactory unless it brought with it successful fulfilment of the demands from above. Failure to meet these expectations could result in dismissal or demotion, while in the second half of the 1930s even death was a possible result.

The consequences of perceived failure were clearly serious for middle- and lower-ranking officials. What made this situation particularly dangerous is that failure was not something that could always easily be discerned. There were two aspects to this question. First, the demands emanating from above were not always clearly expressed and consistent. The language used was often vague and exhortatory, with greater utility as a mobilisational weapon than as an instruction for action. Demands to weed out of the party 'enemies with party cards in their pockets' was a general statement of little value unless it was accompanied by more specific instructions about how such people could be identified and what was to be done with them. Unfortunately, such detail was not always provided. On other occasions, instructions that were inconsistent, and even mutually contradictory, could be given. Vague and conflicting instructions left room for local initiative, but this also meant that ample grounds were created for criticism of the failure of lower-level officials to carry out the instructions from above. The second aspect is an extension of the first: there were no clear criteria for success. The vague and open-ended character of many of the instructions, the changing and contradictory nature of many subsequent demands from the centre, and the propensity on the part of central leaders continually to increase the level of their demands, mean that there were never clear criteria for measuring the success or otherwise of the performance of lower level officials. These factors substantially heightened the level of insecurity on the part of such leaders and made the long term tenure of their positions much more problematic than they would have been in an organisation of a different type. The high levels of turnover of these leaders at various stages of Soviet history reinforced this sense of insecurity.

Faced with such an uncertain political environment, lower-level leaders sought to protect themselves as best they could from the consequences of perceived failure. Simply working hard and achieving some successes was an inadequate defence against the arbitrariness of higher level authorities because of the problems outlined above. Two tactics were deployed in an endeavour to protect themselves: formation of a vertical political machine joining middle- and lower-level leaders with those at higher levels who could afford them assistance and protection, and establishment of a horizontal political machine based in the local area. The creation of vertical political machines has been a feature much commented upon by observers of the Soviet scene. Much of the discussion has concerned Stalin's rise to power and the way in which he courted (and in some accounts captured) party leaders at lower levels, tying them to his banner and using them to steamroller the opposition. This has usually been seen in terms of the strategy adopted by Stalin to achieve victory in the elite conflict of the 1920s and 1930s, but it was also a case of the construction of protective networks on the part of those lower level leaders. Their aim was to ally themselves with a higher-level protector in the hope that by supporting the latter in the policy and realpolitik realms, he would protect them from any potential attacks from above. Despite the formal prohibition on fractionalism, these sorts of informal organisational structures characterised the party throughout its life.

The other tactic involved the organisation of an informal political machine at the local level. This sort of structure has been referred to as the 'family group' both in official party documents and by observers of Soviet affairs. The essence of the family group was an informal association between local figures, often involving the leaders of the major bureaucratic structures in the region, who combined together in order more effectively to run the affairs of the region. While such groups were usually rooted in the party structure, they tended to cross institutional boundaries, uniting the leaders of the main organisational hierarchies in the region – party, state, security apparatus, trade unions, komsomol and productive enterprises. Their operating characteristics and mode of functioning were based on personal relationships rather than formal party rules. They were often little more than personalised cliques, with a local leader's cronies united around that leader in an effort to administer local affairs, often to their own material advantage. Local leaders sought to use these informal structures not just to run local affairs, but also in an attempt to control the information flow to the centre. If, through their personal networks, they could not run local affairs effectively and fulfil the demands made upon them, they could hope that through their control over all of the local command posts, they could project a positive face on their achievements and prevent the centre learning of their failings.

The development of these family groups running local affairs was not an isolated development; during the 1920s and 1930s it became the normal mode of functioning. Combined with the vertical machines, these horizontal organisations were the essential building blocks of the party structure. The degree of autonomy they were able to exercise depended upon two factors: the adequacy of the technical control apparatus within the party, including the communications network, and the willingness of central party leaders to leave local elites in substantial control of their own affairs rather than adopting an intrusive approach. During the pre-war period, the effective links between centre and regions were much weaker and more *ad hoc* than we have often assumed[5] with the result that the capacity of the centre to exercise continuing control over affairs at lower party levels was seriously restricted. While the centre could become involved in the affairs of any lower level party organisation at any time it wished, it could not exercise close supervision over all lower level elites in a continuing fashion. The centre's involvement was therefore *ad hoc*, almost idiosyncratic, rather than continuous and regularised. When the technical links between centre and regions improved after the war, chiefly as a result of improved communications facilities, the Khrushchevite centre adopted a more intrusive policy. This period was marked by a propensity on the part of the central party leadership to play an activist role in local cadre questions, reflected in the frequent removal and shifting of lower level party leaders. The circulation of cadres appeared to many at this level to be a veritable merry-go-round of local elites. It caused significant disruption to many careers and to the way in which local party machines may have functioned, but it did not destroy the essential principle of the control of local affairs by family group structures; frequently it merely changed the leading figures of those machines while leaving the principle of machine control intact.

The fall of Khrushchev brought a new policy to this question of relations between centre and regions. Partly in an attempt to assuage the anger of the regional leaders at the constant instability resulting from Khrushchev's cadre policy and partly in an endeavour to garner the support of this group, the Brezhnev leadership introduced the 'stability of cadres' policy. Resting on the motto 'trust in cadres', this policy meant the centre left the regional leaderships substantially to their own devices. Even when local leaders were manifestly not performing their party leadership roles satisfactorily, they were rarely removed. When a leader was removed or when a vacancy occurred as a result of death or retirement, the centre usually appointed to these positions people from within the same regional apparatus within which the vacancy occurred. The effect of the non-intrusive personnel policy and of internal appointment instead of the transfer of new cadres in from outside, was a consolidation of the control of the existing family group structures. The combination of the control of these informal machines and the general decline in emphasis upon discipline in party life contributed substantially to the growth of corruption during this period. And because these family group machines cut across institutional boundaries, further blurring the already hazy lines between party and state, their effects on the party, in terms both of reduced responsiveness to the centre and the corrosion of formal party norms, also applied to the whole administrative system. This was a problem that was to loom large in the Gorbachev period.

### Party legitimation

The basis of legitimation of the Soviet party in part reflects its status as an administrative party, closely interwoven with the state administrative structure. In practice there were three principal legs to the legitimation programme. The first was the claim that the party was successfully guiding the country in the construction of the communist future. It was this claim which underlay the party's domination of the state administrative structure as well as its legislative arm; if the party was the special organ which could guide the way forward to the bright future, its effective control over that process through dominance of the state machine was justified. In this sense, the party's place in the administrative structure rested upon a teleological conception of the unique historical role the party was to play.

This conception of the party's historical role was related to the second leg of the legitimation programme, the ideology of Marxism-Leninism. The set of principles, axioms and beliefs encapsulated in this notion sought to provide the philosophical justification for the party's dominance. It involved assumptions about historical progress, the forces producing that progress and the structure of society through which party leaders professed to see the world and which enabled them thereby to understand that world and make decisions that would be best designed to achieve the communist aim. In this sense, the ideology not only justified continuing party dominance, but provided the key for the implementation of policy designed to reach the ideologically prescribed goal of communism. It was thus within the ideology that the teleology was rooted.

But the third leg of the legitimation programme, popular mandate, was relevant here. Since 1936, the Soviet system claimed to be democratic, resting on popular consent. Projecting an image of a people united behind the party in their quest for the communist future, the post-war system regularly staged elections in which more than 99 per cent of the voters supported the party. They were said to have recognised the party's ability to lead the country forward and its achievements in the construction of communism. They thereby gave public validation both to the teleology and to the ideology from which it sprang. The popular mandate was seen as the concrete manifestation of the validity of the other two legs of legitimation. This was to be a major problem in the late 1980s.

One effect of the administrative nature of the party is that the party could not escape the consequences of failures within the administrative realm. This means that as the perception of crisis grew in the final stages of the Brezhnev period and during the Andropov-Chernenko leadership interregnum, it also infected the party. Concerns about declining levels of economic growth, increasing social malaise and the sapping of the energy and vitality of the system as a whole created a crisis for the party and its new leadership. If it was to retain its position of dominance, it had successfully to meet these challenges. If it failed to do so, its entire basis of legitimacy, resting as it did on successful performance, would fall apart. And with it was likely to go the party's dominance. Although largely unspoken, this seems to have been recognised by at least some of the party leaders in 1985.

# 2　The personnel solution

At the time of the election of Mikhail Gorbachev as General Secretary of the Central Committee on 11 March 1985, many of the problems which were to stimulate the drive for change were already evident to observers of the Soviet scene. The slowdown in economic growth that had been under way for some time was becoming particularly acute. The postponement of important investment decisions under Brezhnev, and the consequent need for large-scale re-investment in and re-equipment of productive capacity, was exacerbated by the need to shift to more expensive sources of power and to move towards an intensive style of development instead of the extensive style which had prevailed when labour supplies in the industrial regions were plentiful. A social malaise was also evident, reflected in declining health levels and the growth of such social diseases as alcoholism, marriage break-down, youth alienation, poverty and corruption. In the policy sphere, a sense of drift had prevailed, fuelled but not caused by the succession of national leaders between 1982 and 1985. In the domestic realm, therefore, the need for policy initiatives was clear. Similarly, internationally, the relationship with the West had run into a dead-end and the Afghan war showed no signs of an early successful resolution. But these problems, serious as they were, were part of a subterranean foundation upon which the forms of Soviet politics were played out with little apparent direct effect of the former upon the latter. The surface forms of Soviet elite politics continued their regular patterns with little hint of the build-up of pressures occurring below them.

A surface normality hiding mounting problems was also evident in the party. In the years prior to Gorbachev's election, the leading organs of the party continued to meet on a regular basis: regular CC plena were convened twice a year, with extra meetings called in March 1981 following the XXVI Congress and in February 1984 because of

Andropov's death, and the Politburo maintained its approximate weekly regularity. At lower levels too, party bodies continued to meet with the approximate regularity expected of them. The party continued to function normally, as it had in the past. Membership continued to increase at a regular rate during the first half of the 1980s, although it began to dip as the middle of the decade approached, as table 2.1 shows.

But there were also signs of stagnation and malaise in the party. One was the age of the leadership, reflected most starkly in the succession of aged and ill men who filled the position of General Secretary before Gorbachev's election. This was clear evidence of the party's failure to ensure the replenishment of its leading ranks with members of younger generations and thereby to renew the vigour and vitality of its leading organs. Moreover this problem was replicated at lower levels of the party structure, where Brezhnev's 'stability of cadres' policy ensured the ageing of those in responsible positions throughout the country. This was accompanied by a lack of dynamism in the party's operations. Although party bodies met on a regular basis, little emerged from their deliberations in the way of effective policy-making and, on those occasions when decisions were made, implementation of those decisions often was deficient. Furthermore the anti-corruption drive launched by Andropov during the last years of Brezhnev's rule had uncovered significant evidence of corrupt practices in various parts of the party structure. Gorbachev and his supporters recognised these symptoms from the outset.

### Shaping the Gorbachev leadership

Gorbachev's emergence as General Secretary was a function in large part of the realisation by his leadership colleagues that this sense of drift could not continue. They understood that change was necessary if the USSR was to survive as a superpower. Thus Gorbachev was brought to power by a moderate reform coalition, and he soon set about strengthening this coalition. The speed with which Gorbachev was able to recast the personnel of the leading organs of the party surprised experienced observers of Soviet affairs. The accepted wisdom among most observers was that the election of a new General Secretary was not usually accompanied by an immediate major reshaping of leading personnel. The General Secretary, having inherited a leadership, had to work with it and only over a period of time was he able to fill leading organs with people beholden to him.[1] Gorbachev showed that while

Table 2.1. *Party membership 1980–1985 (figures as at 1 January)*

|      | Full        | Candidate | Total       | % increase |
|------|-------------|-----------|-------------|------------|
| 1980 | 16,398,340  | 683,949   | 17,082,289  |            |
| 1981 | 16,732,408  | 698,005   | 17,430,413  | 2.03       |
| 1982 | 17,076,530  | 693,138   | 17,769,668  | 1.95       |
| 1983 | 17,405,293  | 712,610   | 18,117,903  | 1.96       |
| 1984 | 17,718,842  | 724,679   | 18,443,521  | 1.80       |
| 1985 | 18,041,881  | 701,730   | 18,743,611  | 1.63       |

*Source: Spravochnik Partiinogo Rabotnika* Moscow, 1984, Part 2, p. 336 and *Ezhegodnik Bol'shaia Sovetskaia Entsiklopediia* Moscow, 1984 and 1985, pp. 12 and 13.

this view may have been accurate for earlier successions, the unique circumstances of his rise to power gave him unprecedented opportunity to change the personnel of leading party organs.

Two factors were important. The first was the perception, widely shared both at leading levels of the system and more broadly within the populace at large, that the time had come for the introduction of more vigorous policies and a more activist political executive. The malaise of the last years of the Brezhnev period followed by the Andropov and Chernenko interregna generated a sense of urgency which facilitated significant personnel turnover. The second factor was a function of the Brezhnevian 'stability of cadres' policy, the age of the leadership. At the time of Gorbachev's election, of the ten full members of the Politburo, one was almost eighty, four others were in their seventies, three in their sixties and apart from Gorbachev only one (Vorotnikov who was fifty-nine) was in his fifties; the average age was about 67.5 years. Of the six candidate members, two were in their eighties, three in their sixties and only one in his fifties; the average age was about 68.5 years. Of the five CC Secretaries who were not members of the Politburo, three were in their seventies, one in his sixties and one in his fifties, while the average age was about 67.6 years. The oldest member of the leadership was candidate member Kuznetsov who had been born in 1901, while Gorbachev was the youngest member at fifty-four years of age. Such an age profile clearly gave significant scope for imminent membership renewal. What was most important about this in the immediate sense was that the age of these people combined with recognition of the need for a change in policy made the removal of many of them appear to be an appropriate step. Age itself was not the key, but what it appeared to mean for the new set of priorities which were widely deemed to be necessary.

Gorbachev soon set about reshaping the Politburo and Secretariat.[2] Within twelve months he had fundamentally altered their composition. At the April 1985 plenum, three new full members joined the Politburo, Ligachev and Chebrikov who had both supported Gorbachev in March and Ryzhkov who was to become Chairman of the Council of Ministers in September and was to remain for some years an important supporter of reform within the leadership. There was also one new candidate member, Defence Minister Sergei Sokolov. There was also a new addition to the Secretariat, Viktor Nikonov whose earlier career in the agricultural sphere suggests that he had personal links with Gorbachev. At the July 1985 plenum, Politburo candidate member Shevardnadze (until the end of 1990 probably Gorbachev's staunchest supporter within the leadership) was promoted to full status and Gorbachev's reputed rival Romanov was removed from the Politburo. Romanov was also removed from the Secretariat while Zaikov and Yel'tsin were added. At the October 1985 plenum, full member Tikhonov retired from the Politburo while Talyzin joined as a candidate; Ryzhkov left the Secretariat in connection with his appointment as Chairman of the Council of Ministers. At the February 1986 plenum on the eve of the XXVII Congress, Yel'tsin became a candidate member of the Politburo and left the Secretariat (in connection with his appointment to head the Moscow party organisation) while Grishin resigned from full membership of the Politburo. The old Brezhnevite Rusakov also left the Secretariat at this time.

Following the congress, in March 1986 Zaikov became a full member and Sliun'kov and Solov'ev candidate members of the Politburo while long-time candidate members Kuznetsov and Ponomarev were removed. At the same time five new members were added to the Secretariat: Biriukova, Medvedev, Dobrynin, Yakovlev and Razumovskii, the last four of whom were to remain close Gorbachev collaborators for some time. By the end of March 1986 there were twelve full members and seven candidate members of the Politburo, respectively two and one more than at the time of Gorbachev's accession. Five of those twelve and five of those seven had joined the Politburo since Gorbachev's election, a renewal rate of some 52.6 per cent inside twelve months (the last changes to the composition of the Politburo in 1986 occurred in March). Apart from Gorbachev, only five of the combined full and candidate membership of the Politburo had been members of that body when Brezhnev died in November 1982 (Shcherbitskii,

Gromyko, Kunaev, Dolgikh and Demichev). At the end of 1986 the Secretariat numbered eleven, two more than at the time of Gorbachev's election, of whom seven had been elected between March 1985 and March 1986 (Yel'tsin had been a member from July 1985 until February 1986). Of the other four, three (Gorbachev, Dolgikh and Zimianin) had been members of the Secretariat at the time of Brezhnev's death. Some 61.5 per cent of the membership of the Politburo and Secretariat joined those bodies in the twelve months immediately following Gorbachev's election. This is a rate of renewal at the top of the political structure unprecedented in Soviet history.

The reworking of the membership of these leading party organs substantially strengthened Gorbachev's position by consolidating the moderate reform coalition in power. The new leadership continued to function through the leading organs of the party, with a broad policy consensus focused principally upon *uskorenie*, or acceleration, of the economy. The Politburo met on a regular basis[3] and its discussions covered all major policy questions. The influx of new members does not seem to have altered the work routines of this body, although as the period wore on differences between its members became more marked (see below). Similarly, the CC met on a regular basis, and despite the suggestions that there may have been some resistance from within this body to Gorbachev's election,[4] the CC continued to perform its traditional role in Soviet politics throughout this period: a forum for discussion and unanimous acclamation of decisions adopted. However, during 1986 evidence began to accumulate suggesting that the reform coalition was coming under strain. An open dispute occurred between members of the leadership at the XXVII Congress in February–March 1986. In his speech Moscow First Secretary and Politburo candidate member Boris Yel'tsin criticised the way the CC apparatus (run by Ligachev) had been functioning and called for a reorganisation, and he supported a letter that had appeared in *Pravda* criticising leadership privileges; Yel'tsin used this to call for the abolition of benefits that were not warranted. CC Secretary Ligachev responded, not by defending privileges, but by attacking the way *Pravda* had raised the issue.[5] Although it was not publicly evident at the time, this represented a deep and bitter personal dispute between these two figures that was to rupture the leadership consensus upon which the initial stage of the reform programme rested. The strain under which this consensus was maintained during 1986 is reflected in the inability of the leadership to convene a CC plenum in the last half of that year, an inability directly linked to the radicalisation of the political prescription supported by Gorbachev at this time.

While outwardly at least the leading organs of the political system continued to function in the way they had under Brezhnev, there was an important change in the profile of one institution, that of the General Secretary. The position of General Secretary experienced some redefinition during this period. Three aspects of this are important, one clearly concerning the institutional contours of the post, and the other two the *modus operandi* of the General Secretary himself. The first concerned Gorbachev's failure to take up the position of Chairman of the Presidium of the Supreme Soviet. His immediate three predecessors had occupied this position in addition to their post as General Secretary, and it had been widely accepted that this now constituted part of the institutional contours of the leading post in the system. In his speech to the Supreme Soviet in July 1985 at which Andrei Gromyko was elected to fill this post, Gorbachev argued that while combination of the positions of General Secretary and Chairman of the Presidium of the Supreme Soviet had been justified in 1977, given the new tasks this was no longer 'expedient'. Rather the General Secretary 'should concentrate to the maximum on organisation of the work of the party's central organs and on pooling the efforts of all party, government and non-government organisations for the successful implementation of the planned course.'[6] The intention seemed to be clear: the task of the General Secretary was now deemed to be concerned primarily with party matters, so that the head of state position was no longer necessary.

The changes in the *modus operandi* of the position are reflected in the personal performance of Gorbachev during this period. In stark contrast to his immediate predecessors, the style of General Secretary which he embodied was an activist one who was willing to take the lead on issues, to define options and to present arguments in favour of specific courses of action. As the frequency with which he delivered major speeches in the first eighteen months of his tenure suggests, he intended to lead from the front and provide a positive leadership figure. The profile of the position was thereby restored to something akin to what it had been like before the malaise set in in the early 1970s. But the other aspect of this was no less important. Gorbachev embarked on public walk-abouts, ostentatiously seeking to make contact with and take advice from the ordinary populace. He was projecting an image of a General Secretary who was in touch with the populace and, by implication, had a potential power base independent of that traditional bastion of the General Secretary, the party apparatus.

Despite the changed profile of the General Secretary and the open hints of leadership ⸱conflict between Yel'tsin and Ligachev, the appearance of the course of elite politics in 1985–6 remained one of surface normality. The changes that had occurred and the evidence of greater policy virility than had been evident in previous years were attributed to the new General Secretary, not to any fundamental change in the outlook or assumptions of the leadership as a whole. This was an accurate view, because it was not until the General Secretary began directly to challenge some of those assumptions towards the end of 1986 (in the form of recognition of the need for structural change – see below) that the basic consensus upon which the moderate reform coalition had come together began to fray. The moderate reformist consensus rested upon agreement about the traditional nature of the problems being faced and the consequent appropriateness of traditional remedies. This was as clear with regard to the perceived deficiencies of the party as it was to broader societal problems.

### The reform coalition consensus: the problem

From the outset of Gorbachev's incumbency, complaints about the way the party was functioning characterised the Soviet press and the speeches of leading figures. One prominent aspect of this was corruption. Widespread rings of corruption were uncovered in many republics, including Kazakhstan, Kirgizia, Turkmenistan, Moldavia, Uzbekistan and Azerbaijan.[7] While this took many forms, its roots were identified in the domination of party life by 'family groups',[8] the locally-based personalised networks which dominated party life. From the outset the conduct of party affairs in a narrow departmentalist way, where local favouritism prevailed rather than a responsible concern for broader issues, was criticised in the press. Stern measures were called for against those 'leaders whose wounded pride sometimes overrides their sense of party and professional duty and workers who, consumed by self-conceit, succumb to ambition and embellish the real state of affairs'.[9] While calling for the fearless exposure of shortcomings and the rejection of 'false idealisation', Gorbachev criticised the conduct of personnel policy on the basis of 'personal loyalty, servility and protectionism'.[10] Such personal connections and the abuses they produced also were identified by Tajik First Secretary Nabiev when he referred to 'the patronage of a higher-ranking leader who, for patently unprincipled reasons, 'rescues' an unworthy worker. Ties of kinship, friendship, local favouritism . . . come to light.'[11] Personal patronage, protectionism and the promotion of toadies undercut the ability of party organs to function effectively.[12]

Even when the conduct of personnel matters was not explicitly charged with being tainted by nepotism and localist considerations, concern was expressed about the deficiencies in cadre work. In some cases, it was charged, work with cadres was not well thought out, was not designed for the long term and was not informed by the opinions of party organisations.[13] A superficial approach led to the appointment of inefficient people and frequent turnover,[14] while a lack of system and proper supervision led to flaws in personnel matters.[15] Such problems had an adverse effect upon the performance of party organs. In a report on the Dzhizak oblast party organisation, it was declared 'Most instances of economic failure are linked with errors by party organs in the selection of economic cadres and lack of exactingness toward them on the part of primary party organisations.'[16] There was clearly perceived to be a direct link between satisfactory cadre work and acceptable party performance.

The structuring of local power along personalised lines had direct implications for the way in which the party as an organisation functioned. Abuse of position, protectionism and local favouritism were associated with party organisations being characterised by inertia, breach of discipline and the absence of a political approach to the solution of socio-economic tasks. Conceit, arrogance and rudeness were attributed to some leaders in this context.[17] More bluntly, in a criticism of the Azeri Ministry of Procurement which clearly applied to the party as well, it was charged that

> people are not always chosen for their practical, political and moral qualities and there is a lack of proper exactingness. Workers who have compromised themselves are often protected and shielded from responsibility. All this creates an unprincipled, servile atmosphere, leads to various kinds of negative phenomena and abuses, and generally has a negative effect on the sector's work . . . [we must] resolutely oppose any attempts to use official positions for personal ends and any disregard for our laws and for party and moral norms.[18]

This was usually linked with a particular type of leadership attitude. In the words of Ukrainian First Secretary Shcherbitskii

> It is very bad when the wounded self-respect of a leader sometimes proves to be above awareness of party and official duty, or when a

functionary suffering from excessive conceit or arrogance gives way to ambitions, overestimates his services and possibilities, indulges in self admiration, embellishes the state of affairs, tolerates obsequiousness and boot-licking, immediately rejects fair remarks or even takes vengeance for them.[19]

Leaders were called upon to ensure that their words matched their deeds.[20]

This sort of situation was associated with a formalist approach to meetings. Gorbachev attacked such formalism whereby the speeches and by implication the decisions of meetings were worked out in advance, a practice which thereby turned such gatherings into purely ritualistic and ratificatory meetings.[21] He called for criticism and self-criticism of performance and the provision of objective information to the centre rather than 'paradeness, ballyhoo . . . [and] the embellishment of reality'.[22] Such an approach involved the stage managing of meetings in order to avoid the possibility of awkward questions arising and to gloss over controversy. In the words of a *Pravda* editorial: 'In some places people try to "prepare" the discussion in such a way as to avoid any tricky issues in it. Speeches are usually made only by "staff" speakers, usually in a predetermined order. Things even go as far as the editing of draft texts of speeches.'[23] In discussing agriculture in Riazan oblast, it was declared 'mainly pompous speeches are to be heard from the platforms of oblast meetings and obkom plena. These sessions and meetings are still held without pointed criticism and self-criticism and without in-depth analysis of shortcomings.'[24] An emphasis upon the ceremonial aspects of meetings at the expense of their substance was characteristic of this approach. Here was a main mechanism for the 'embellishment of reality' criticised by Gorbachev. Important in this too was the attempt to pull a veil over events in the local region by failing to keep higher levels of the party accurately informed about the local situation. Gorbachev complained about the way in which the party's central organs often were not given accurate information about the state of affairs in the localities,[25] and this was clearly a problem also for all the intervening levels of the party structure. The normal processes of party life could be manipulated to obscure the vision of higher levels. At the XXVII Congress of the party in February 1986, Gorbachev criticised the 'propensity for excessive organisation, the habit of speaking vaguely, and the fear of revealing the real state of affairs', window-dressing and complacency, the speaking only of successes and papering over of shortcomings, and careerism, toadyism and unbridled laudation of those of senior rank.[26] All forms of 'window-dressing', of hiding abuses from view, should be eliminated.[27]

From the beginning, the role leaders played in the party and in the drive for change was recognised, but the performance of many of these people was judged to be deficient. Higher standards of performance were demanded of leaders, and yet too often their poor performance was being accepted without concern; some demonstrated an unacceptable 'vulgarity, arrogance, high-handedness and impatience regarding criticism'.[28] Leaders had to be judged by their performance, and their deeds had to match their words.[29] In the words of Leningrad party boss Solov'ev 'The main demand which the party makes under modern conditions on the party committee secretary and the staff officer is ensuring that nowhere, under no circumstances, does word part from deed since any discrepancy here causes palpable damage to the authority of our policy and cannot be tolerated in any form.'[30] Party organisations had to work in a new style, and in this the party leader played a crucial role. In mid-1986 Gorbachev declared, 'I should like to stress the tremendously important role of the leaders of party bodies in asserting the new style. How consistent and vigorous the reconstruction of party work will be depends on the position they take, on their manner of acting and behaviour.'[31] Or in the words of a *Pravda* editorial entitled 'First Secretary' soon after Gorbachev's comments,

> It is they who are obliged to set the tone in work and display a broad political horizon, profound understanding of the tasks, organising abilities, high responsibility, a critical and self-critical attitude to assessments, and party-mindedness in the highest sense of the word. How consistently and vigorously work is done on the spot largely depends on their stance and their way of acting and behaving.[32]

A negative example of a leadership role was provided by the first secretary of Frunzenskii raikom in Moscow, Griaznov, who 'was accustomed to stagnation, encouraged ostentation, ignored collective opinion, lost the feeling of party comradeship, and only pretended to be carrying out restructuring.'[33] Some leaders in Kazakhstan were accused of finding it 'difficult to rid themselves of elements of excessive administration and a commander-like style'.[34]

Criticism of the deficiencies of republican party leaders was a significant characteristic of the republican party congresses leading up to the XXVII Congress of the party in February 1986. Particularly important in this regard was the criticism levelled at former leader of the Uzbek party, Sharif Rashidov. According to his successor Inamzhon Usmankhodzhaev, it was due to Rashidov that

> a depraved style, when show and self-congratulation, the ignoring of criticism and self-criticism, loss of modesty, and in a number of instances even simply of party and human decency, caused the spread of intrigues, sharp practices, formalism, indifference, abuses of official position and embezzlement, took root in the Central Committee of the Communist Party of Uzbekistan and in oblast, city and raion party committees.

The basis of this was the promotion of supporters and favourites.

> In these conditions, all manner of grabbers and rogues, bribe-takers and embezzlers of public funds, traitors to our party cause, felt free. A juggling with facts and deliberate deception of the central organs for the purpose of receiving awards and honours occurred. Sh. Rashidov protected people like Yakh'yaev and Odilov, who turned out to be major state criminals, and at the same time reviled and cruelly persecuted honest communists who tried to expose the offenders and speak the truth.[35]

The criticism of Rashidov was particularly harsh and damning, coming as it did at a late stage of the anti-corruption campaign that had been continuing in Uzbekistan for some time; the new leadership was clearly trying to distance itself from its tarnished past. Criticism was also mounted against a number of other republican leaders at this time, including those of Ukraine, Kirgizia, Belorussia and Turkmenistan.[36] While some of the charges made against the former, and sometimes current, leaderships of these republics reflect the dynamics of anti-corruption campaigns, they were also representative of a more widespread concern about the performance of leaders at all levels.

The failure of first secretaries to provide adequate leadership was reflected most clearly in the continuation of the old ways of working, of failing to renovate the style of party work and adjust to the new conditions and demands. At the June 1986 CC plenum Gorbachev was critical of the way in which in some circles the view still prevailed that work should continue as before. Initiatives ran into a wall of indifference, if not outright opposition. In some organisations people were waiting to see what would happen before committing themselves, while in others blind faith was placed in the centre. In other cases people wanted change, but they did not know how to go about implementing it: 'Sometimes words are substituted for deeds, no action is taken in response to criticism, and self-criticism takes the form of

self-flagellation.'[37] Passivity, words instead of deeds, the generation of
mountains of paper and formalism in meetings[38] were all typical of the
old approach which needed to be eradicated. So too was 'the armchair
method of work',[39] the propensity of leaders to remain in their offices
and to thereby make decisions divorced from the reality of the
problems confronting them. But this also involved illegalities, such as
the generation of fictitious projects, the misappropriation of funds and
bribe-taking.[40] The linkage between poor work and corruption was
clear.

The complaints about the way in which the party was operating
which resounded through the press in 1985 and 1986 amounted to
a condemnation of the party's organisational culture. This culture,
consisting of a set of values and practices which had become embedded
as party lore over the life of the party in power, sustained the
phenomenon of family group control and the patterns of operation
consistent with it. It was the established patterns of thinking and action,
the culture of the party, which needed to be changed. During the first
eighteen months or so of Gorbachev's tenure as General Secretary, there
seems to have been a general underestimation of the strength and
sources of this culture and of what was necessary to eradicate it. The
heart of the solution the Gorbachev leadership pursued was thoroughly
traditional in the Soviet context, personnel.

### The reform coalition consensus: the solution

The established Soviet remedy to deficiencies in party
operation was to change personnel, to replace those in positions of
responsibility who were unsympathetic to the new mood or unable to
adjust and improve their performance by those more attuned to the
demands of the new times. This approach was pursued with some
vigour in these early stages of Gorbachev's tenure. The sweeping
changes at the apex of the party have already been noted. At the level
immediately below this, turnover was also significant. The CC elected
at the XXVII Congress continued the earlier trend of increased size (477
cf 470 in 1981), but the number of full members (307) was twelve less
than elected at its predecessor. More importantly, some 40.7 per cent of
full members were elected for the first time in 1986 compared with only
25.7 per cent in 1981. This was the highest turnover rate since 1961.[41]
Within the CC, fourteen of the twenty-three department heads were
replaced during this time.[42] Of the fourteen Union Republican party
leaders, five had been replaced by the end of 1986.[43] Among the 157 first

secretaries in the krais and oblasts, fifty had been replaced between March 1985 and July 1986; this follows figures of thirty-three replaced during Andropov's short tenure and seven under Chernenko. Turnover at lower levels was also significant, particularly in those areas like Uzbekistan, Kazakhstan and Turkmenistan where a purge was accompanying the anti-corruption campaign. In sum, levels of turnover among responsible officials were high during this period.[44] But the removal of dead or obstructive wood was not the only means of approaching the personnel problems that were seen to be at the heart of the party's unsatisfactory performance.[45]

A major theme of discussion during much of this period was the need for improved work with cadres. While some of this was directed specifically at some of the abuses noted above, such as calls for the conduct of cadre policy on principles other than personal favouritism, an important element concerned the need for better training and preparation of party cadres. This was particularly evident in the month following Gorbachev's election when a series of republican party plena discussed work with cadres and emphasised the need to boost the training of party cadres.[46] This led into the April 1985 CC plenum at which Gorbachev gave a speech in which he addressed the question of personnel policy in terms which laid out the main lines whereby that question would be pursued in the following twenty months.[47] These lines were the demand for increased exactingness and the associated strengthening of supervision (kontrol'), increased publicity and popular involvement in political work, criticism and self-criticism, and, something which became stronger later, collectivism in leadership. These were all traditional themes of political life and reflect the traditional approach adopted at this time to resolving the acknowledged problems of the party.

The demand for increased exactingness was directed at gaining higher standards of performance on the part of party members. Responsible officials were expected to be characterised by high standards of both moral conduct and personal performance. They were to be models of the fulfilment of civic duty, of labour for the welfare of society and of the Leninist style of work. In Gorbachev's words, 'It is necessary to increase the responsibility of each party member for his attitude to his public duty, for the fulfilment of party decisions, for the honest and pure image of a party member. A Communist is assessed by what he does. There are no, nor can there be, any other criteria.'[48] The catalogue of inappropriate ways of acting noted above, and in particular the deficiencies in performance on the part of individual leaders, were all the reverse side of this call for exactingness; they were evidence of the failure to apply high standards to personal performance. The demand for increased exactingness could be realised through changes in personal attitudes (see below) and through a heightening of supervision. The latter was a traditional theme of party life, usually taking the form of calls for verification of the fulfilment of party decisions. But in this case its more common form was the call for the strict accountability of cadres, the constant monitoring of performance of all party members, particularly responsible officials.[49] In the words of Leningrad leader Solov'ev, there can 'be no organisations in the party which are beyond supervision and closed to criticism and there are no and must be no leaders protected against party liability. This requirement applies to all leaders, all organisations and establishments and every communist without exception.'[50] It was through supervision that an atmosphere of exactingness was created in party organisations.[51] It was within this context that considerable attention was devoted to the process of 'attestation'. Begun in the Georgian party, this was a means whereby party members were regularly to have their qualifications and perfomance scrutinised with a view to evaluating their continued membership of the party or occupation of a responsible position.[52] But despite this rhetoric, no effective institutional measures were implemented to strengthen either exactingness or supervision.[53]

The emphasis upon supervision was linked with calls for increased publicity in the work of the party and for the populace to play a more active role in political life. Political institutions were called upon to become more integrated into the mass of the populace and to encourage greater openness and publicity in the work of their organisations in order to break down the distance that existed between organisations and people.[54] Greater openness was seen as a potent weapon against such abuses as 'window-dressing' and 'superficiality, protectionism and formalism'.[55] In an attempt to strengthen popular involvement in these matters, the new party Rules adopted at the XXVII Congress made provision for non-members to participate in the discussion of the the qualifications of individual candidates for entry to the party.[56] The involvement of the broader non-party masses in party affairs was thus seen as a means of overcoming abuses in party life. However, with the exception of the provision for participation in the discussion about entry qualifications of individual candidates, no effective institutional mechanisms were established to facilitate popular involvement.

A traditional theme of party life, and one which historically was designed to combat abuses in the party, was criticism and self-criticism. The aim of criticism and self-criticism was to ensure that all within the party continually questioned their own actions and opinions and, rather than complacently drifting along, continually compared their performance with the party's norms and aims. This was to be supplemented by being continually subject to the critical gaze of others, so that none could escape from the collective party morality which embodied the membership as a whole. For Gorbachev, criticism and self-criticism 'are as necessary for us as air'.[57] No party organisation should be immune from criticism and no party leader fenced off from party responsibility. The consequences of these injunctions being ignored, declared Gorbachev, was the situation that had prevailed in Uzbekistan where a leadership that had spoken only of successes and had encouraged careerism and sycophancy had produced a deterioration in the economic and social spheres, embezzlement, bribery and the transgression of socialist legality.[58]

Criticism and self-criticism were essential to a healthy party, but it was useful only if it was used correctly. In some instances, it could be used by people to cover up abuses and defend themselves against honest criticism. According to one editorial, 'Misdirected criticism, usually directed upward and couched in general, stereotyped forms will hardly be of any use, nor will criticism used just for the sake of appearances and form . . . '[59] Criticisms voiced by individual party members should not be played down or ignored, but investigated and, if justified, acted upon.[60] However, it was claimed, criticism and self-criticism were not well developed in all organisations; in some cases criticism was only conducted from above, being poorly developed at grassroots level.[61] This charge is doubtless true and may reflect the passivity of the party membership, a complaint which recurred during this period.[62] But it also reflects conscious opposition to criticism and self-criticism on the part of responsible leaders at various levels. There were cases of the crude suppression of criticism[63] while the comments of Ukrainian leader Shcherbitskii reflect reservations about responsible officials being subject to criticism from below: 'Authentic Bolshevik criticism has nothing to do with labelling, personal attacks, peremptory shouting, or a rude reprimand. While providing conditions for sound and constructive criticism, it is necessary, at the same time, to nip in the bud attempts by malignant and anonymous people to besmirch honest functionaries dedicated to the cause.'[64] While there was clearly some justice in Shcherbitskii's comments, they may also reflect some nervousness about the potential implications for responsible leaders like himself of the unleashing of criticism from below.

Although criticism and self-criticism was potentially an important weapon against the sort of abuses of power that went with family group control, no important institutional innovations were made which would have facilitated its use against such abuses. Certainly the Rules adopted at the XXVII Congress contained new provisions designed to reinforce the operation of criticism and self-criticism: higher standing party bodies were to be kept regularly informed about the work of subordinate party organisations and about the situation in the localities, and party organs were systematically to inform their organisations 'about the realisation of critical remarks and proposals of communists'.[65] However, in the absence of new institutional mechanisms designed to facilitate the operation of these principles, the strengthening of criticism and self-criticism was dependant upon the personal disposition of party members, and particularly those in responsible, leadership positions.

Collectivism too was a traditional theme of party life, and one which usually found increased prominence at the time of leadership succession. But what was new about the approach to collectivism at this time was the close connection drawn between it and notions of personal accountability. This was most clearly expressed about the time of the XXVII Congress. The new party Rules adopted at the congress added a fifth element to the traditional four principles of democratic centralism. The new element was 'collectivity in the work of all organisations and leading organs of the party and the personal responsibility of every communist for the implementation of his duties and party com-missions'.[66] This explicit linkage between 'the collective nature of leadership . . . [and] personal responsibility for the assigned sector'[67] clearly reflects the way in which collectivism was seen to be aimed against abuse of power and position. This was made even more explicit in the new party Rules, which declared collectivism to be 'a reliable guarantee against the adoption of volitional, subjective decisions, manifestations of the cult of personality, and the infringement of Leninist norms of party life'.[68] This combination of collectivism and individual responsibility was directed at preventing the type of one-man dominance that often went with family group control by establishing the collective principle as the norm in party life and by making all individually responsible for their own actions; this was clearly to include any violations of the collective principle.[69]

The common factor behind these four principles designed to

overcome the problems in the party, exactingness, openness, criticism and self-criticism and collectivism, was accountability. All were concerned with rendering responsible officials and ordinary party leaders accountable for their behaviour. The key to eliminating the problems in the party was thus perceived to be altering the behaviour of party members. But while the principles that should shape behaviour were clear, the means whereby that reshaping could be brought about were not. Gorbachev spoke about the need for the psychological restructuring of cadres in the spirit of the new demands and for changing the mentality of cadres and developing within them the desire and ability to think and work in new ways.[70] According to Shcherbitskii, economic demands call 'for a profound reform in the psychology of cadres, it calls on the cadres to learn, and to learn rapidly, to think in terms of the present day, and to work properly'.[71] Short-comings flowed from the way in which 'a number of workers still have not changed their ways of economic thinking'.[72] A change in thinking and mentality was essential to overcoming the problems.[73]

This perception was certainly accurate, but alone it was insufficient. It constituted a demand that people think and act in new ways, exercising initiative and independence, and that leading cadres render themselves accountable for their actions. But this strategy was deficient in two ways. First, the 'psychological restructuring' of large numbers of party cadres would not be achieved quickly, and therefore did not accord with the prevailing sense of urgency signalled in the economic programme of *uskorenie* (acceleration). Second, despite the emphasis given to education and training, the process of 'psychological restructuring' was left up to individuals to achieve. No effective mechanisms were set up to assist this process.[74] Moreover, no institutional means were established either to deal with those who refused to respond to the call for a change in their thinking or to establish meaningful ways of implementing the principle of accountability. Without institutional changes, accountability could be pursued only through rhetorical means, and when this failed, there was no weapon available to reassert it. Indeed, as late as the XXVII Congress Gorbachev seems to have seen such measures as unnecessary: he declared the party to be a 'healthy organism' which was perfecting its style and methods of work and eradicating its problems.[75] A healthy organism clearly did not need radical institutional surgery.[76]

This does not mean that institutional changes had no part in the continuing process of political debate. The redefinition of the position of General Secretary has already been noted and, in the debate on the party Rules preceding the XXVII Congress, some institutional changes were suggested. Among these were a maximum tenure of two terms in elected party office (with the possibility of a third for exceptional people) and minimum turnover levels;[77] Gorbachev openly supported a maximum tenure in one post of ten years for party secretaries.[78] There was also talk about eliminating the 'formal' aspects of party elections, including the issue of multi-candidate competitive elections.[79] However, in practice the institutional changes made in the party were minimal, and in effect they did not increase democratisation or the possibility of rank-and-file control: in the new Rules the principle of secret ballot was waived in favour of the possibility of open ballot for a range of leading positions including party secretaries in small party organisations, the right of a defeated minority in the CC to appeal to the rank-and-file through the conduct of a party-wide discussion was withdrawn, and the responsibility of all party organs and PPOs to report to higher standing bodies was strengthened.[80]

Two other aspects of the debate at this time, both reflected in the party's Rules, were also interesting for what they portended in later years. The first was the provision that the party was to act within the state Constitution (# 60), a provision which formally subordinated the party to the law of the land in a way it had never been before. In line with this, a party member who broke the law was declared to be responsible before the state as well as the party (# 12). In 1986 such provisions were largely symbolic, part of the drive to establish a socialist legal state in which law was supreme. However, they did raise interesting questions about the legal basis for the party's actions and the basis of its property ownership which were to become more important when its constitutionally entrenched monopoly position was abolished in 1990.

The other aspect of the debate was the old problem of *podmena*, or substitutionism. Successive party leaders had railed against this since the party had come to power in 1917. Gorbachev too criticised this, calling for the party to exercise 'political' influence based on the authority, expertise and prestige of party members rather than through crude administrative means.[81] However, no institutional changes were made which would have facilitated the accomplishment of this aim. Indeed, the new edition of the Rules emphasised the role and responsibilities of party members in the economic sphere, thereby at least in spirit violating the expressed desire to eliminate overlap and substitutionism. However, this, too, was something that was to be taken up much more vigorously in later years.

The weakness of the campaign to rectify the problems in the party was thus the absence of any institutional means of enforcing the notions of increased accountability which were at its heart. The source of this weakness seems to have been an initial underestimation of what was needed to overcome the problems. Initially Gorbachev seems to have believed that what was needed was an 'invigoration' of the system,[82] a strategy consistent with his economic programme of *uskorenie*, although he did also talk about 'the extension of socialist democracy and people's self-government'.[83] But these seem to have been seen in traditional, campaign terms rather than as meaning significant institutional change. However, as the economic programme faltered and the search for economic solutions began to embrace more radical alternatives, so too his realisation about what was needed in the party became more radical. In the months following the party congress, Gorbachev seems to have become convinced of the need for institutional changes in the party's operating procedures. In September 1986 Gorbachev declared that future success depended upon 'how quickly the CPSU will restructure itself, all its links from primary party organisations to the Politburo and the CC'.[84] This could have meant simply the sort of psychological restructuring Gorbachev had earlier focused upon, but given the proposals he made at the January 1987 plenum, it is likely that he had institutional change in mind.

An alternative explanation for the limited nature of the approach initially championed by Gorbachev is that while he was personally convinced of the need for wide-ranging institutional change, he had to moderate his public position because of the reservations of his leadership colleagues. It is certainly true that even though Gorbachev had substantially strengthened his personal position through the personnel changes he engineered at the top of the party during his first year of office, he had to take note of the views of his colleagues. The moderate reformist coalition which had brought him to power and which he had done so much to strengthen rested upon agreement about the need for change and the appropriateness of the sorts of traditional measures to bring this about referred to above. While events were to show that some members of that coalition (most particularly Yel'tsin, Shevardnadze and Yakovlev) were willing to embrace more radical, far-reaching change, this was not true of all members. Gorbachev must have realised from the start that commitment to change was not shared equally among all members, but the strength of his own position was such that he could be confident of carrying a majority with him on most issues. Had he been convinced of the need for radical change from the start, why not press for this as soon as the final personnel changes for 1986 (and his own position had thereby been further strengthened) had been introduced in March of that year? Gorbachev *may* have been hiding his plans from hostile elements in the leadership until he had consolidated his position, but as later events showed, he does not appear to have had a clearly formulated programme of change in his head. Furthermore it is not clear that his position was stronger at the end of 1986 when he launched the campaign for political reform than it was nine months earlier. Developments seem to fit better with the view that Gorbachev's policy position became radicalised in the second half of 1986 by his realisation that the earlier measures were not working.[85]

So Gorbachev came to power with a broad consensus behind him which accepted the need for change. But that consensus rested upon the assumption that major structural changes did not have to be made in order to achieve the economic improvement that was desired. Furthermore initial ideas about change, its course and dimensions, were vague; agreement was therefore to what was essentially a lowest common denominator programme. Such a programme not only facilitated the initial broad-based agreement, but it left sufficient ambiguity to render uncertain the extent to which new policies would fall within the consensus. Thus, while in one sense this consensus muted disagreement, its ambiguity also provided the basis upon which disagreement could rest. This created a somewhat paradoxical situation as this period continued. According to the established criteria of kremlinology, throughout this period Gorbachev's position was becoming stronger. He presided over the reshaping of the membership of the party's leading organs, and the consolidation of his personal position by the promotion of such supporters as Shevardnadze and Yakovlev. Furthermore the language that was used to refer to Gorbachev[86] increasingly suggested that he was becoming rather more powerful than the *primus inter pares* formula would imply. Indeed, in terms of tenure, Gorbachev was the longest serving senior secretary and therefore clearly superior to his Politburo colleagues. However while this evidence of his consolidation of power[87] was accumulating, the radicalism of the policy prescriptions he was edging towards began to erode the leadership consensus. His inability to convene the CC plenum scheduled for late 1986, and which eventually met in January 1987, was evidence of this. Leadership conflict escalated, although during this period it remained behind closed doors. It was to come further into the open with the rebuff Gorbachev suffered at the January 1987 CC plenum.

# 3    The move to institutional reform

By the end of 1986 Gorbachev had become convinced of the need for institutional reform in the party that involved not simply the changing of individual psychology, but structural change in the party's organisational machinery. He had been conducting informal consultations with party leaders for some time about the solutions he was to unveil at the forthcoming CC plenum, and he found considerable resistance to his proposals.[1] The result was the postponement on three occasions[2] of the plenum, which did not open until 27 January 1987. In the weeks prior to the plenum, the main public focus of party life was events in Kazakhstan.

On 16 December 1986 party first secretary in Kazakhstan, Dinmukhamed Kunaev, an old Brezhnev protégé, was removed and replaced by Gennadii Kolbin. Kolbin was a Russian, and the reaction in the Kazakh capital Alma Ata was almost immediate. There were demonstrations and violence in the streets, as supporters of the former leader registered their protest at the change in leadership. The degree to which the popular reaction was in response to the appointment of an ethnic Russian or was something organised by the well-developed Kunaev political machine remains a matter for conjecture, but this was significant in party terms for two reasons. First, despite some moderation in practice,[3] this appointment seemed to signal continuing commitment to maintaining a central interventionist personnel policy. Secondly, leading personnel decisions appeared no longer to be the concern only of those in responsible positions within the party structure, but were now open to question and debate on the part of wider sections of the populace.

In the immediate aftermath of the leadership change, the Kazakh press discussed party affairs, with the record of the Kunaev leadership an important theme. In a discussion on the need for improving party control,[4] the themes enunciated in the initial period of Gorbachev's leadership were once again emphasised: the development of intra-party democracy, collective leadership, criticism and self-criticism, monitoring and a responsible attitude to work. Continual monitoring, the verification of implementation and the personal responsibility of every apparatus worker were prominent themes. What was required was actual, detailed checks on implementation:

> The life of party organisations and labour collectives must not be judged just from written or telephoned reports. But people in some places are in no hurry to abandon the armchair style of leadership, and they substitute paperwork and numerous circulars for live contacts with people. Just such a flawed practice was 'introduced' by Gurev oblast's Makhambetskii party raikom, which produces a large number of decisions. But the apparatus is, of course, unable to monitor their execution. The raikom constantly asks for local written reports. The circulation of paper has literally clogged up all components.

Much depends on the moral and psychological climate in labour collectives and this is largely determined by the personality of the leader. Party control must not only be 'from above' but also 'from below'; it is not true that only higher levels can call the chiefs to account.

> A special role in persuading people to work in the new way belongs to the implacability of communists toward all negative phenomena – use of official position for mercenary purposes, mismanagement, red tape, padding of data . . . Many instances of the deliberate distortion of report data and of deception of the state have been exposed in the republican ministries of consumer services, light industry, local industry, construction, and construction materials and in certain others. This data padding is the result of inadequate party control over the work of ministries and departments.

The theme of this article reaffirmed the former position that problems in performance were the result of the unsatisfactory personal attitudes of many in the party. This was reinforced, in a pointed fashion, by an interview with a veteran of the war[5] who argued that his generation had believed that the only privilege a communist should have was to be where things were most difficult. However, he declared, some seem to have forgotten this precept. 'Leaders appeared who began their activity based on the principle of 'looking out for number one' – concerned with fitting out their own private residences and filling their offices with imported furniture.' The party's ranks must be purged of these people. Many became accustomed to everything being decided for them from somewhere up on high, leading to inertia, passivity and indifference. This picture would have had real resonance in a Kazakhstan recently emerged from the Kunaev era.

This was reinforced by a *Pravda* article[6] which reported the comments of many people in Kazakhstan on the tenacity of connections and the way they ensured that people who performed badly did not suffer as a result. Instead of being demoted or expelled, they were often simply shifted to other jobs. According to some people from Dzhambul oblast, 'There is no memory of former Sarysuskii raikom first secretary A. Nurkenov ever having done a good deed. He messed up the economy of what was once a leading raion, he suppressed criticism and self-criticism, and he 'raised' many toadies and fawners. Then what? He was appointed chairman of the agro-industrial complex workers trade union obkom.' The problem was seen to lie at the higher rather than lower levels, with unsuitable methods of cadre selection 'on tribal lines or on the basis of where people came from.' The article continued, 'There was a failure to make a prompt, principled assessment of the actions of the former leaders of the Alma Ata party gorkom and gorispolkom who distributed apartments without regard to precedence – in response to verbal or written orders from certain senior personnel, including people from the Kazakhstan Communist Party Central Committee'. There were reported to be many instances of scores being settled, of revenge and persecution. 'Again the ringleaders are the 'quicksand' types who have moved from seat to seat as a result of old connections or because they come from the same area as someone else. On the pretext of restructuring and strengthening of discipline, they would deal with any cadres who got in their way and would blacken their names.'

Kolbin was aware of these problems and he addressed them in a speech to a seminar on restructuring reported in early January.[7] He called on party organisations to take real decisions rather than just declaratory ones, to work at implementation and to conduct their affairs in an ordered and systematic way. A procedure had to be established whereby each PPO made use of the reports by individual communists on their performance of their party and state duties. Heavy demands must be made of all comrades. Every leader had to be accountable, so a practice had to be instituted 'whereby the appraisal report on each worker on the nomenklatura of a party or other organ is periodically reviewed'. This should be done at no more than two-year intervals, and the reports must reflect both the good and bad points:

During the review procedure, the party appraisal report on a Central Committee nomenklatura worker must be prepared by the Central Committee branch department, reviewed by the department and the branch secretary, and then submitted to the Secretariat or Bureau, which decides on confirming the appraisal, noting that the leader was present at the discussion, that he agrees with the remarks, and that the appraisal report should be sent to the organs on whose nomenklatura he is – the CPSU Central Committee or a union ministry.

Each leader is accountable to his superior organ and to the collective that he leads. Leaders must report to their subordinates at least once every three months 'and must admit openly their shortcomings both in production affairs and in personal behaviour, including the behaviour of members of their family. In the event of excessive "modesty" in these matters, the enterprise's party organisation secretary or trade union committee chairman must expose the shortcomings which leaders have tried to conceal or play down.' Every leader is responsible for the behaviour of his family – family members cannot enjoy greater benefits because of the leader's position. There should be no protectionism, no 'you scratch my back and I will scratch yours', no 'lordlings' who encourage a toadying approach. There must be closer contact between the leadership and the rank-and-file, with the former being more responsive to the latter. Kolbin related this back to the CC resolution on Perm obkom.[8]

As a result of these obvious failings in the performance of the Kazakh party, a plenum of the Kazakh CC decided to hold a certification of senior officials in the CC 'in order to evaluate their political, professional and moral qualities, their degree of preparation for fulfilment of the duties they bear and of the development of their initiative in the matter of restructuring party work.'[9] Such a vigorous exposure of the failings of the Kazakh party under Kunaev was clearly designed to bolster the position of new first secretary Kolbin and to justify the removal of many old officials and their replacement by the new leader's supporters. But it also served to add force to the arguments about the need for structural change in the party that Gorbachev was to make at the coming CC plenum.

### Democratisation

When the CPSU CC plenum opened on 27 January 1987, Gorbachev delivered a major address focusing upon the problems in the party and what he saw to be the necessary solutions.[10] This was a crucial step in the process of party reform because it combined a continued emphasis upon attitudinal change with the first concrete proposals from the party leadership for structural reform. The early part of Gorbachev's speech contained a stinging attack on the way the party had been operating. Among the charges he directed at the party's performance were conservatism and inertia, lenience and lack of demandingness, toadyism and personal adulation, red tape, formalism, intolerance and suppression of criticism, ambition and careerism, administration by decree, permissiveness, mutual cover-ups, careerism, departmentalism, parochialism, nationalism, substitutionism, a weakening of the role of party meetings and elective bodies, embezzlement, bribery, report-padding and violation of discipline. The degeneration of personnel and breaches of Soviet law had taken ugly forms in Uzbekistan, Moldavia, Turkmenistan, Kazakhstan, Krasnodar krai, Rostov oblast, Moscow and in the Ministries of Foreign Trade and Internal Affairs. There had been an under-estimation of the importance of political and theoretical training in the selection, placement and distribution of personnel, and the filling of offices with those unfit for such posts. High moral standards of personnel were needed. In Gorbachev's view, the key to eliminating these problems was greater democratisation. He argued that many proposals had been forthcoming regarding the formation of leading party bodies, and that these could be summarised in two points:

1 In the election of secretaries of party bureaux and committees in the PPOs, full scope must be given to the views of *all* communists. The responsibility to the electors on the part of those elected must be enhanced.

2 Secretaries, including first secretaries, of district, area, city, region and territory party committees and the central committees of union republican parties should be elected by secret ballot at plenary sessions of the respective committees, with members of the committee having the right to enter any number of candidates on the voting list.

These proposals were an important step in the direction of democratisation. They emphasised accountability, the former by focusing on the breadth of opinion that must be tapped for the filling of responsible office, and the latter by opening the way for multi-candidate competitive elections. Moreover, there was to be provision for those candidates to be chosen by the electorate rather than being handed down via the nomenklatura mechanism from above. But the potential effect of this was immediately qualified by the injunction that the decisions of higher bodies were to remain binding on lower bodies.

Another shortcoming of these provisions was that although Gorbachev did say that further democratisation should apply to the formation of the leading central bodies of the party, the CPSU CC was not included in the list of party bodies to which multi-candidate elections of secretaries should apply. But this does not mean that Gorbachev was satisfied with the performance of the CC; in his speech he criticised the CC and its *modus operandi*. Too often important issues were not discussed in this forum, where the meetings were frequently brief and formal with many members unable to participate effectively. A fresh influx of new forces into this body (and the Politburo) was needed, although this had to be combined with the maintenance of continuity of leadership. The key was to expand the role of elective bodies in general. According to the General Secretary, there had been an excessive growth in the role of executive bodies at the expense of elected organs. While plena may have been held regularly, their work was often excessively formalised, or it discussed only secondary issues or measures that had already been decided. This resulted in a lack of proper control over executive organs and their leaders, who often viewed elective bodies as nuisances. This view, declared Gorbachev, was also sometimes present in the relationship between committee members and permanent staff. Executive organs must not be allowed to supplant or dominate elective organs.

Gorbachev's speech to the plenum was a major challenge to existing practice in the party. He had called for a much more vigorous electoral process characterised by multi-candidate elections, the conscious participation of all party members in the discussion of candidates, and the strengthening of elected bodies (committees) at the expense of elected organs (bureaux) and the apparatus. But reflecting the opposition Gorbachev had encountered in his preliminary soundings with regional leaders and in the need continually to postpone the plenum, these proposals met a cool reception with the plenum refusing to endorse Gorbachev's specific proposals. The plenum resolution[11] acknowledged the need to democratise the work of party organs, to democratise party elections, to open up the work of party bodies to the gaze of all, to strengthen the accountability of elected and appointed leaders, to further develop criticism and self-criticism, to ensure that elected organs were characterised by full collectivism, equality and freedom of discussion, to exercise control over executive organs and the work of the apparatus, to do away with substitutionism, and to ensure the high moral quality of party members. But by failing to endorse the principle of multi-candidate elections, the CC refused to implement the measure that was essential to the realisation of accountability, which was in turn fundamental to the achievement of these aims.

But if the drive for democratisation was blunted by opposition at the top, it now received impetus from the lower levels of the party. Within two weeks of the end of the plenum, positive reports occurred in the press about the election by secret ballot from among two candidates of a new first secretary of Izhmorskii raikom, Kemerovo oblast.[12] This was cited as an example for other party organisations to follow, even though it was acknowledged that there were aspects of the procedure that could be improved: the candidates could have been allowed to present their views rather than having others speak about them, and perhaps the list of candidates could have been determined by the electors themselves rather than the raikom or gorkom.[13] During the remainder of 1987, some 120 secretaries were elected in a competitive ballot.[14] However, none of these elections was for a post higher than the city level, and although there was a choice between a number of candidates, those candidates were still chosen from above rather than nominated from below.[15] Despite the coverage given to some of these competitive elections, during this period most posts were still filled in the traditional fashion.

The blunting of Gorbachev's push for institutional reform meant that the main avenue open to those who sought to engineer such change in the party was the press. As a result, in the period following the plenum, the press was characterised by criticisms of shortcomings in the way the party had been functioning, and particularly, following the line enunciated at the plenum, in cadre work. Sometimes this was attributed to the influence of one leader, as in the criticisms by Turkmen first secretary Niiazov who complained that his predecessor (Gapurov) had prevented the implementation of control measures and thereby ensured that the concealment of performance became a 'universal phenomenon' throughout the republic.[16] On other occasions the sorts of criticisms made by Gorbachev at the plenum were aired,[17] and although the solution was seen to lie in increased democratisation, rarely was this given a concrete form by open advocacy of the notion of multi-candidate elections.[18] The failure to openly press for multi-candidate elections reflects the extent of opposition to such a process throughout the party. This opposition rested on a clear understanding of the potential danger multi-candidate elections could pose to the nomen-klatura system of personnel placement in the party and to those holding responsible positions within that structure. In principle, multi-candidate elections alone need not have posed any threat to the established structure and processes. If the candidates for election were nominated from above, through the nomenklatura, the choice between such candidates posed no threat. However, if those candidates could be nominated from the floor of the electoral meeting or directly from within the electorate, higher party officials had lost control of the personnel system. This would have meant the destruction of that system and of the personalised networks which thrived on it. Those who had power and position to lose, were unwilling to give this up without a fight.

Those who supported Gorbachev's drive for democratisation also realised the power implications of these measures. His ally Gennadii Kolbin also had the incentive of discrediting his predecessor Kunaev. The picture he painted of the situation in Kazakhstan under Kunaev was a graphic illustration of the sort of leadership structure which, in the mind of Gorbachev and his allies, was at the heart of the party's problems.[19] According to Kolbin in March 1987, there had been serious mistakes and distortions in cadre policy. 'It was founded on the principle of local allegiance and manifestations of national protectionism in the placement of cadres.' He attributed the rioting in Alma Ata to the appointment of someone (himself) from outside who was not part of this network attached to the old leadership, and he announced that they were struggling to eradicate protectionism, nepotism, family or home-town favouritism and abuse of official position. Privileges have already been taken away from the old caste.

> Protectionism is the most terrible vice in cadre affairs. No other evil inflicts so much damage on public interests. Unlike crimes or some illegal deal, protectionism at times has a more open and innocent nature, penetrates all spheres of public activity, and puts down firm roots. Since protection is exercised mostly by high-ranking and influential persons, it becomes exceptionally pervasive and ensures success for those taking advantage of it. As a rule, they suffer no pangs of conscience. Selfish interests and advantage – these constitute its sole guiding rule. The pernicious nature of this evil is further exacerbated by the fact that it provides a breeding ground for bribery, cliquishness and toadyism in relations. The existing shortcomings in the style and methods of work of leading organs are to a large extent nourished and bred by the corresponding group interests.

This was the situation at the top of the Kazakh hierarchy, in Kolbin's view.[20]

Similarly in Dnepropetrovsk obkom, the first secretary was accused of exercising a 'bureaucratic, office-style' of leadership with little consultation or contact with the rank-and-file.[21] In the obkom bureau

> the creative atmosphere of collegial and comprehensive discussion of urgent problems gradually began to recede into the background, giving way to arbitrary not always well-considered, individual decisions. This applied particularly to the promotion and reassignment of cadres. Many appointments were decided in secret, after which the bureau members were presented with a *fait accompli*.

It is clear that the way in which party life in the command centres of the party throughout much of the country was being presented showed that all too common was a situation in which the elected party organs, and particularly party committees, were in practice of secondary importance to the non-elected party apparatus and to the first secretary. The latter frequently went his own way, consulting the committee only when he felt like it if at all.[22]

Echoes were still being heard of the corruption scandal in Uzbekistan. At the plenum of the Uzbek CC,[23] the criticisms that were made of the CPU's work at the XXVII Congress of the CPSU were acknowledged as having been correct and it was claimed that positive changes were occurring, albeit slowly. Bureau member and CC secretary R. Abdullaeva was removed, accused of having violated the principles of selection and placement of cadres, of not being objective in assessing the work of certain leaders, of having sheltered her protégés and of ignoring the work of party committees. In the view of first secretary of Tashkent obkom T. Alimov, this was possible because

> The Central Committee Bureau has not yet managed to overcome indecisiveness or abandon its wait-and-see position. Miscalculations and omissions in ideological work have been in evidence for a long time. This has been spoken of many times at bureau meetings and plena. There have been repeated visits of Abdullaeva herself. She did not admit to any errors. We bureau members must display more firmness and rid ourselves as quickly as possible of our accustomed approaches. This applies especially to the Central Committee secretaries, and above all to first secretary I. Usmankhodzhaev.

At lower levels of the Uzbek party too, committees needed to play a more active role instead of being passive in the face of an activist local secretary.

There were also problems at the top of the Azeri party, as expressed in the CC plenum in April.[24] It was declared that although the party was coming to grips with the deficiencies that had characterised it,

> the inertia of old habits in cadre policy is still strong. Trust is frequently replaced by mindless credulity, which is essentially lack of control and all-forgiveness. The promotion of cadres for reasons of personal loyalty or friendship or by virtue of coming from the same region or being related has not been successfully eliminated. A kind of closed ruling elite has formed in Agdzhabedinskii raion. As they replace each other the leaders there take turns holding a range of nomenklatura posts. Having worked a year or two or even just a few months, they are dismissed at their own request and soon reappear in another official post.

Sometimes, having taken up a responsible post, a person 'begins to be concerned not so much for business as for how to derive creature comforts and material benefits from his post. A kind of displacement of the scale of values occurs.' Where there is no collegiality in leadership, 'ostentation, keeping quiet about shortcomings, gross distortions in work with cadres, lack of principle, embezzlements, and exaggerated data invariably appear with time.'

Towards the end of April, a *Pravda* editorial[25] discussed the results of the January plenum and its reception in the party as a whole. It reported that party organisations were taking up and discussing the themes raised at the plenum and that increased democracy was evident in the operation of some party organisations. 'Party committee plena and meetings must be held in a new manner. One cannot help noticing that in many places there was much more frankness, professionalism, criticism and self-criticism in the discussion.' However, some were slow to change their style and methods of work, with questions raised in the traditional way, with no militancy or desire to speak openly and honestly. *Pravda*'s evaluation was accurate as far as it went. There was extensive criticism of the state of affairs in the party at some meetings, but even here the course of criticism fitted into the traditional pattern: a question was broached from above and the broad parameters set, after which party bodies at various levels raised these questions within their own particular contexts. There was little extension of the terms of the debate by these lower-level party meetings,[26] and there was no clear pattern of support for the specific institutional changes championed by Gorbachev at the plenum,[27] at least not in the published reports.

The limited way in which these questions were being discussed in party fora was clearly expressed in a letter cited in *Pravda* at the end of May.[28] The writer argued that all party members should be equal before the party Rules and that those in higher positions were not always correct. Everyone should be able to express their viewpoint, but the mentality of not objecting to one's superiors was still strong in the party. The plena of local party committees had clearly changed substantially:

> There was less ostentation and more criticism and professionalism. But one thing clung on quite strongly: criticism of republic, oblast, city or raion leaders was still a rare phenomenon. Particularly criticism of so-called top people. The phenomenon is so rare that at many plena there are simply no cases of criticism. True, a new approach has appeared. At certain plena the first secretary, delivering this report, provides a brief assessment of the work of the bureau members, including his own work. This is a critical assessment, with the accent on what ought to be rectified. That is undoubtedly progress. But why does none (literally none!) of the speakers discuss the shortcomings in the work or behaviour of the first secretary? Does this brief one-line self-criticism really cover everything? I doubt it somehow.

Proceedings should not be scripted; there should be frank, open and principled discussion without excessive deference to authority. People must learn to accept views that are at variance with their own.

On the eve of the June 1987 CC plenum a resolution entitled 'On Serious Shortcomings in the Tashkent Oblast Party Organisation's Work on Party Admissions and Strengthening the Party's Ranks' was published.[29] This acknowledged that the obkom had been taking measures to restructure the activities of party committees and PPOs, to overcome the violations and abuses of the past and to foster an atmosphere of openness, criticism and self-criticism and a responsible attitude to work. But the measures had been half-hearted, insufficiently consistent in nature and had not had the desired impact. They had not taken account of the fact that many shortcomings resulted from the failure of party organisations to keep to principled positions. This was linked with distortions in the practice of forming party ranks and deterioration in their quality. Many party organisations sought artificially to boost membership and took in many 'infected with a private ownership mentality, subject to careerism, with a penchant for receiving flattery and presents, and drunkards.' Many party organisations had stopped monitoring the work of the apparatus, while an atmosphere of permissiveness and mutual cover-ups prevailed in some organisations. More exacting standards needed to be set for entry to the party.

The charges in this resolution are interesting. They imply that deficiencies in the state of health of the party relate to an indiscriminate recruitment policy. The further question of whose interests were served by such a policy was not broached, but this was clearly central to the issue of local power and accountability, which remained the focus of the measures Gorbachev had espoused at the January plenum.

Another resolution was adopted on the Kazakh party in mid-July.[30] It declared that under the old leadership there were serious short-comings in the work of the party organisation, but proper conclusions had not been drawn in the republic. 'Ostentation and glorification continued to thrive, achievements were exaggerated, results were not assessed critically, and failures and shortcomings were hushed up. A false impression of the true state of affairs was thus created and sentiments of national egoism and complacency appeared among some cadres.' Crude mistakes in cadre policy occurred.

> During the selection and appointment to leading posts, nationality, family and regional ties, and personal servility were frequently the decisive factors rather than political, professional or moral qualities. In an atmosphere of cliquishness and back scratching, a considerable number of key posts in party, state, and economic organs, scientific institutions, and educational establishments were occupied by careerists, sycophants and toadies. A moral degeneration of a proportion of the cadres took place.

The party's rules must be applied strictly in cadre questions, and 'Protectionism and the selection of personnel according to family, tribal, parochial and friendship criteria must be resolutely eradicated.'

### Increasing pressure for democratisation

The CC plenum which met at the end of June 1987 discussed the restructuring of economic management. Gorbachev clearly saw this plenum as an important opportunity to press ahead with his reform of the party. In his address to the plenum,[31] Gorbachev declared that the party needed to recognise that a diversity of interests existed in the society and that instead of being 'out of touch with the dominant moods and lagging behind the dynamic processes now developing in society', the party must be restructured in order to give leadership to the economic, social and spiritual processes in society as a whole. He claimed that while there was deep understanding of these processes in the Politburo, there had been shortcomings in practical work and instances of major decisions being fulfilled slowly or incompletely. As a result, the Politburo and Secretariat should regularly review the implementation of key decisions as a means of controlling their fulfilment. The existing system of control was declared to be inefficient, closely linked with departmental and parochial interests, and dependent upon those organisations which were to be controlled in the first place. Seats of inertia and sluggishness remained at the local level, with Armenia and Gorkii oblast being cited as performing unsatisfactorily. Some local officials were accused of shifting the burden of change onto higher authorities and waiting for assistance from those higher up. Gorbachev called on the departments of the CC 'to act in a new way in a new situation, exerting deeper influence on the state of affairs in the republican, territorial and regional party organisations, and supervising enactment of the decisions of the CPSU Central Committee'.

Gorbachev pressed the need for democratisation and openness, and charged that those opposed to democratisation were afraid of being subject to society's control, refusing to accept criticism and believing themselves to be infallible. He also called for combatting attempts to use openness to attain narrow, self-serving aims. In Gorbachev's view, the forthcoming report and election meetings in PPOs should focus on how party organisations were functioning and how individual communists were participating in reform. The most active supporters of social change, those who were aware of the demands of the time and willing to work for change, should become leaders of the party organisations. All party bodies, even those not scheduled for re-election, were called upon to hear reports about their efforts to direct and supervise perestroika. These meetings should be an important stage in the run-up to a party Conference, the first since 1941, to be held at the end of June 1988. The agenda for this conference was to include measures for more democratisation in the party and the tasks of the party organisation in promoting the process of perestroika. The plenum resolution on the conference[32] reaffirmed Gorbachev's view that the task of the conference would be, *inter alia*, to introduce 'measures for the further democratisation of the life of the party and society', and declared that when delegates were elected in April and May 1988, they would be elected by secret ballot at party plena.

Gorbachev's speech and the formal decisions of the plenum are interesting. The main thrust of Gorbachev's comments attributes responsibility for the slow pace of democratisation and perestroika to foot-dragging among lower level officials. The clear reluctance to move too far in this direction on the part of members of the top leadership was not openly mentioned. However, the proposal to convene an all-union conference was motivated in part by a desire to circumvent officially-based opposition by appealing to rank-and-file support. In this sense, Gorbachev's strategy was to outflank entrenched opposition within the party structure by using secret ballot elections to encourage those who supported reform to send sympathetic delegates to the conference and thereby stimulate further change. He also hoped that this would enable the partial renewal of the CC by the conference, strengthening the position of pro-reform forces by replacing the 'dead souls' with more committed members.[33] But given this strategy, Gorbachev's silence on the question of multi-candidate elections is surprising. It may be that, tactically, he had to remain silent on this because of the strength of opposition forces at the top of the party. Certainly his espousal of multi-candidate elections in January had placed the initial reform coalition under considerable strain, with some members of it possessing real reservations about the implications of such a move. As that reform coalition became even more unravelled toward the end of 1987 with the Yel'tsin affair (see below), the balance of forces within the Politburo became even more unfavourable for a radical reform programme.[34] Once again the only way of maintaining momentum for change in the period leading up to the conference was through the press.

Deficiencies in the leadership and the failure of ordinary members to expose such deficiencies was one cause of complaint. The first secretary of Kursk gorkom was dismissed for tapping the telephone conversations of the head of the gorkom's general department whom he suspected of being the source of leaks from meetings, yet the younger people in the apparatus had remained quiet about this breach of the law.[35] According to Ukrainian party leader Shcherbitskii,[36] many obkom secretaries and bureau members were not setting an example in developing democratic forms of work, in criticism and self-criticism. Moreover, 'The role of plena and party meetings has been belittled, they are often orchestrated, and have not become a tool for invigorating communists and for developing a genuinely collective opinion'. In Armenia,[37] despite continuing concern by the CC CPSU,

> party committees and PPOs make a superficial and uncritical assessment of the state of affairs and display self-satisfaction and complacency. Not every opportunity is used to overcome such negative phenomena as bribe-taking, speculation, acquisitiveness and protectionism. However, instead of resolutely combatting these and other shortcomings, they have delayed, revelling in individual successes. Expressions of optimism from the platform can be said to have prevailed everywhere.

Similarly, in an interview Turkmen first secretary Niiazov[38] acknowledged that until recently the judgement of leaders was made according to 'kinship, hometown favouritism, and, finally, servility and sycophancy', and that there had been instances of 'lawlessness, protectionism and patronage', of corruption and bribery.

At the Leningrad obkom plenum[39] party leader Solov'ev called on the obkom bureau to be more efficient in ensuring implementation of decisions, a development which would lead to increased demands being placed on gorkoms and raikoms. These, some of which were restructuring themselves very slowly, were to be certified during the year. He then declared that the party oblast organisation had reacted positively to the January plenum. It had recognised the need to move away away from petty tutelage and *podmena* in the economy, and from departmentalism and parochialism in the activity of sector departments and gorkom and obkom secretaries. He also noted the need to improve the structure of the party apparatus and the performance of PPO secretaries. The January plenum was not discussed in terms of Gorbachev's proposals for democratisation.

In mid-1987 elections were held for the soviets under a new electoral law providing for competitive contests.[40] A raikom first secretary was interviewed in the press on the results of the competitive elections.[41] He reported that some leading personnel had not been elected, but that they were those people who continued to operate in the old way; some party workers in the apparatus sought to act in the old way during the campaign and had suffered accordingly. He said that there had been some attempts to manipulate meetings and act in a commandist fashion.

While the press was full of such criticisms, there were also reports of successful change in the party in accord with some of the demands of the January plenum. In the Estonian party it was declared[42] that although the style could still improve, 'there is less petty tutelage, inappropriate interference and paper-shuffling'. In the Central Asian republics the continued existence of problems was acknowledged along with improvements in the party's work style.[43] According to *Pravda*[44] many party committees were changing their style of work in accord with the CC instruction, with fewer sessions, a more businesslike approach to the conduct of meetings, a reduced number of resolutions and documents sent to lower level organs, the absence of joint resolutions with soviets, greater attention to the opinions of the people and the collective, and greater availability of officials to the populace. In addition, the apparatus had been renewed to a significant degree in party committees; in some Moscow raikoms it had been renewed by more than 60 per cent over the last two years, a level of change reflecting the activity of Boris Yel'tsin (see below).

Nevertheless the tone remained one of continuing criticism of deficiencies. In Khabarovsk kraikom[45] secretaries and chiefs of departments were only slowly eliminating ingrained stereotypes in their work, were poorly eradicating the wilful command style of leadership, were engrossed in economic questions, and had not switched over to political methods of work. Some party committees were criticised[46] for failing to exercise satisfactory leadership over subordinate party organs. According to an editorial in the party press,[47] 'Restructuring in party work is not proceeding without mistakes and failures. Sometimes people seek to eschew obsolete forms but do not know how to act differently. As a result, formalism appears once again.'

In late October the CC adopted a resolution[48] based on the decision of the June plenum that party committee plena and meetings of communists were to be held to discuss the reports of elected party organs and their secretaries on the leadership of restructuring. Committees were called on to make an exacting evaluation of their own activity to ensure that it did not lag behind developments in society. Those 'who are delaying restructuring must be named'. Plena and meetings were to be held between November 1987 and January 1988. CCs, kraikoms and obkoms were called upon to ensure 'that the reports of elected party organs and their secretaries are conducted in a spirit of Bolshevik openness, glasnost' and constructive criticism and self-criticism, on a truly democratic basis, without allowing meetings to be turned into orchestrated sessions.' Effective leadership of perestroika is the criterion whereby the performance of party organs is to be evaluated. The report of the resolution then turned to the question of democratisation: 'During the reports measures must be elaborated to ensure in-depth democratisation in every party organisation and the assertion in the party milieu of an atmosphere of true comradeship, freedom of discussion and unity of communists' actions. Opinions must also be exchanged on questions of the further development of democracy in the party and society as a whole.' No mention was made of specific measures to achieve this end.

The central criticism of the performance of lower level party organs was maintained. Tatar obkom was accused[49] of failing to act upon the numerous criticisms of and complaints about its performance, particularly 'complaints about violations of party principles with regard to cadre selection, unworthy behaviour by officials, selfish abuses, waste, embezzlement, and incorrect distribution and illegal acquisition of housing'. The embellishment of reality through false reporting, red tape and bureaucratic attitudes, the refusal to monitor individual responsibility and the rejection of criticism and persecution of critics was attacked. Above all, the obkom was accused of paying insufficient attention to letters from below which had complained about these problems.[50] Vyborgskii raikom in Leningrad was accused[51] of failing to give adequate leadership to perestroika and to oppose those who obstruct it. The committee was not actively involved in the struggle for perestroika, instead spending too much time on planning at the expense of living work with people.

In mid-November, at an early stage of the wave of party plena that occurred in late 1987–early 1988, *Pravda* returned to the centrality of party principledness for the success of perestroika.[52] It declared that merely raising one's voice against those responsible for evil was inadequate; action had to be taken against them. However, it cited a report of a study from Novosibirsk which showed that many party members 'prefer not to make criticisms because sometimes nobody reacts to them and no measures are taken and the critics only suffer unpleasantness'. More support needed to be given to criticism and self-criticism. At report and election meetings, what was needed was strict demandingness, not compliments and mutual applause. It is clear that

> mutual relations among workers based on servility and sycophancy have to this day not been eliminated in the apparatus of some party, soviet and economic bodies. Here you still find a collection of rules which can essentially be described as 'Know your place'. There are leaders who are unashamedly proud of the obedience of their subordinates, who unthinkingly carry out any assignments but are totally incapable of initiative. This kind of style does not accord with the spirit of the times. Party-minded, civic activeness is today demanded of everyone.

PPOs must be at the forefront of this. The message in *Pravda* was clear: there must be more rank-and-file activism and criticism of their leaders.

In the last months of 1987 and the early months of 1988, reports appeared about the plena that were held by party organisations throughout the country. For the most part these reports presented a balanced evaluation of both the recent performance of the party organisation and the conduct of the plenum itself. While criticisms of deficiencies in performance were aired, rarely were they full-blooded and they were almost always balanced by praise of the good points or emphasis upon the way in which the party was acting to rectify those problems. In Belgorod oblast,[53] for example, the organisation's past record was said to be one of 'Corruption, bribery and nepotism affecting the highest echelons of power, that now familiar style whereby hospitality meant banquets, an exchange of experience meant snacks of black caviar, an awkward customer was fired with a twitch of the chief's eyebrow, and blind allegiances and endless toadyism were honoured.' But, said the report, the plenum had been well prepared; the report's main points were published well in advance, party members were able anonymously to fill in questionnaires about their leaders, and there had been frank, uninhibited and constructive discussion. There had also been criticism of the patriarchal party custom whereby a secretary's authority was extended into literally all spheres of life, petty tutelage and a commandist style of leadership. The Tashkent party organisation was reported[54] to have taken to heart the criticisms made of it by the CC and to be conducting a certification of all members of the party organisation. The plenum itself differed from 'the old sessions 'rehearsed' down to the minutest detail' and was characterised by the rejection of attempts to browbeat critics at the plenum.[55] In the Kemerovo obkom plenum,[56] the gorkoms and raikoms were said to 'sometimes lack energy, efficiency and initiative, and have not fully overcome elements of bureaucracy and the strong-arm decree style of work.'

An unsatisfactory leadership style was a cause for frequent complaint. The Kazakh plenum was again the scene of criticism:[57]

> For decades the weeds of protectionism, nepotism and the omnipotence of old bonds had choked cadres to an appreciable extent. Not every weed has been uprooted. At the beginning of last year, [1987] while attempting to normalise the moral and psychological climate in the republic and treat cadres with the greatest possible care, the Central Committee Bureau was in no hurry to rearrange leading personnel. After all, some of them had originally been promoted through knowing the right person and, despite this, were holding posts they did not deserve. Now the plenum has admitted that life has shown this attitude to be a mistake. Not at all because these people are deliberately sabotaging the perestroika process, although this has been known to happen. No, most of them have been objectively unable to work in line with the demands of the time, as they are prevented from doing so by the burden of old stereotypes and obligations to those who wrongly gave them leading posts.

In Belorussia[58] there had been 'relapses into the old style. There are still people who love to command, to supplement everyone and everything, instead of developing people's activeness and coordinating their activity through party organisations.' In Magadan

> it was noted at the plenum, an authoritarian and administrative-command style prevailed in the work of the bureau and the obkom apparatus. The oblast party headquarters must be credited with having changed its methods of leadership. Collective leadership, glasnost, and businesslike, principled criticism are now taking root in the work of the bureau.[59]

In Alma Ata[60] 'Communists have mounted a decisive offensive against the phenomena of stagnation, protection, nepotism, violations of the principles of social justice and socialist legality, and bureaucracy', but 'The administrative-pressure style of work has still not been eradicated in the obkom secretariat and bureau, words do not tally with actions, little is being done to verify on the spot the effectiveness of the measures adopted, mistakes are being committed in cadre work, and not enough is being done to improve the situation in the economic sphere'. In Azerbaijan it was declared that 'positive changes have taken place in the cadre corps during the period under review. The struggle against manifestations of protectionism, promotions to leadership positions on the basis of family ties, home town favouritism, or personal loyalty, and other violations of party principles of cadre policy had been intensified. A number of related officials had been dismissed from leadership positions, including officials in the Central Committee apparatus, soviet and law enforcement organs, and the trade network. More than 400 officials on the Azerbaijan Communist Party Central Committee nomenklatura had been relieved of their posts in the last two years, one-fourth of them for having totally failed to cope with their work.[61]

Some criticism was directed specifically at particular institutions. In Belorussia[62] CC departments were accused of adhering to narrow departmental interests, getting bogged down in current economic matters and usurping others, losing perspective and being unable to predict and regulate the processes taking place, and sometimes failing to analyse events in committees and departments within their supervision. The Estonian CC departments were accused of failing to monitor the fulfilment of party decisions sufficiently closely.[63] In Poltava[64] weaknesses in democratisation were caused 'primarily by the lack of mutual exactingness and strictness in the activity of the obkom bureau', while in Ukraine more generally the CC and Bureau were accused of being too concerned with decision-making and not enough with the verification of their implementation.[65] In Zaporozh'e[66] the obkom was accused of giving insufficient attention to the economy and of lacking a real picture of what was happening on the ground. The party apparatus did not do sufficient to remedy this. Furthermore according to the report, 'The present party apparatus structure fetters initiative and the possibility for manoeuvre, it was noted at the plenum. It almost seems to be purpose-built for a highhanded administrative work style.' The plenum declared that the structure and staff of the apparatus should be decided by the bureau of the relevant party committee, not by the CPSU CC, and that this proposal should be discussed at the XIX Conference. In Leningrad too the apparatus came under criticism,[67] for isolation from the PPOs, slowness in mastering political methods of leadership, and for podmena. But the work of the apparatus had also improved:

> The style of the obkom apparatus' work is changing, there has been a significant cutback in document circulation and the number of conferences and sessions held, the number of questions referred by departments to the bureau and secretariat has been reduced by almost one-half, and party gorkoms and raikoms have been given more independence in determining forms of work on resolutions from higher-ranking organs.

There was also a problem with the way the plenum itself was conducted in some areas. The Lithuanian CC plenum was characterised[68] by an absence of a critical thrust: 'Many speeches, prepared in advance, smacked of self-justification, or were devoted to petty issues, or resembled . . . economic shopping lists.' But such a smooth atmosphere did not always go undisturbed. The case of Armenia is a good one. The CC CPSU plenum of June 1987 had criticised the Armenian party for a whole series of abuses, but when first secretary K.S. Demirchian addressed the plenum of the Armenian CC, his report, while containing some critical elements, was largely complacent.[69] He was followed by a string of speakers whose comments also were not critical. But then two speakers, both from within the Armenian party, launched stinging attacks on the Demirchian leadership. One declared that there was widespread bribery and protection of well-placed individuals by the republican law enforcement organs while the other accused the party leadership of bribery, protectionism and corruption and called on Demirchian to resign. The result of these speeches was widespread condemnation (by twenty-four speakers) of the second of these critics and calls for his expulsion from the party. These events were the subject of a later report in *Pravda*[70] which came out in support of the two critics. This report was used to highlight the bribery, corruption, embezzlement, and lack of criticism and party principle that had existed at all levels of the Armenian party.

In some plena, certain individuals were singled out for criticism. In Latvia it was the members of the CC Bureau for failures in their leadership style and performance.[71] In many plena the first secretary indulged in a self-criticism, acknowledging faults in his recent performance.[72] However, in most cases such criticism seems to have been bland and ritualistic.[73] Criticism was also often directed at lower level party authorities,[74] and this tended to be much more severe than that directed at individuals at the top. The contrast between the strength of the criticism directed at lower levels and the absence of such criticism from below of those above them was striking.

Many of the plena adopted ritualistic invocations of democratisation as the cure for their ills. Some posed specific proposals for enhancing democratism in the party. At the Donetsk obkom plenum, one member proposed the direct election of raikom and gorkom secretaries by all party conference delegates rather than just the members of elected bodies,[75] a proposal endorsed for discussion by the Zaporozh'e obkom plenum.[76] The Poltava organisation was called upon, *inter alia*, to boost the role of plena, to create an atmosphere at plena that was conducive to free and frank exchange of views and an objective evaluation of the work performed by bureau members and secretaries, and to increase accountability.[77] In the resolution from the Ukrainian plenum,[78] there was even a call for the 'widespread use of competitive principles' in the 'development of democratic forms of work with cadres.' It was also announced at the Ukrainian plenum that during 1987, 42 per cent of secretaries were elected from among several candidates, although not all of these may have been elected in a secret ballot.[79] In Azerbaijan first secretary Bagirov declared 'A number of party raikom secretaries were elected by secret ballot from among several candidates',[80] a formulation whose vagueness is perhaps more graphic than what is actually said.

The centre published its evaluation of these meetings in mid-February 1988.[81] It declared that the reports published in November–January reflected

> a fundamentally new phenomenon in party practice. For the first time on an all-embracing scale the elected organs were obliged to carry out a searching evaluation of their own activity and report not 'in general terms', but in concrete detail; to report sincerely and exhaustively; to report on the cause and in the name of the cause . . . In the majority of party organisations the discussion of the reports, as envisaged by the

corresponding CPSU Central Committee resolution, took place in a spirit of the utmost frankness, true democracy, glasnost', profound analysis and constructive criticism and self-criticism. Often, judging by reports from the localities, it was tough going both for those who were criticised and for those doing the criticising.

Many who had been found unable to cope or who had compromised themselves were removed from office, while communists 'openly condemned the tendency to put on a show, formalism, and the attempts, in the guise of stepping up monitoring, to revive command and control methods and petty tutelage over everyone and everything, phenomena that are manifesting themselves in the course of the resolution of new tasks'. However,

> even at meetings, conferences and plena of special political signifi-
> cance it proved impossible to avoid 'going over old ground'. It
> emerged that in many party organisations and their leaderships
> perestroika is still replaced by futile but reassuring talk, while sharp
> words and truthful criticism are relegated to the smoking room, so to
> speak, the open air. Say what you like out there, people say, but don't
> mount the platform! Once again those who are skilled in turning
> businesslike discussions into orchestrated 'measures' made their
> presence felt in some places. Many people are finding it hard to get rid
> of the habit of using the platform for routine self-praise and reports of
> victories and for parasitical requests and compliments to presidium
> members . . . in the course of the report campaign higher party organs
> repeatedly had to resort to extreme measures – stopping and in
> essence revoking discussions that did not hit the target and holding
> them again. As a rule both the primary party organisation secretaries
> and the representatives of party committees who were present were
> called strictly to account for the low standard of meetings.

This evaluation of the meetings followed the standard and well-established Soviet format of the discussion of party affairs: there were some areas that needed improvement, but overall the performance of party organs was satisfactory.[82] In this sense, the report did not constitute that thorough-going analysis and critique of party life central to Gorbachev's concept of intra-party democracy. Furthermore the reports of these meetings hardly reflect a party which was bubbling with democratic enthusiasm.[83] Rather they suggest that for the most part local leaders were able to control proceedings, certainly allowing a greater degree of criticism than may have been evident in the past, but not the sort of full-blooded democratic party life that Gorbachev had espoused in January 1987. This impression is strengthened by the figures for competitive elections: during 1987, competitive elections with more than one candidate were held in 253 PPOs throughout the country;[84] in the report and election campaign, only 3 obkom first secretaries, 20 other obkom secretaries and 20,500 PPO secretaries were removed.[85] It is difficult not to conclude that, at least for many parts of the party, the rhetoric of democracy was used to clothe the maintenance of traditional power structures.

But if the report and election campaign served to underline how little progress democratisation had made inside the party since the January 1987 plenum, the obvious continuing dissatisfaction with the way lower level party organs were performing continued to provide impetus for this campaign. It was now maintained through the debates leading up to the party conference and by the process of election of conference delegates.

### Preparations for the XIX Conference

Between the announcement of the conference and the opening of that assembly, a wide-ranging debate on party reform took place within the pages of the party press, particularly during late 1987 and the first half of 1988 when the elections for delegates were to occur. *Kommunist*, the theoretical journal of the CC, was a leader in this debate.[86] Among the issues discussed were: multi-candidate elections and tenure limits for all party posts;[87] mandatory turnover levels;[88] age limits for office-holding, with sixty-five suggested for members of the Politburo and Secretariat;[89] the loosening of Politburo and Secretariat control over the proceedings of CC plena to enable more CC members to take part in those proceedings;[90] CC plena should be more open;[91] direct election of all secretaries by the conference/congress/plenum;[92] election of the General Secretary should not be the preserve of a small group but should be conducted through national ballot, or secret ballot by congress delegates, or by general party referendum, or by the party congress followed by nomination as state president and confirmation in that post by nationwide secret ballot;[93] the party apparatus should be reduced in size;[94] and the nomenklatura was criticised for the way it rendered officials free from notions of accountability.[95] One letter published in *Pravda*[96] argued that elected organs were passive because their composition was decided by the apparatus, which presented a list to the conference/plenum which merely adopted it, and therefore those who fitted in with the apparatus rather than the real fighters for causes tended to be elected.[97] Therefore, the author argued, all secretaries should be elected by secret ballot directly at the conference. Another correspondent, published in the same issue of *Pravda*, declared that such a process of electing the first secretary would give him a mandate independent of the committee as a whole and thereby reduce his responsibility to it. Another correspondent referred to the 'cult of the leader' that existed throughout party organisations, with the leader's opinion being imposed upon the collective,[98] while another complained about the concentration of too much power in the hands of a first secretary and saw a limited tenure of two terms as a possible answer to this.[99] There was also criticism of podmena[100] and a call for ' "party pluralism", that is freedom of debate within the party on all questions of party and state life, with a guarantee against accusations of revisionism, opportunism, the creation of, 'anti-party', blocs and so forth, and with these guarantees being written into the party Statutes'.[101]

This debate reached its formal pinnacle with the publication at the end of May 1988 of the CC Theses for the conference.[102] Among the theses were the following:

1 Freedom of debate on all issues, followed by concerted action after a majority decision is reached.
2 Precise delimitation of functions between party and state.
3 Radical restructuring of PPOs to ensure they carry out their functions and exercise their democratic rights.
4 The life of party organisations must be characterised by openness, debate, criticism and self-criticism, party comradeship and discipline, collectivism and personal responsibility.
5 More exacting demands must be made of party entrants and the opinion of work collectives must be considered in the question of party entry.
6 The social and political posture of every communist must be reviewed at open party meetings before the next congress.
7 In the formation of elected party bodies, there must be genuine competition, wide discussion of candidates and voting by secret ballot. In elections to all party committees, communists will be able to nominate more candidates than there are positions to be filled. This will apply at all levels from the raion and city to the CC CPSU.
8 All party committees must have a standard term of five years. No communist may hold an elected post for more than two terms unless a three fourths vote of the party committee concerned permits a candidate to stand for a third term. Voting must be by secret ballot.
9 Collectivism must prevail in the working of the CC. New forms

of collective work of CC members between plena should be considered.

10 There should be provision for partial replacement of CC members between congresses.

11 Party functionaries must be strictly subordinate and accountable to elected party bodies, while bureaucracy, communist conceit and unwarranted secrecy in party life must be eliminated.

12 Personnel questions should be resolved in a principled way through election.

13 Control and auditing work within the party should be concentrated in one organ.

These Theses constituted a wideranging programme for change in the party. However, they were not as radical as some of the proposals that had arisen in the party-wide discussion. On three points in particular there seemed to have been a drawing back from more radical positions: the Theses made provision for competitive elections without making them compulsory, they allowed for nomination of candidates by the rank-and-file without making this mandatory, and there was no provision for the direct election of bureaux and secretaries by the conference/congress. Nor did the Theses draw the logical conclusion from their support for competitive elections – the right to organise factions inside the party.[103] In this way the Theses constituted a compromise; they drove the reform debate further, but when it came to the more radical areas of reform, they were permissive rather than mandatory. They permitted reform to take place if local power-holders desired it, but they provided sufficient room for those power-holders to avoid the implications of the proposals if they so wished. The election of delegates to the Conference showed that many local power-holders were only too willing to use their power to subvert the thrust of these reforms.

The procedure for election of delegates had been broadly specified at the June 1987 plenum.[104] Delegates were to be elected by secret ballot at plena of union republican CCs, krai and oblast committees; in Ukraine, Uzbekistan, Belorussia and Kazakhstan they would be elected by oblast plena. In practice, nominations were made at the grassroots, in the PPOs and labour collectives, and were sent to the raion and city party organisations for approval before being voted upon at the krai, oblast or republican levels. This meant that the middle and upper levels of the apparatus could act as a sieve, preventing unsatisfactory candidates from appearing on the ballot paper. Such manipulation of the delegate-selection process was widespread.

In most parts of the country, the election of delegates proceeded in much the same pattern that Soviet elections had always followed. Party leaders handed down a list of candidates, equal in number to the positions to be filled, which the electors voted in to office. Any nominations of which the leaders did not approve were not included in the ballot. However unlike in the past, this process did not always go smoothly. In Moscow, a large number of outspoken supporters of perestroika initially were to be excluded from the ballot, but as a result of public pressure and the intervention of Gorbachev, some were finally included in the vote and gained election to the conference.[105] In Sakhalin, popular discontent with the performance of the local first secretary led to mass meetings (one with some 4,800 in attendance) which culminated in him being sacked as first secretary and losing his mandate as a conference delegate.[106] In Omsk there was a public protest by some 8,000 people about the way the local authorities had chosen their own people as delegates without consulting the rank-and-file,[107] while in Yaroslavl public protests led to the dropping from delegate status of a former obkom secretary who had been nominated by the current oblast leadership.[108]

This sort of rejection of nominations from above, while it did not occur in many instances across the country, received national publicity through the press. It was accompanied by warnings about the way the selection process was being manipulated.[109] According to one reader's letter, 'the party apparatus locally is doing everything possible to put forward the candidates it has selected. This is considerably assisted by the accepted procedure of the multilevel selection of candidates at party committee, raikom and republican central committee bureau levels. Instead of electing candidates in PPOs, the alleged discussion and support of appointed candidates is often organised.'[110] Gavriil Popov, future mayor of Moscow, criticised the way the apparatus sought to protect its own interests by subverting the democratic process and remaining deaf to Gorbachev's view of the way delegates should be chosen.[111] The apparatus was accused of playing 'games' with delegate selection.[112]

Despite these criticisms, the official evaluation of the conduct of the delegate selection process was positive. According to first deputy chief of the CPSU CC Organisational Party Work Department, E. Z. Razumov,[113] 'no deviations at all from the delegate election procedure established by the CPSU Central Committee or violations of the prerogatives of local party committees were allowed to occur.' He declared that the CC has no information at all indicating that the procedure it laid down for election of delegates was violated in any substantial way. True, not all party committees proved sufficiently prepared for solving those questions in an atmosphere of openness, broad glasnost, and genuine consultation with the party and nonparty masses. Unfortunately, there were some irregularities and instances of formalism.

And again, in some cases plena 'limited themselves to the number that party committees were entitled to elect according to the set norm of representation. This procedure may or may not be to everyone's liking, but there were no deviations from the procedure established by the CPSU Central Committee or from party statutes.' The complacency of Razumov's evaluation simply reflects the deficiencies in the official procedure for delegate selection and the scope provided for manipulation of that process. Despite the calls for the Conference not to be dominated by old-style apparatchiks,[114] the course of the delegate selection process ensured that delegates acceptable to the power-brokers in the party apparatus would be in the majority.

### The reform coalition splits

The Conference was widely seen by both those supporting more radical reform and those who were more cautious as a crucial forum in the struggle over change. This was evident in the party leadership, where the rivalry between these two forces had become sharper during 1987–8. Paradoxically, through personnel changes, Gorbachev seemed substantially to strengthen his position during these eighteen months. Despite the apparent rebuff in the policy field sustained at the January 1987 plenum, the changes to the leadership made at this gathering seemed to strengthen Gorbachev. The plenum removed two long-time Brezhnev appointments, Kunaev from the Politburo and Zimianin from the Secretariat, and elected Yakovlev as a candidate member of the Politburo and Sliun'kov and long-time Gorbachev associate Luk'ianov as CC secretaries. At the June 1987 plenum Sokolov was removed as a candidate member of the Politburo, while Sliun'kov, Yakovlev and Nikonov were promoted to full membership and new Defence Minister Yazov became a candidate member. All three new full members of the Politburo had former associations with Gorbachev. At the October plenum Aliev was removed from full membership of the Politburo, while at the February 1988 plenum Yel'tsin was removed from candidate membership and Masliukov and Razumovskii became candidate members. At the same plenum, Baklanov became a CC secretary. This means that by the eve of the party conference only four full and two candidate members owed their current positions on the Politburo to promotion achieved before Gorbachev came to power; only two CC secretaries were in the same position. A significant proportion of those promoted under Gorbachev appear to have had former links with the General Secretary and all owed, at least in part, their advancement to the party leader. This should have meant that Gorbachev had a commanding position within the party leadership. But while there was no challenge to Gorbachev's position, the period between the January 1987 plenum and the XIX Conference was not one of the unalloyed consolidation of Gorbachev's reformist position within the party leadership.

The radicalisation of the political agenda of which Gorbachev's competitive election proposals were part (see below) deepened the differences within the elite.[115] These proposals represented a direct challenge to the power, position and privilege of responsible officials at all levels of the party, and these people transmitted their concern to sympathetic ears at the top of the party structure. Such concerns would not have been allayed by the unremitting criticism of the way the party, and particularly the party apparatus and those who filled responsible positions in it, was functioning, but given the blunting of the push for institutional change, such criticism had been the only means through which further reform could be prosecuted. The chief defender against these charges was Ligachev. While Ligachev supported the need for moderate reform and was willing to see the definition of this move in a radical direction,[116] he was much more cautious than others within the leadership and as a result of his institutional position at the head of the party apparatus was more willing to speak and act in defence of it. However, it would be misleading to see Ligachev as the leader of a consistent, coherent and clearly-defined opposition within the leadership. All members accepted the need for change, but individually their views of how far and how fast such change should be varied. Apart from Gorbachev, only Yakovlev and Shevardnadze proved in the long run to be committed to the continuing radicalisation of reform, and even these people at times had reservations and uncertainties. Among other members of the leadership, such uncertainties were stronger and more marked, and as the policy agenda became radicalised, such uncertainties naturally became stronger and more politically important.[117] The contours of leadership politics were thus fluid, characterised by tendencies in favour of further radicalisation of reform and more cautious about this question. From mid-1987, the policy front upon which tension between these different tendencies focused broadened. An important element of this was historical, and in particular the interpretation of Stalin and his role.[118] This is something which Ligachev in particular became involved in, reaching its peak with the infamous Andreeva letter of 13 March 1988 which vigorously criticised the blackening of the Soviet past and the unbalanced criticism of its achievements.[119] Differences also emerged over foreign policy,[120] while the radicalisation of economic policy during 1987[121] and the open outbreak of ethnic disputes[122] were further potential causes of leadership difference.

Throughout 1987 the tension between these two tendencies in the leadership was exacerbated by the abrasive effect of Boris Yel'tsin. Since becoming Moscow gorkom first secretary, Yel'tsin had behaved in an unorthodox fashion. Some elements of the populist style that was later to be his hallmark were already evident, but more important in the view of many was the ruthless way in which he approached personnel questions within the Moscow machine. Shortly after his arrival, he sacked the mayor of Moscow, six gorkom secretaries, fifteen of nineteen section heads, and twenty-two of thirty-three raikom first secretaries, and then shortly after brought in another round of such personnel changes.[123] To many in responsible positions this seemed to be a cavalier way of dealing with important matters, and because it directly involved the role of the apparatus in personnel questions, it brought Yel'tsin into direct conflict with Ligachev. This was reinforced by the evident personal dislike between the two men and by Yel'tsin's continuing concerns about how the apparatus was functioning under Ligachev's leadership. He had raised this matter at the XXVII Congress, and did so again at the October 1987 plenum at which the rivalry came to a head. In that plenum Yel'tsin mounted a bitter attack upon Ligachev and the way the apparatus operated, upon the speed of reform and upon the increasing glorification of Gorbachev.[124] Yel'tsin's criticisms were rejected by the plenum and he was subsequently removed from his positions as candidate member of the Politburo and first secretary of Moscow gorkom.[125]

The effect of Yel'tsin's withdrawal from the leadership was to remove the most radical force for speeding up the course of change. In this sense it weakened the tendency favouring more radical change and strengthened that which counselled caution. It also complicated Gorbachev's task; by laying bare the radical critique of continuing caution, it forced Gorbachev to balance his criticisms of the slowness of reform by criticisms of more radical demands if he wished to keep the cautious elements behind the move for continuing reform. The danger to this process was brought home to Gorbachev by the Andreeva affair and Ligachev's reputed involvement because it demonstrated the significant reservations that this key figure in the leadership had about at least some aspects of the unrolling reform programme. But the Andreeva affair also demonstrated the limits to which the campaign for more extensive reform could be prosecuted successfully through the press. If the continuing criticism of lower level party performance which had been such a highlight of the press in the eighteen months following the January plenum had shown the limited success achieved in getting the party to function in a new way, the Andreeva affair showed that the principal channel through which such a change was being pursued, the press, was not unalterably wedded to the course of radical reform. Recognition of this served to heighten the perceived importance of the forthcoming party conference and the reformers' conviction that institutional change was essential. In retrospect, it is clear that such a view of the conference was accurate: the conference was the decisive turning point in the effort to change both the organisational culture and mode of functioning of the party.

# 4    The programme for change

From the time it was first announced in June 1987, the XIX Conference was seen as an important event in the party's life. As the first such gathering since 1941, this alone would have ensured that it was seen as an unusual development. But the conflict that had been continuing in the party over the reform programme gave it an added importance. Both sides realised the potential significance the Conference had. For Gorbachev, whose more radical proposals had effectively been swept under the carpet at the January 1987 plenum, the calling of the Conference was a means of circumventing the opposition of those in the middle and upper ranks of the apparatus by appealing to the rank-and-file which, he believed, supported his democratisation proposals, and by gaining the removal of some of the more cautious elements from the CC. For supporters of the reform proposals more generally, the Conference was seen as a means of advancing those proposals and of reversing the series of rebuffs that democratisation had sustained in the preceding eighteen months. Clear rebuffs there had been: the shelving of Gorbachev's specific measures in January 1987, the sacking of Yel'tsin at the end of 1987, and the domination by the apparatus of the delegate selection process for the Conference were all setbacks, and were clearly seen as such, by supporters of democratisation. For opponents of the more radical measures of democratisation, the Conference was seen as an opportunity to stem the impetus for democratisation that had been set in train in January 1987. The compromise nature of the CC's Theses suggests that the top leadership was evenly balanced in its attitude towards the reform process. Neither side really foresaw the extent of the stimulus to change in the party that the Conference would provide.

### The XIX Conference

The keynote address to the Conference was delivered by Gorbachev.[1] The speech touched on all the areas mentioned in the CC Theses on party democratisation as well as ranging more widely over the question of state democratisation and the need for 'radically reforming the political system'. He emphasised the need for the party to overcome the 'definite deformations' that had emerged in its work and activities, the bureaucratic centralism and command style of administration that had displaced its democratic traditions. He called for decentralisation and democratisation, because one unit cannot take adequate decisions on a range of questions better tackled at lower levels, and said it was necessary 'fully to restore in the party an atmosphere of fidelity to principle, openness, discussion, criticism and self-criticism, conscientious discipline, party comradeship, unconditional personal responsibility, and efficiency.' Higher standards for party membership were declared to be necessary, and essential in obtaining certification conducted 'in the framework of a normal democratic process, at open party meetings, and not by commissions of three or five persons, not through discussions behind the scenes, nor by issuing testimonials which are not to be made public'.

Gorbachev also discussed a number of concrete proposals for reform of the party structure. He supported multi-candidate, competitive elections for all committees in the party, including the CC, and the holding of elective office for only two successive terms with a third permitted only in exceptional circumstances. He called for consideration to be given to enabling lower level organisations, at the same time they were electing congress or conference delegates, to make suggestions regarding potential candidates for election to higher level party bodies (committees and bureaux). Increasing the profile of elected organs in the party was also declared to be important. Party secretaries, bureaux and the party apparatus must always be under the control of elected party bodies, and these must in turn resolve all major questions in an open and democratic way. He devoted particular attention to the CC, although his discussion of this body was clearly meant also to apply to committees at lower levels. The members of the committee should be more active in party work, including the work of the Politburo, which ought to present regular reports on its work at CC plena. The means for CC members to become more continuously involved in party work was to be through the creation of commissions for the structuring of such activity. The party apparatus too should be reworked, with its present division by spheres of management being forsaken in favour of restructuring in line with the party's current functions. It should also be reduced in size. Finally, Gorbachev suggested a change in the position of party first secretaries. In an attempt to boost the prestige of the plenary assembly of the soviet at the expense of the executive committee, he suggested that the party first secretary be elected chairman of the soviet. This proposal meant that, once elected as first secretary, that person should stand for election as soviet chairman. If the deputies to the soviet did not elect the party first secretary as soviet chairman, 'the party committee and the communists will obviously have to draw the necessary conclusions'. This seemed to suggest that, effectively, the identity of the party leader could be determined by the deputies to the soviet and therefore in principle, potentially by non-party members. However this proposal to unite the two positions of party and soviet leader in the one individual directly contradicted another significant theme of Gorbachev's speech, that of a clear demarcation between party and state and the withdrawal of the former from the day-to-day management of the economy.

For Gorbachev, the party's withdrawal from daily management functions was not seen as a rejection of its traditional leading role in Soviet society, but an effort to define that role in a new way. It was an attempt to come to grips with the old problem of podmena, of the party making the decisions that the state should make. What was envisaged was that the practical decision-making should be located in state organs while the party would continue to exercise overall leadership through its members in these organs. This required, in Gorbachev's view, a clear demarcation of functions between party and state and the restoration of full authority to the soviets of people's deputies. The latter was to be achieved by the combination of party first secretary and chairman of the soviet, the election of the soviets in multi-candidate competitive elections, and the construction of a new national legislative structure. This was to involve a new Congress of People's Deputies to 'be convened annually to decide on the country's more important constitutional, political and socio-economic issues'. The Congress was to elect from among its number a smaller Supreme Soviet, which was to be a standing body combining all legislative and monitoring work and was to decide all legislative and administrative questions. There should also be a new, executive, presidency in the form of the Chairman of the Supreme Soviet. Gorbachev also emphasised the notion of a socialist law-governed state, in which the law was supreme; the party was to operate in accord with the law.

Gorbachev had put forward a broad agenda for reform, and many of its components came under vigorous examination at the Conference. In particular, his proposal to combine the positions of first secretary and soviet chairman was widely attacked. This was symptomatic of the Conference, which was unlike any party gathering which had preceded it. The *pro forma* speeches that had dominated all such party gatherings after 1925, with the speaker elaborating on the successes achieved in his or her area and requesting increased resources to overcome pending problems or keep up the good work, were largely absent. Instead speakers engaged in the real cut and thrust of debate. Contemporary shortcomings and failures (rather than those in the past, as formerly had been the pattern) were highlighted and criticised, the sacking of specific national leaders was called for from the floor, and other leaders including Gorbachev were criticised to their face. Perhaps the most poignant moment was when Boris Yel'tsin appealed, unsuccessfully, for his political rehabilitation.[2] Much of the course of the Conference was broadcast nationally on Soviet television. By showing the vigour with which the debate was pursued, this projected into Soviet homes both an image of the party as much more divided than its public face formerly had acknowledged, and of the sort of organisational culture which Gorbachev wished to see characterise party life. In this sense the proceedings of the Conference alone would have had a radicalising effect and thereby stimulated the course of party reform. But also important were the direct results of Conference decisions.

The Conference resolution dealing with democratisation of the party[3] reproduced most of the main points made by Gorbachev in his speech. PPOs' independence was to be enhanced, a more demanding approach to party entry (which was to be based on the individual's attitude to perestroika rather than 'according to quotas') was to be adopted, party meetings should be reanimated, the CC was to be more involved in the work of the Politburo (which was to report on its activities to CC plena), CC commissions were to be established to deal with different aspects of domestic and foreign policy, stenographic reports of plena should be published, and both elected bodies and individual members should be subject to recall by party members if their performance was considered unsatisfactory. There was to be provision for party conferences to be convened mid-way between congresses to renew committee personnel by up to 20 per cent. According to the resolution, 'The formalistic approach to the selection and placement of key personnel, an approach based on sticking to a rigid list of approved cadres, is losing its effectiveness', and therefore personnel policy must be updated and based on a democratic approach and elections. All posts must be filled by multi-candidate elections and secret ballot, while tenure in elected offices was to be restricted to two five year terms (the proposal that a third term in office be possible was dropped). Provision was made for lower level party organs to make recommendations that specific individuals be elected to party organs at higher levels, such recommendations to be carried by the delegates to the conferences and congresses that elected those higher organs. The resolution also provided for the combination of the control and auditing apparatus in an attempt to strengthen central supervision over lower level party life.[4] The party apparatus was declared to be strictly subordinate to elected organs and was to be reduced in size and made to operate more efficiently. The resolution also established the state structure outlined in Gorbachev's speech and emphasised the democratic nature that needed to characterise state organs.

Other resolutions emphasised the need to combat bureaucracy through a strengthening of democracy,[5] the need for an expansion of glasnost,[6] and the need to strengthen law and legality and the foundations of a law-governed state.[7] The decisions of the Conference posed a direct challenge to the party and its established way of operating, although it is not clear that all realised the dimensions of that challenge. The criticism of the nomenklatura style of personnel management and its replacement by competitive secret ballot elections to posts of limited tenure posed a direct threat to the established structure of power and privilege in the party. It directly threatened the power over personnel which was at the heart of the power of the party apparatus. The construction of a new legislative structure and the intention to withdraw the party from day-to-day management, allied to the desire to strengthen legal norms, threatened the dominant position the party had enjoyed in Soviet society for so long. The strengthening of glasnost threatened to open the party up to the public gaze and to public criticism even more than it had been in the immediate past, a prospect rendered even more alarming by the implications of the decision regarding competitive elections to state organs: the party may have to compete electorally. Opponents had had some success in moderating Gorbachev's proposals. Competitive elections were still only possible, not mandatory, and even when they were held nomination by the rank-and-file was not essential. The call for a review of the qualifications of all party members was dropped, and the original proposal regarding press freedom was watered down.

Nevertheless, as the Conference decisions were realised in practice, their full import was to have a dramatic effect on the party.

## The implementation of conference decisions

Implementation of these decisions began at the CC plenum at the end of July 1988. During his speech to the plenum,[8] Gorbachev repeated many of the decisions of the Conference, but he also enlarged on a couple of these issues. He declared that the provision on limited tenure was to take effect from the next set of elections, even though there would be no formal provision for this in the party Rules until they were changed at the next congress. He repeated the view that commissions should be created to enable CC members to be more continually involved in the party's work and that the party apparatus should assist elected bodies to fulfil their functions as society's political vanguard and should therefore be relieved of administrative and managerial functions. Using political methods of guidance, the party apparatus was to focus on key directions of domestic and foreign policy. Reflecting this function, its structure and composition should be changed. The establishment of commissions and the reworking of the apparatus were both directly linked with the proposed withdrawal of the party from an immediate administrative role. The resolutions of the plenum[9] confirmed many of the decisions on these issues made by the Conference and called upon party organisations to operate on the basis of them without waiting for formal amendment of the party Rules.

At the plenum a new report and election campaign to be held towards the end of the year, as recommended at the Conference, was announced.[10] This was seen as an important step in the process of democratisation: in the words of the resolution, the campaign was to 'make a maximum contribution to the further democratisation of all internal party life, to foster in party organisations an atmosphere of creative discussion, freedom of opinion, broad criticism and self-criticism, greater initiative, personal responsibility and conscious discipline of communists'. For those supporters of reform who saw the apparatus as holding up that process, the campaign was a further opportunity to weaken the apparatus by calling forth the support of the rank-and-file to break its power. According to Razumovskii, who was to become Chairman of the new CC Commission on Party Construction and Cadre Policy, the democratic means of resolving cadre questions was a combination of full glasnost, the filling of office by election and full control from below. In his view, 'this changes the very concept of the "nomenklatura" about which there are so many arguments at present. The party's cadre corps will henceforth be determined not by membership of some kind of "list", but by the free, totally unrestricted expression of the communists' will and the effective functioning of the democratic institutions of our political system.'[11] It is clear that the new provisions governing party elections were widely seen as directed at reducing the power of the apparatus.

The conditions under which the campaign was to be conducted were spelled out in August when a new 'Instruction on the Conduct of Elections to Leading Party Organs' was adopted.[12] This provided for the election of all leading party organs up to and including the CC (but excluding both primary organisations with fewer than fifteen members and the promotion of candidate to full members) by secret ballot following wide discussion of each candidate individually. Individuals were to be restricted to a two term maximum. The Instruction also provided for 'the possibility' of more candidates than there were seats on the ballot paper, competition thereby remaining possible and desirable but not mandatory. Furthermore all decisions about the identity of candidates in the discussion and nomination phase of the process were to be made by open voting. The Instruction also made provision for 'meetings of representatives of delegations' to convene before the nomination session with a view to considering candidates for the soon to be elected organ (# 17) and for the possibility of the cooptation onto committees of candidates for whom a majority would vote in a secret ballot, such cooptation to take place either on the recommendation of or with the agreement of higher standing organs (# 23). Provision for recall of non-performing people was made and five-yearly conferences with the power to renew committees by up to 20 per cent (including a national conference and the CC) was foreshadowed. The Instruction thus set in place the machinery to implement some of the democratisation measures adopted at the party Conference. But there were still clear limitations: although members could nominate candidates from the floor, the possibility of prior arranged lists existed, there was still provision for cooptation from above, much of the procedure of nomination took place in open session, multi-candidate competition was not mandatory, and the provision remained that election required only 50 per cent of the vote which, in a party election, it seemed almost impossible for a member of the apparatus to fail to attain.[13]

The report and election campaign does not appear to have been the unambiguous and powerful force for democratisation for which its proponents had hoped. Competitive elections did occur. According to

*Pravda* at the outset of the campaign, 'it is becoming more and more firmly established that communists are putting forward as leaders two and even more candidates'.[14] According to Shcherbitskii, in Ukraine nearly 66 per cent of party group organisers and secretaries in shops and PPOs were elected from two or more candidates.[15] In Moscow oblast it was reported that 25 per cent of party group organisers, 50 per cent of shop party organisation secretaries and 'almost all' PPO secretaries were elected in competitive elections.[16] Across the country as a whole, it was reported that 33 per cent of party group organisers and 50 per cent of shop and PPO secretaries were elected from two or more candidates.[17] According to Gorbachev, 1,117 gorkom and raikom secretaries and a number of secretaries of obkoms were elected in competition.[18]

These figures do not clearly establish a consistent pattern of competitive elections across the country. However, the absence of many figures for levels above that of the PPO is suggestive of the limited nature of the competitive process; once the process no longer involved direct rank-and-file participation, it was much more subject to manipulation from above. The absence of competition was also referred to by official spokesmen. According to Moscow gorkom first secretary Zaikov,[19] 'In some places there has also been reluctance to nominate more than one candidate, and attempts were made to foist convenient cadre decisions on communists.' In February A. K. Masiagin, consultant to the CC Department of Party Construction and Cadre Work, declared:

> Let us take the election of secretaries from among several candidates – this is enshrined in the resolutions of party conferences and Central Committee plena and recorded in instructions. However, are there many multi-candidate elections? Not very many as yet. What is the problem? When you ask about this, comrades say: What is the point of a second candidate? Everyone trusts the leader. But if they really do trust him, why be afraid of competition?[20]

Individual reports of single candidate elections[21] suggests that this practice remained widespread. Another reflection of the concern that some clearly had about competitive elections was provided by Moscow gorkom first secretary Zaikov.[22] He said 'Now we have fully switched to the principle of leaders being elected, we cannot allow principle to be replaced by narrow pragmatism, we cannot allow group interests to prevail over social interests, we cannot allow demagogues and careerists to force their way into leadership.' This was a thinly veiled statement of the dangers of competitive elections as perceived by someone who had everything to lose should they be implemented in full. It was a sentiment that was widely shared within the party apparatus.

Similarly there is no compelling evidence that these meetings were characterised by the wave of criticism and self-criticism for which Gorbachev had hoped, although clearly some meetings were. In late August, Politburo member Vorotnikov warned against persecution for criticism,[23] but the reports of the meetings do not suggest that vigorous criticism of the leadership was a feature of them. Turning again to Masiagin:

> How are the progress reports of many party committees and bureaux usually structured? The raikom reports back, and the PPOs are criticised; the obkom reports back, and the raion committees are on the receiving end. You will appreciate that everything is arranged topsy-turvy fashion. And we can in no way overcome this strange tradition if, instead of giving an account of ourselves, we deliver a lecture to our subordinates. It must be acknowledged that some changes have occurred, particularly in the reports made by elected organs to the 19th party Conference on the leadership of restructuring. But there has not really been a breakthrough.[24]

Despite the report about the nomination of a candidate from the floor and his subsequent election as first secretary of Pskov obkom,[25] and the vague statements about competition, party meetings during the 1988 report and election campaign generally do not seem to have been greatly different from those in earlier campaigns. The references to the 'businesslike' way in which the meetings were conducted[26] does not suggest the turmoil and conflict of the full-blooded democratic gathering.

According to Shcherbitskii, as well as very positive meetings,

> there were also meetings and conferences that followed old scenarios, that not all the meetings and conferences managed to escape the framework of habitual schedules and stereotypes and to avoid lapsing into discussions of merely production issues. Now and again, the speakers used the platforms to read dull accountability reports and to criticise in a soft way, and the adopted decisions were general and ambiguous.[27]

Many party organisations remained dominated by their leaderships who were able to manipulate the meetings to serve their own ends,[28] while *Pravda* itself acknowledged that the campaign had shown cases of meddling from above and too little independence having been given to lower organs.[29] According to six prominent reform supporters in an open letter to Gorbachev after the campaign had ended, it had been so structured that it was almost impossible to replace existing cadres with 'talented organisers'.[30]

On 24 August Gorbachev presented a draft plan for the creation of CC commissions which was adopted by the Politburo on 8 September.[31] At the September CC plenum, six commissions were foreshadowed and their chairmen named:[32]

Party Construction and Cadre policy – G. P. Razumovskii
Ideology – V.A. Medvedev
Social-economic policy – N. N. Sliun'kov
Agrarian policy – E. K. Ligachev
International policy – A. N. Yakovlev
Legal policy – V. M. Chebrikov

All the chairmen were CC secretaries at the time of their appointment to head the commissions, and all except Razumovskii were full members of the Politburo; Razumovskii was a candidate member and Medvedev was made a full member at the CC plenum. Perhaps the most important appointment here in terms of the continuing tension within the leadership over the course of perestroika was that of Ligachev. He was moved out of the ideological sphere into agriculture, an area which carried much less weight in decision-making circles than the ideology portfolio.

Full composition of the commissions was confirmed at the November plenum.[33] The commissions were declared to be means of enhancing collectivism in party leadership and of drawing members and candidate members of the CC and members of the Central Auditing Commission into regular work on the most important issues of foreign and domestic policy. They were to study problems and to prepare proposals for the CC for improving both the activities of the party and the realisation of party decisions. They were to analyse how the party was performing and make practical recommendations to party organisations and committees regarding their work. The commissions were also to prepare and present analytical materials and documents to the Politburo and CC. They were to meet when required, but no less than once every three months.

The relationship between the new commissions and the party apparatus was not clearly enunciated in the decision establishing the commissions. It did say that in their work they were to be 'supported by' the departments of the CC (and party scientific and educational institutions), while the 'organisational-technical conditions' for their work were to be ensured by the General Department and the Chancellery (*Upravlenie delami*) of the CC.[34] But at the same time the commissions were created, it was decided[35] to restructure the CC apparatus by reducing the number of CC departments from twenty to nine. The nine were to be Party work and cadres policy, Ideology, Social-economic policy, Agrarian policy, State and legal policy, International, Defence, General and Chancellery. The staff of the reorganised departmental structure was to be reduced by some 40 per cent.[36] Six of these departments correspond to commissions and were intended to do the basic housekeeping and policy research functions for these commissions, as the departments formerly had done for the Secretariat. Of the other three departments, Defence would have been designed to maintain a watching brief over the military and the general defence area while maintaining contact with the Main Political Administration, the party's organisational structure in the military. The other two would principally have performed service functions for the party's central organs. Significantly for the avowed aim of removing the party from the day-to-day administration of the economy, the Agrarian Policy Department was the only specifically economic department not to disappear as an independent entity.

Changes were also made to the party apparatus at lower levels. According to the CC it was advisable that the apparatus of the union republics, kraikoms and obkoms have departments for Organisational-party and cadre work, Ideology, Social-economic, Agrarian, State and law, General and Chancellery. Gorkoms and raikoms were to have Organisational, Ideological and General departments; gorkoms in major industrial centres could have a department for Social-economic development and those in major agricultural districts could have an Agrarian department. Obkoms, kraikoms and republican central committees could have a maximum of five secretaries, raikoms and gorkoms three. However despite the recommendations on structure, the local organs were to have the right to form their apparatus in the way which they believed best suited their particular circumstances. The staff of the apparatus of these committees was also to be reduced by up to 30 per cent with the precise percentage depending upon the category into which the party committee fell.[37] The funds thereby saved were to go into raising the salaries of those who worked in the apparatus. Once again the changes were justified by the claim that the apparatus was being brought into line with the changed functions of the party, in particular the exercise of political rather than administrative leadership.

The following months saw a number of reports about the reduction of the apparatus in various parts of the country. The reports suggest that restructuring took place along the lines suggested by the CC,[38] with a reduced number of departments, fewer staff and the establishment of commissions. There is no real discussion of how this change was carried out, although the tone of at least one interview with an oblast first secretary suggests that this was not always a smooth process.[39] Certainly many of the CC commissions do not appear to have begun work for some time after their formal creation: the first meetings of the CC commissions occurred on the following dates (all in 1989): Ideology, 27 January; Agrarian policy, 10 February; Party construction and cadre policy, 27 February; Legal policy, 13 March; International policy, 14 March; and Social-economic policy, 18 March.[40] It is likely that the changes to the structure of the party apparatus, at least in the short term, produced significant confusion.

The November 1988 plenum also reviewed and adapted the proposed amendments to the Constitution and the new election law which would bring into effect the state structure envisaged by Gorbachev.[41] The Constitution was accordingly amended in early December[42] and the election law adopted.[43] The challenge that these changes in the political system constituted was recognised in the party. In late December 1988 Shcherbitskii argued that the party needed to retain the initiative in resolving people's problems in order to combat those groups which sought to spread alien ideas of national selfishness and anti-Sovietism.[44] A month later, in discussing the forthcoming election campaign for the Congress of People's Deputies, he declared, 'the present election campaign is, on the one hand, a serious test for the political platform set forth in the CPSU Central Committee's appeal to the party and the Soviet people and, on the other, an opportunity to engage new masses in restructuring'.[45] The fear that the party was lagging behind developments in society, a fear openly stated by some,[46] increased the sense of threat and gave greater weight to the statements of people like Gorbachev that the party was necessary for the success of perestroika.[47] It is reflected in the election speech of Politburo member Vadim Medvedev:

> In a society that is renewing itself a party that is renewing itself must operate – operate as a political vanguard imparting a general direction to development, but not as a force directly controlling absolutely everything . . . The party is open both to internal debates and to the discussion of any questions with all social organisations and movements and with the non-party masses. It cannot be otherwise.

However, this presupposes that healthy principles be clearly separated from bogus anti-social aims, not to mention extremist actions – the imposition of views alien to working people's interests and attempts beneath the guise of democracy to resort to methods of pressure and diktat and to sow enmity and distrust . . . The party does not lay claim to a monopoly in seeking the best paths of social progress, it does not believe that it possesses the ultimate truth. But communists have something to defend firmly and adamantly. Namely our socialist values, our socialist choice, and our commitment to the ideas of social justice and of ensuring a better life for all Soviet people.[48]

A number of other answers to this challenge were being offered in party ranks. One, contained in a *Pravda* editorial in early October 1988,[49] called for the combatting of the pluralism of views that was developing in society through a re-emphasis on the study of Marxism-Leninism. This, it was claimed, would combat such views at the intellectual level. Another view, associated with the prominent Rector of the Higher Party School Viacheslav Shostakovskii, was the restoration of Leninist norms in the party.[50] Many saw the restoration of such norms as involving the acceleration and expansion of democracy in intra-party life. Following Gorbachev's conception of perestroika, this was envisaged as involving increased participation by the rank-and-file, an expansion of the role of the plenary bodies and committees at the expense of executive organs, and a freer flow of information.[51]

But the hope that democratisation might save the party rested on uncertain foundations. The 1988 report and election campaign had shown that apathy was common among the rank-and-file.[52] The report of the district and city party conferences held at the beginning of November[53] gave a generally positive view of developments at these levels, citing cases of competitive election[54] and of the failure of some who had not performed to gain re-election; the failure of some to gain re-election was attributed to 'command-administrative methods of work, lack of competence, separation from people, gap between word and deed, and abuse of official position'. But the report also referred to the continuing existence of many deficiencies in the operation of many of these gatherings. The limits were still clear; according to the report and despite Gorbachev's comments cited above, no gorkom or raikom secretary was elected by competitive ballot.[55] Furthermore there were reports that party membership was falling at an accelerating rate, at least in some areas.[56] But also important was the reserved commitment to democracy at the upper levels.

## Leadership tensions

The tension which had marked the relationship between the more radical and more cautious tendencies in the leadership in the months prior to the Conference remained evident both during that gathering and after it. Reference has already been made to the vigorous exchange of views and the Yel'tsin–Ligachev clash at the Conference. But perhaps more important for this general question was Ligachev's speech in which he declared the correctness of the position of that section of the leadership which he said had been crucial in Gorbachev's election as General Secretary: Chebrikov, Solomentsev, Gromyko and himself.[57] Here Ligachev was openly hinting at Gorbachev's need for the support of some of the more cautious elements in the leadership to retain his position. There was some moderation of some aspects of the drive for more radical change at the Conference: the failure to make any personnel changes and the step back from the theses regarding a membership review and press freedom show this. Also consistent with such opposition is the way Gorbachev sprang the timetable for the proposed institutional changes on the Conference at the last minute, giving that body no time to debate that timetable and its implications. Those who may have voted for the changes from a desire to adhere to the convention of party unanimity while believing that those changes could be blunted through a prolonged timetable for introduction were caught off guard by Gorbachev's manoeuvre. But this tactical victory did not remove from the leadership those concerned about the direction and speed of the changes.

Nor did the changes to the leadership at the September plenum remove the influence of more cautious counsel, despite the significant personnel reshuffling: Gromyko and Solomentsev were removed as full members and Demichev and Dolgikh as candidate members of the Politburo while Medvedev became a full member and Luk'ianov and Biriukova became candidates; Dolgikh, Dobrynin, Biriukova and Luk'ianov ceased to be CC Secretaries while Chebrikov became one. In addition, Ligachev was downgraded, with his secretarial responsibilities shifted to agriculture, and the new CC commissions were created, effectively displacing the Secretariat, which had been Ligachev's power base. At the same time Gorbachev replaced Gromyko as Chairman of the Presidium of the Supreme Soviet, or state president, with his long-time friend Luk'ianov as his deputy. These changes seemed dramatically to strengthen the position of the reformist tendency: some cautious members of the leadership had been replaced,

Ligachev had been downgraded, Gorbachev had been promoted through acquisition of the presidency, and putative supporters Medvedev and Yakovlev had taken over some of Ligachev's former responsibilities in ideological and foreign affairs. Furthermore, the driving force of the party apparatus, seen by many as the location of the stiffest opposition to reform, the Secretariat, had been significantly downgraded. But in the context of the radicalisation of the political agenda from mid-1988, such changes could not remove the influence of the more cautious, conservative tendency in the leadership.

# 5    Reform out of control

During 1989 the worst fears of those who had foreseen the potential of the changes wrought at the XIX Conference were realised. The working out of those reforms created a political situation which the party and its leadership could no longer control. From the end of March 1989, the party leadership was reactive, trying to keep up with changes which were occurring faster than it could control and propelled by political forces for the most part outside that leadership and of the party as a whole. This year saw the explosion onto the Soviet scene of a whole range of autonomous political groups whose activity called into question the party's constitutionally enshrined political monopoly and its capacity to continue to encapsulate the main stream of political activity within its bounds. While such activity had begun in 1988, most spectacularly with the mobilisation of ethnic forces in the Nagorno-Karabakh affair, it was in 1989 that non-nationalist political groups began to crowd onto the political stage. The principal vehicle for this was the changes to the national political structure adopted at the XIX Conference.

### The parliamentary challenge

The elections for the Congress of People's Deputies began on 26 March 1989.[1] The period leading up to the election saw an extensive nomination process in which, for the first time since the revolution, the populace was involved in an electoral campaign in which there was the possibility of real choice. Party managers in many areas realised the potential dangers that this held and sought to manipulate the nomination process in such a way as to deny a place on the ballot to unacceptable candidates. In many cases this simply meant candidates not chosen by the party apparatus, but in some places it had a sharper political point: it meant those who sought to push the reform process

78

further and faster than conservative elements desired. This sort of struggle occurred both in the popular constituencies and in those closed lists for public organisations;[2] the difficulties experienced by Boris Yel'tsin in a Moscow constituency and Andrei Sakharov in the Academy of Sciences are good examples of the difficulties encountered by some non-establishment would-be candidates. In many constituencies across the country, a real contest occurred between different candidates, but in many others there was no competition at all with the same number of candidates as there were seats to be filled. The Central Committee had not provided an example of competition for others to follow by nominating at its January plenum 100 candidates for the 100 seats that had been allocated to the party.[3] Even Gorbachev, who had publicly championed the cause of competition, avoided facing the voters by gaining a position on the CC's list.

When the voting was held, there was substantial voter disillusionment with the traditional style of party candidate. Although some 87 per cent of the delegates elected to the Congress were party members and many leading party figures were elected in their own right, many prominent party figures failed to gain election. In some cases official party nominations were defeated by a rival candidate, but also an astonishing 44 per cent of party candidates who stood unopposed failed to gain the required 50 per cent of the vote and therefore were not elected. Among those defeated were the mayors of Moscow and Kiev, party first secretaries in Kiev, Minsk, Kishinev, Alma Ata and Frunze, the Latvian prime minister, Lithuanian president and prime minister, some 38 regional and district party first secretaries, and almost the entire leadership in Leningrad, including first secretary and Politburo candidate member Solov'ev (who had stood unopposed). In the Baltic republics, candidates were elected only if they were supported by the local nationalist popular fronts, while in Moscow the disgraced former Politburo candidate member Boris Yel'tsin won a crushing victory (89 per cent of the vote) over his apparatus-supported rival.[4]

The party's public reaction to the election was moderate. In the evaluation provided by a *Pravda* editorial[5] it was argued that

> The CPSU's political line of restructuring and democratisation enjoys tremendous support. This was confirmed by the election campaign. Being for the first time ever the real makers of a political process, the working people deliberately gave preference to the loyal fighters for perestroika. It is gratifying that numerous party and komsomol leaders of different ranks are among those who won the mandate of people's trust . . .

But the editorial also noted that 'people lose their trust in officials who detach themselves from the masses, disregard their needs and opinions, and are slow in restructuring themselves. Why, for example, did leading party and soviet officials fail to gain the required number of votes at the elections in Leningrad? The same also happened in Kemerovo, Kiev, Tomsk and some other cities and oblasts.' The lesson to be drawn from this was that

> Only radical changes in the style and methods of work, only a struggle waged in collectives against bureaucratism and the inertia of administrators' ardour will ensure advancement of the cause and the party officials' prestige among the masses. This is well realised by many communists in leadership positions. They no longer wish to tolerate the lagging of their enterprises, regions, departments or sectors. Those who do nothing to overcome the difficulties will, sooner or later, find themselves by the wayside. Party committees (and this is a sign of the times) are stepping up demandingness toward communists regarding end results . . . By getting rid of inert workers who discredit the party with their lack of professional skills or their inaction, party committees are supporting authoritative and talented personalities. Moreover, this work is being done with mandatory consideration for the people's opinion. The time demands renewal of the content and methods of party work.

The basic message of the *Pravda* editorial was that the party was lagging behind and out of touch with the course of developments in society. This explanation was also given in a number of regional party meetings.[6] However not all party meetings appear to have been characterised by a vigorous investigation of the problems the election highlighted. According to a report of a meeting in Kiev gorkom, there was a 'desire to avoid objective evaluations of the causes of the defeat of high-level leaders in the elections, and the fear of fundamental criticism which goes back to the times of stagnation' among some participants, leading them to blame the press.[7]

On 25 April a CC plenum was held. This meeting had been preceded by considerable behind-the-scenes arm twisting on the part of the Gorbachev leadership, resulting in the submission of formal requests for retirement by 110 members of the CC and the Central Auditing Commission. These requests were accepted, with laudatory comments about the service of these people being uttered by plenum speakers. However although no one voted against these retirements from the central organs, nor against the election of replacements, it is clear from the tone of the speeches of some of those who were going that their departure was reluctant. It may have been just as well for the mythology of party unity that, unlike elections to positions, votes to accept resignations did not have to be by secret ballot. The CC fell from 301 to 251 members, and in the process saw the representation of party apparatus workers drop from approximately 45 per cent to 34 per cent. The CC had a new membership that, in the eyes of some observers, seemed to favour reformism rather more than that which it replaced.[8] But the plenum also addressed the issue of the party's performance in the election to the Congress of People's Deputies. Although not all speakers devoted large parts of their speeches directly to this issue, it was this which provided the stimulus and background for many of their comments on other questions.

The comfortable argument that it was those who had been unable to improve their work style and make it relevant to contemporary conditions, an argument which could be used to direct responsibility away from the party as a whole, was heard at the plenum. Others sought to externalise the blame, in particular focusing on the press. According to Mesiats from Moscow obkom,

> on the one hand television, radio and the press, including the party press, provide a forum for publicists and other persons who sometimes proceed from positions which are essentially incompatible with perestroika and our socialist way of life, and on the other hand, a psychological stereotype of the party worker as an impediment to perestroika is being moulded and has already taken shape. The corrupt nature of the party apparatus, its privileged position, its lack of knowledge of the situation at local level, and its inability to exercise leadership is being emphasised. All this is affecting the prestige of party and soviet cadres and creating an unmanageable situation.[9]

In a more pointed fashion, some placed the responsibility, indirectly, on central policies. Glasnost was being misused, according to some, to sully the party's name. In the view of first secretary of Vladimir obkom R. S. Bobovikov,

> Against the general background of the mainly negative assessment of history, the tendency to develop a psychological habit of regarding the apparatus worker and the party and economic leader as being the main brakes on perestroika, and invariably bureaucrats, stands out clearly. It has become universally fashionable to draw inappropriate generalisations from individual negative examples. Any mention of the apparatus causes people nothing but irritation . . . We must stop people trying to pin the mistakes and crimes of individual communists, leaders included, on the entire party and its policy. We must stop the discrediting of the elected party aktiv and the groundless censuring of the management apparatus.[10]

Such a negative appreciation of the party's past was, according to Krasnodar kraikom first secretary Polozkov, leading to resignations from the party by people who felt their efforts were not appreciated.[11] Polozkov also claimed that the 'socialist pluralism of opinions proclaimed by our party' has led to disunity rather than the consolidation and strengthening of its ranks.

Democratisation too was criticised. According to Volgograd obkom first secretary V. I. Kalashnikov, democratisation and glasnost' had 'brought to the surface of public life the dross of demagoguery, egoism, nationalism and anti-Sovietism'.[12] For Polozkov, 'It is, after all, an undeniable fact that, on the pretext of democratisation, those elected are frequently neither the best nor the most authoritative – drunkards, drinking cronies, and people who have just been released from jail and have been deprived by the courts of the right to hold such offices. And yet nobody intends to take any measures in this connection.' In the view of a number of speakers, democratisation had led to the emergence of the informals (unofficial organisations which had emerged in 1987–88), many of which adopted a purely negative and anti-Soviet position. In one of the more extreme speeches, Azeri first secretary A. Kh. Vezirov, referred to the way the '"independent" periodicals . . . want to deprive the people of immunity in the face of ideological subversion and to foster a kind of ideological AIDS in our people.'[13] The answer to this problem for some was seen to lie in the combination of democracy with discipline and a strengthening of law and order.[14]

But the real thrust of much of this, at least by implication, was the lack of effective leadership coming from the centre. Failures in the election were directly attributed by Kalashnikov to deficiencies at the top: 'Both the Central Committee Secretariat and the apparatus were clearly lax in their election work', while there were problems with the CC's 'slack monitoring of the fulfilment of decisions' and with the Secretariat's work generally. The CC was accused of failing to give leadership, especially in ideological matters (Mel'nikov from Kemerovo and Mel'nikov from Komi), while the Politburo was called upon to set an example in the clear resolution of ideological questions (Polozkov).

The failings of the party apparatus as opposed to the elected organs appears to have been a greater point of concern. According to Mel'nikov from Kemerovo, 'There are shortcomings in the work of the party apparatus. Now, in connection with the reorganisation, there are even more of them because the flow and general volume of business has basically not changed, but functions are changing. And bureaucracy exists everywhere.' Only the party can successfully combat bureaucracy today.

> But at the same time the situation is reminiscent of the well-known fable in which the criminal shouts 'stop,thief!' louder than anyone else. The struggle against the party is warming up and this matter goes deep. Having put forward the slogan of resolutely combatting bureaucracy, in effect we fattened up the bureaucratic apparatus. We increased wages to excessive levels for some categories, for the same poor work, low efficiency, and low quality of labour. This apparatus is today, from the lowest to the highest echelons, becoming the most active critic of the party apparatus, of all our work.

It was support for the bureaucracy which cost the party the election in Kuzbass. According to Mesiats, in contrast, the reorganisation of the apparatus was beginning to bear fruit,[15] although he did complain about the existence of many vacancies in the oblast apparatus, a fact attributed to low wages and increased pressures. But according to Mel'nikov from Komi, the CC apparatus was too preoccupied with the reorganisation and was not sufficiently on top of the situation at the local level. Furthermore

> We have every reason to believe that some of the information from below that we prepare sometimes does not reach Politburo members, or reaches them in a toned down, soothing form. The Central Committee apparatus is clearly shielding the general secretary from the acuteness of the situation prevailing at the grass roots, Mikhail Sergeevich. For some reason Central Committee personnel have formed the opinion that everything is being held up by party obkoms, gorkoms and raikoms. This idea is given every support by the mass news media. Often only those who oppose local party organs are regarded as supporters of perestroika. Here to some extent I see the Central Committee apparatus as out of touch with grassroots party links.[16]

Despite a salary increase, in Polozkov's view, the apparatus was not performing satisfactorily. Gennadii Kolbin, Kazakh first secretary, criticised the continuation of old methods in personnel work, at the same time suggesting a centralised approach to filling positions for top leaders and a democratic method at lower levels, while according to Vezirov from Azerbaijan a high standard of work was evident in the personnel sphere.

Other speakers sought to explain the election performance by reference to a diverse array of other factors. Conservatism and the party's association with economic problems (Bobrovikov), the lack of readiness of party committees for decisive action (Mesiats and Mel'nikov from Komi) and the low political standards among the population (Saikov) were among those mentioned. But the single most important recurrent theme was the failings in leadership provided from the centre. Not all were as publicly forthright as Polozkov who, after complaining about economic shortages and disruption said:

> It was fine to hear it said here that the comrades who have personally written an application to resign from the Central Committee in connection with their retirement on pension deserve total acclaim and have performed, let us say it bluntly, an altogether noble and moral act. And yet the comrades who have allowed such a debacle in the country in terms of, for example, soap and detergents and have thus discredited the party and undermined the prestige of the Central Committee and the government, so far none of them has displayed the courage and civic conscientiousness to resign, at least of their own accord. And why does the Politburo not give a hint about this to the comrades who are specifically responsible for such sectors?

The trend of opinion was there: lack of leadership. So too was recognition of a source of the problem. To quote Mel'nikov from Komi:

> New elections lie ahead. At conferences today gorkom and raikom secretaries are stating that in such an atmosphere they will not participate in these elections, because there is a 100 per cent guarantee that they will not be elected . . . We must seek ways of ensuring that both gorkom and raikom secretaries enter the elections, with alternative candidacies of course, on equal terms with them, without the prejudice that they are from the party apparatus, in which people now see only the negative aspects.

The speeches at the plenum clearly convey an impression of a party which recognises that it has suffered a setback and which, in a vague way, sees the reason for this: its being out of step with the shift of opinion in society as a whole. However, this vision was obscured by the belief that the people had used their judgement in supporting those communists who were firmly in favour of perestroika, and that the party had had to struggle against the negative stereotype of the party worker projected through the press.[17] But there was no agreement on the precise reasons for being thus out of step. Was it bureaucracy, the lack of leadership, or the speed with which opinion was shifting? Without agreement on this, there was no chance that the party as a whole could unite around a coherent strategy designed to extricate it from the difficulty. Perhaps, Gorbachev hoped, the changed membership profile of the CC would help to bring that body more into line with his thinking. Perhaps he also hoped that the action programme that emerged in the wake of the April plenum would satisfy the critics and unite the party around a commitment to a viable policy direction.[18] As the speed of events accelerated later in 1989, these were proved to be vain hopes.

On 25 May the first session of the Congress of People's Deputies opened. During the first days of this session, the Congress elected the new Supreme Soviet of 542 deputies and a Chairman of the Supreme Soviet (Gorbachev). Although party members dominated both assemblies, neither was the sort of tame cat body which Soviet legislative organs formerly had been.[19] In both there was vigorous debate and criticism, with the party leadership coming under strident attack both for mistakes in the past and policy in the present. The list of ministers that Ryzhkov presented to the Supreme Soviet was accepted only after considerable questioning of the individual nominees and the replacement of some names by others which the assembly would accept. Even Gorbachev's election as Chairman of the Supreme Soviet was not unanimous (87 of 2,210 deputies voted against him, while 795 deputies had supported the adding of a non-party candidate, design engineer A. M. Obolenskii, to the ballot paper), and occurred only after a vigorous question and answer session, including the demand that he first resign as General Secretary. These developments in the legislative arena, the refusal to accept without question both what the party leadership said and who it nominated for office, was more significant than a temporary rejection of political authority. It was a rejection of the principle of monolithic unity in the party and of the principle that party members had to obey the instructions sent down from higher party levels. This meant that, despite the party majorities in both Congress and Supreme Soviet, they would not be the passive instruments of the party leadership. Indeed, they could become active challengers to the party's leadership position. They constituted the formal institutional structure for a continuing parliamentary-based government that threatened to be independent from central party control. In turn, this had the potential to displace the party from its position of dominance in the political system.

The election and the creation of the Congress of People's Deputies introduced a legal public sphere of politics for the first time since the closing down of such a sphere soon after the Bolsheviks gained power in October 1917. This new sphere was characterised by the emergence of a wide range of small, nascent political parties. Growing out of the 'informal' group movement, these bodies became radicalised and politicised by the election campaign and the prospect of a continuing parliamentary arena within which to be active. Some participated in the election campaign, with the popular front movements in the Baltic republics being particularly successful. But what was important about these new political organisations was that they were challenging the CPSU for the allegiance of the people. For the first time since 1921, there were political rivals to the communist party, and although most of the self-proclaimed parties remained at this stage very small bodies, the principle and the potential challenge that they constituted was important.[20] No longer could the CPSU claim without challenge to represent the interests of all parts of Soviet society. Furthermore following a decision of the Congress of People's Deputies in December 1989 abolishing the quota of seats for public organisations in future elections,[21] the party would have to face this challenge without the in-built advantage of guaranteed seats. Later in the year a more immediate and weighty challenge was to come from the Baltic popular fronts, particularly in Lithuania.

The public threat to the party's position posed by the new legislative organs and its loss of the claim to universalism was reinforced in the minds of many by the miners' strikes in the summer of 1989.[22] This strike activity, which embraced more than 100,000 miners in Siberia and 250,000 in Ukraine, involved a rejection of the authority of local party committees, reflected chiefly in the subsequent development of independent regional miner organisations which effectively displaced the authority formerly exercised by party organisations in mining communities, and an appeal to the leadership of the Soviet government. It seemed to symbolise the party's loss of support among its traditional, and ideological, base, the working class. In this sense it may have been an even greater shock to many party leaders than the election setbacks.

### Debate over party reform

The mood in the upper echelons of the party was graphically demonstrated in a meeting of first secretaries of union republican CCs, kraikoms and obkoms held in July. The meeting opened with an address by Gorbachev[23] followed by speeches from a number of party first secretaries and other political leaders and a concluding speech by Gorbachev.[24]

Gorbachev's comments suggest that he was still dissatisfied with the state of the organisational culture in the party. He called on the party to liberate itself from the habits of the past, for discussion in its ranks to be characterised by 'the fearless confrontation of views, the promotion of alternatives, different approaches to the solution of various problems while retaining unity on questions of principle and strategic aims.' Criticism was essential, he declared, particularly given the peculiarities of the one-party system. Without criticism and self-criticism, party life became impoverished and laid the way open to 'large errors, tyranny and in some cases illegality'. The Leninist views on the relationship between freedom of opinion and unity of action, democratism and centralism needed to be revived.

Some of the first secretaries agreed with the need for more self-criticism in the party – Lev Zaikov (Moscow gorkom) even hinted that problems in this were related to continuing family group control when he declared that while there had been much criticism of those above, there had not been one word of criticism by leaders of their own sub-divisions, of those upon whom they relied for their immediate material and official welfare. N.A. Nazarbaev (Kazakhstan) referred to the way in which some leaders had not escaped 'the stereotype of a negative attitude to different thinking'. However others suggested either that discussions were already sufficiently critical (Bobykin of Sverdlovsk obkom – party meetings were 'stormy, there was no indifference in the discussions')[25] or that criticism of the party and its performance had been excessive (e.g. Masaliev of Kirgizia, Ligachev and Salykov of Karakalpak obkom). Substantial differences of opinion thus remained over the state of the party's organisational culture.

The introduction of multi-candidate elections seems to have had a mixed response. According to Gorbachev, 'this principle has been greeted very slowly in the party'. In the latest report and election campaign, he declared, only half the secretaries of PPOs were elected on an alternative basis, at the district level even less and at the oblast level only a few. First Secretary Postoronko from Ivano-Frankov obkom gave some other figures: in the most recent report and election campaign, 75 per cent of party group organisers and secretaries of shop organisations and PPOs, and 25 per cent of secretaries of gorkoms and raikoms were elected in ballots in which there was an alternative.[26] However, another speaker (Ponomarev of Belgorod obkom) complained of 'pokazhuka democracy', of twaddle, of narrow-minded, Philistine bitterness against local party leaders in the most recent election campaign. Clearly many party leaders had taken advantage of the let out clause in the electoral regulations to avoid a competitive ballot.

The reform of the party apparatus also evoked different reactions.

Gorbachev defended the party apparatus against 'groundless' criticism and said that while it was necessary, it needed to work in a new way. He declared that a new apparatus, with many new members, was being formed, but complained at the difficulty of changing patterns of work: 'Some comrades are so used to the old, that after the liquidation of branch departments they find any type of hole in order to reproduce those functions in organisational or socio-economic departments.' Many of the first secretaries were more critical of the changes introduced by Gorbachev, although they did not mention his name in connection with this. Zaikov declared 'that the reduction in the party apparatus and the change of its structure for the present has given us nothing'.[27] Bobykin from Sverdlovsk complained about the weakness of the influence of the Social-economic department of the CC and referred to the 'premature reduction of the party apparatus' and the weakening of the role of the Secretariat.[28] According to Ryzhkov there had been some confusion in the apparatus, while the failures of those departments and secretaries concerned with ideology were leading to 'the large-scale deideologization of society'.

Ryzhkov also complained about the lack of a clear line of leadership coming from the CC,[29] a criticism echoed by a number of other speakers at the meeting. Such complaints seem to have had a firm foundation in fact, at least as far as they apply to the party apparatus. The commissions did not begin meeting until the end of January,[30] while according to Boris Yel'tsin in early January, the Secretariat had not met since September.[31] Another spokesman said in April 1989 that the Chancellery and General Department were less important than previously, but that the CC commissions were still in the planning and formulation stage and no one was as yet clear about their functions.[32] It is in this context that Ryzhkov called for a review of the distribution of the responsibilities of the Politburo and Secretariat and claimed that Gorbachev needed greater assistance in order to enable him to concentrate more fully on the party and its problems.

The July meeting reflected the extent of opposition among responsible officials to the changes Gorbachev had instituted. Although no one at the meeting openly accused Gorbachev of bringing in measures which threatened the party's institutional existence, it was clear from the tone of many of the comments that the speakers did not approve of many of the changes, were concerned about the effects many of the changes were having upon the party, and blamed Gorbachev for them. Such evidence of uneasiness in what should have been the General Secretary's 'natural' constituency might have been expected to lead to a moderation of Gorbachev's drive for reform. But it had no discernible effect upon his commitment to change. Some of the criticisms, both implied and direct, were ignored, while some of the other points made at the meeting did enter the on-going party debate.

One criticism made in the July meeting which continued to strike a responsive chord in many parts of the party was the failure of leading party organs to give clear leadership. The centre was accused of procrastinating and avoiding making decisions on important questions.[33] This criticism of a failure of leadership applied to party organs at various levels,[34] with some being accused of awaiting edicts from above and complaining about the absence of guideline instructions rather than displaying initiative in their activities.[35] The level of the activity of the Politburo seems to have declined in 1989, at least as reflected in the reports of its deliberations in the press,[36] a development that may reflect heightened levels of conflict within the leadership. This may also be reflected in Zaikov's comment that a Politburo sitting may last seven to eight hours, and 'Sometimes only one question will be studied before we adopt a decision. We virtually all express our views, then debate and argue, disagreeing with certain standpoints, and then coming to a decision.'[37] The activity of the CC commissions remained desultory,[38] and it seems that by the end of 1989 the Secretariat had again begun meeting, reflecting the dissatisfaction with the performance of the commissions.[39]

The CC did meet in plenary session more frequently in 1989 than earlier years: 1985, 4 times; 1986, 3; 1987, 3; 1988, 5 (including two directly linked with the Conference), and 1989, 8. Plena were also held in February and March 1990. The sharp increase in 1989 and early 1990 reflects less the CC thinking ahead and formulating a coherent strategy than reacting to the changed contours of institutional power in the Soviet political structure; five of the plena in 1989 and one (March) in 1990 concerned forthcoming meetings of state organs and the need for the party to formalise positions on matters coming before those bodies.[40] All of the meetings were of short duration. But what gives most cause for hesitation in interpreting the greater number of meetings as reflecting a more activist leadership role in decision-making was the conduct of those meetings. In at least two plena, those of April 1989 when 110 members of the CC and the Central Auditing Commission resigned, and February 1990 when it was resolved to eliminate the party's 'leading role' from the Constitution, significant numbers of the participants had clear reservations about these courses of action. Nevertheless, the opponents of proposed measures generally voted in favour of those measures.[41] They appear to have felt constrained by considerations of party discipline and the party ethos of monolithic unity to vote for these measures, just as had been the case in the pre-1985 period. Without the possibility of the manifestation of real opposition through negative votes, it is doubtful that the CC could muster the necessary authority to provide vigorous leadership for many in the party under the new conditions. Some even doubted its interest in the problems facing the party and society more broadly, citing its failure to take positions on many leading questions.[42] Reflecting sensitivity to the criticism of the performance of leading party organs, Gorbachev proposed major structural changes to these early in 1990. These are discussed below.

The restructuring of the party apparatus was also going slowly, a fact which ensured the possibility of a return to authoritarian methods of resolving questions in the view of one observer.[43] A discussion of the apparatus in *Pravda*, cited a comment from the July conference: 'We reject the defamation of the party apparatus. We need an apparatus, capable of performing its functions in a skilled manner and offering elected organs comprehensive assistance.' It went on to argue:

> Has the reorganisation of the party apparatus achieved its goal? Not entirely in our view. The 'ideology' behind the restructuring of the apparatus was not thought out fully; voluntarism and pressure from above intervened in this process once again, as before. Figures were given and the apparatus structure was adjusted to fit these indicators rather than its new functions. The press, covering the report and election conferences, cited numerous complaints from local party workers that the new party apparatus structure was 'triggered' from above without considering the opinion of the grassroots links and the specific situation at local level. At the same CPSU Central Committee conference certain first party committee secretaries stated unequivocally: Cutting back the apparatus and changing its structure has not yet produced any results; this action seems premature.[44]

Another critic suggested that too many apparat workers were unable to operate in the new conditions and what was needed was a renewal of the leading cadre corps.[45] However, some were willing to suggest that excessive criticism of the apparatus was occurring and having baleful effects. According to a department head from Donetsk obkom, 'criticism of the apparatus "in general" is developing into defamation of the party'.[46] One correspondent even argued that the poor performance of apparatus workers was due to the fact that they modelled themselves on 'leaders'.[47]

Some argued that the reform of the apparatus had seriously hindered its capacity to carry out its functions. According to Ul'ianovsk obkom secretary O. Kazarov, the party apparatus has been streamlined and the sectoral departments abolished, but the 'workload on the apparatus, in view of the new political tasks as well, has doubled or tripled. Whereas before there were twenty-eight personnel in the obkom's industrial sector departments, now there are just seven in the Social-economic Department. And although these are mostly people of the highest qualifications, they simply lack the time to do a great deal.'[48] According to Polozkov, while the apparatus had been reduced by 33 per cent and the branch departments eliminated, no one had taken over their functions, with the result that the load on the party apparatus worker had increased two to three times. He cited the case of the kraikom department for agrarian policy which now had thirteen staff instead of the twenty-six it had had earlier, but which, because the state organs had not taken up their functions, spent its time trying to get supplies through. The failure of state organs to take over economic activities was condemning the party apparatus to continue the same tasks it had formerly performed.[49] A similar story was told in Moscow.[50]

Among some party leaders at the republican levels, there was a feeling that the central apparatus was still too intrusive in their affairs. According to Belorussian leader Sokolov, while there had been many positive changes in the work of the CC apparatus, 'we in the provinces would like them to proceed more quickly and certain senior officials of the Central Committee apparatus not to try to explain in their own way or even touch up decisions of the CPSU Central Committee Politburo and Secretariat'. They leave little room for low level initiative. Nor should leading positions in republican and oblast party organisations be decided by the CC apparatus in Moscow; currently 146 posts of leading Belorussian workers were on the CC CPSU schedule, while there should not be more than ten.[51]

### The national structure of the party

The question of the national structure of the party came onto the agenda of party debate at this time. The stimulus for this was the growing strength of the national movements in the Baltic republics, a factor which forced the local party leaderships to confront the issue of maintaining a profile in a rapidly changing political arena. These leaders soon saw the alternatives: remain closely tied to Moscow in the public's mind and thereby lose authority in their home societies, or cut loose from Moscow in the hope of being able to clothe themselves in nationalist garb. In June the Latvian first secretary Vagris had argued that while he would not go so far as to espouse a federal relationship between republican and central party organs, republican organs must be given 'independence in solving many questions'.[52] At the July meeting the Latvian and Lithuanian first secretaries hinted at the need for the federalisation of the party. The position as viewed from the Baltic capitals was clearly stated in the Draft Programme of the Communist Party of Estonia. This declared:

> The policy of the sovereignty of Estonia presupposes the restoration of the CPE as an independent political organisation. The CPE is a component of the CPSU, however, not just in the capacity of its territorial organisation but as an independent party of a sovereign union republic which participates in working out the overall political strategy of the CPSU on an equal footing with the communist parties of the other union republics. All issues of party activities in the republic fall within the jurisdiction of the CPE; it is completely free to determine its structure and its composition and to use its funds. The CPE operates on the principle of self-capitalization and has a separate budget; it determines the structure of its income itself, having substantially reduced the contribution of membership dues to it. Independence of the CPE presupposes its protection both in the new CPSU code of party life and the CPE Statute.[53]

This position virtually involved the confederalisation of the party, not its federalisation. But the real pacesetter in these developments was the Lithuanian party.

In February 1989 at its 17th plenum, the CC CPLith had favoured greater independence from the CPSU but continuation of its activity within the CPSU.[54] By the following plenum four months later, explicit calls were being made for the CPLith independently to conduct cadre policy, economic and financial activity and questions of internal party life and foreign ties, and for a congress to be convened later that year to formalise such a situation.[55] By October, the official position was clearly contradictory: the CPLith was to be an independent party with its own programme and statutes, but also to be an integral part of a renewed CPSU.[56] Despite pressure and persuasion from the centre[57] at a congress in December, the Lithuanian party declared itself an independent political organisation with its own programme and rules and said that it would seek equal partner relations with the CPSU.[58] A less extreme position was taken by the Moldavian party, which was to 'expand the independence of the republican party organisation and perfect its structure and functions as an integral part of the CPSU',[59] while the Ukrainian party decided 'unambiguously in favour of CPSU unity, to dissociate ourselves from the idea of constructing the party on principles of federalism'.[60]

The position of the leadership group around Gorbachev was to reject calls for federalisation while acknowledging the need for greater autonomy on the part of the union republican parties.[61] Initially the mechanism for this was to be the drawing up by republican and oblast parties of their own 'socio-economic action programmes', although these had to be consistent with the Programme of the CPSU. By the time of the lead-up to the elections for republican and local soviets in early 1990, all party committees were allowed to have their own election platforms to suit local conditions.[62] But such autonomy, although a significant modification of established practice and of the notion of democratic centralism, was insufficient for Baltic leaders. The continuing danger of being left behind by the sweep of nationalist sentiment encouraged the Lithuanian Communist Party to declare itself independent of the CPSU on 20 December 1989 as noted above,[63] an action followed three months later by the Estonian party. On 7 April, the Latvian party split into pro- and anti-independence wings,[64] just as the Lithuanian party had done when it declared itself independent.[65] Gorbachev continued to reject the right of these parties to act in this way and reaffirmed the importance of a unitary rather than a federal party,[66] while allowing for increased autonomy in the resolution of local issues and an expanded role in the discussion of national issues.[67] As the drive for national independence strengthened, the success of this line became increasingly unlikely.

Another aspect of the national structure of the party which came up for debate concerned the Russian republic. At the July meeting, two party leaders from the RSFSR called for a special party organisation for the republic, arguing that the party in Russia needed a similar set of structures to the party in the other republics. This principle was accepted at the September 1989 CC plenum[68] and realised at the 9 December 1989 plenum with the formal establishment of the Russian Bureau of the CC.[69] This body, which was to meet when needed but no less frequently than once per month and was to use the apparatus of the CC, was to coordinate the activities of oblast and krai party organisations of the RSFSR directed at the realisation of party policy, and to supervise the implementation of decisions. According to Gorbachev at the plenum,[70] it was decided to structure Russian affairs in this way rather than through the creation of a separate Communist Party of

Russia because of Russia's importance for national affairs. For this reason it was to be headed by the General Secretary and would unite that part of the CC apparatus which concentrated on party work in the republic. Furthermore, noted Gorbachev, this was to be only the first step in the formation of new party structures for the republic. The CC's Draft Platform adopted at the February 1990 plenum acknowledged the need for 'the creation of an appropriate leading organ' in the RSFSR and foreshadowed the convocation of a republican party conference prior to the XXVIII Congress to discuss the question of the development of the party in the RSFSR.[71]

The establishment of the Russian Bureau appears puzzling given the emphasis upon the need for increased autonomy on the part of the republican parties. The establishment of a republican organ which remained intrinsically part of the central apparatus was not consistent with this emphasis. Moreover, such a solution had been tried under Khrushchev and rejected as unsatisfactory in 1966.[72] Furthermore there was considerable pressure from within Russia for the establishment of a constituent party for the Russian republic, not just a Bureau.[73] The reason for the adoption of such a course may lie in part in the drive for independence in Lithuania. The speech in which Gorbachev announced the formation of the Russian Bureau included an attack upon the proposals for the federalisation of the party, and the establishment of a new party organisation for Russia may have been seen as simply creating another institution with an interest in pressing such proposals. But also important was the balance of power in the party: Gorbachev was unwilling to see a separate Russian party established because of the real danger that this would become dominated by conservative sections of the party based in Leningrad and in the countryside. The Bureau was a compromise to prevent this from occurring. But as events were to show, this was to be only a temporary palliative.

### Recognition of political diversity

As well as pressure for recognising national diversity in the party structure, pressures also developed for recognition of political diversity. This took the form of demands for the making of provision for pluralisation of opinion in the party. Three elements combined to place this on the agenda of party reform. First, the introduction of multi-candidate elections in the party made little sense unless potential candidates were able to disagree over issues. Second, the way in which some party members who were also deputies to the new legislative organs ignored party discipline and were openly critical of the party and some of its decisions without suffering party discipline was a clear indication that the line against pluralisation of opinion in the party was becoming untenable. Third, the debate over federalisation in the party and the differences in views expressed by party leaders in Moscow and Vilnius in the context of Gorbachev's continued rejection of the independence claims of the Lithuanian party, clearly projected an image of different views within the one party structure. Indeed, the encouragement given to republican and oblast party organisations to design their own programmes, albeit within the bounds of the CPSU Programme, confirms this view. All of these dictated that the monolithic ethos associated with the banning of fractions and the meaning of democratic centralism that had emerged in the 1920s had to be rethought.

This view was not unanimously adopted in the party. Vadim Medvedev acknowledged in the middle of 1989 that although there was diversity and ideological struggle within the party, what was not wanted was organised tendencies, parties within the party obstructing the implementation of a single policy.[74] There were also calls for closer ideological cohesion,[75] for the combination of democracy with discipline,[76] and that those who disagreed with the party should leave its ranks.[77] However this sort of view was more than balanced by calls for such organised tendencies to be allowed.[78] There was also a strong argument favouring greater protection of minority rights within the party, in particular their right to maintain their views once a decision with which they had not agreed had been made. The current situation was well summarised by Maliutin: 'The conformity of opinion in the party in the old form no longer exists, but no mechanisms protecting party pluralism have been worked out. This, in turn, provides an opportunity for the broadest interpretation of both the right of a communist to his personal opinion and the confines of this right beyond which incompatibility with party membership occurs.' The answer was protection of minority rights by party statute.[79] As one writer declared, 'a decision adopted by the majority must be binding on the minority but must not deprive it of the right to uphold its own viewpoint subsequently'.[80] This view was the basis for acceptance of the right of platforms to exist in the party.[81]

Concrete realisation of this was the emergence of the first public fraction in the party since the 1920s, the Democratic Platform, in early 1990.[82] Interviews had occurred with the major spokesman of this group prior to its public emergence,[83] and it is clear that the views expressed in those interviews struck a responsive chord in party ranks. At the February 1990 plenum Gorbachev accepted that the renovation of the party implied 'the rethinking of the principle of democratic centralism, with the accent on democratism and the power of the party masses'.[84] The CC Draft Platform accepted as fundamental to the party, *inter alia*, 'pluralism of opinions, freedom of criticism, diversity of approaches and platforms . . . and the minority's right to uphold its views subject to mandatory fulfilment of decisions made by the majority.' However, the Platform declared, the renewal of democratic centralism along these lines was to forestall 'the formation of fractions with their own internal organisation and discipline'.[85] An important development in the legalisation of different views was the publication in *Pravda* of the Theses of the Democratic Platform.[86] These were published as part of the on-going discussion leading up to the XXVIII Congress, but what set them apart from the other contributions to this discussion that appeared in the party daily is that they were openly associated with an organised fractional grouping and therefore clearly contradicted the established tradition of party life opposing organised groupings with programmatic aims.

The main thrust of the measures for domestic restructuring of the party thus constituted a major challenge to the traditional power axis in the party. Increased autonomy by lower level party bodies, elections in which the electors freely chose the candidates, organised fractions with programmatic positions and the severe curtailment of the secretarial apparatus all represented direct attacks upon the nomenklatura system whereby the party had structured its personnel relations, and power configurations, since the introduction of this system formally in 1923. Gorbachev recognised this, as his speech to the July meeting suggests when he referred to the way in which the democratisation unrolling in the society 'demands from the party a decisive end to the formal-nomenklatura approach to cadre work'. So too did other leaders.[87]

### Intra-party democratisation

The pressures for democratisation in the party continued during this period. In January 1989 it was decided to undertake publication of the protocols and stenographic reports of party conferences, congresses and plena, a development which would have opened up contemporary leadership debates to an even more public airing than they currently received.[88] There were many references in the press to elections for party posts being conducted on a competitive basis,[89] but in overall terms this represented only a small proportion of the posts filled; one report about the 1988 round of party elections noted that some 8.6 per cent of raikom and gorkom secretaries, 6 per cent of raikom and gorkom first secretaries and 1 per cent of obkom secretaries were elected on a contested basis from two or more candidates.[90] Furthermore in many cases there were a large number of nominees for positions which were reduced by party authorities to a choice of only two at the time of voting: for example, in the Karelian obkom twenty candidates were reduced to two.[91] One correspondent noted that readers of the reports of plena where organisational matters were considered were 'perplexed' because they saw

> that of a host of candidacies considered at the initial stage the same couple invariably find themselves at the final stage – the gorkom first secretary and the obkom second secretary, the obkom second secretary and the chairman of the oblispolkom, a former obkom secretary and another former official. That is, the actual people who were closest to the first secretary who has quit his post and under whom the oblast frequently simply failed to achieve particular success.[92]

For some, competitive elections were only instances of 'apparat games' in which matters continue to be decided in the old way.[93] This reflected the continued difficulties in shifting personnel work from nomenklatura principles to democratisation;[94] reliance on personal connections continued to be a feature of personnel matters.[95]

The process of democratisation in the party was advancing slowly.[96] This is reflected in a comment in *Pravda* about the report and election meetings:

> analysis of the report and election meetings that have started shows that in many areas they are held in the old fashion – following the well-trodden line that has been covered for decades. And people do not even dream about moving away from that line. The same old self-justifying reports are heard, without even the slightest hint of work and the situation in the collective being analysed. The standard-issue speakers with their prepared criticisms of associated plants and their smug approval of their own work. In fact this work boiled down to collecting membership dues and holding meetings with agendas repeated year in, year out. And it is typical that in certain areas communists are even less active then they were last year.[97]

There were still calls for the direct election of congress delegates by rank-and-file party members,[98] for the dominance of the elected organs over the bureaucracy,[99] for criticism of leaders[100] and for the publication of transcripts of CC plena.[101] Indirectly Ryzhkov admitted how far democratisation had to go when, in discussing the February plenum, he declared:

> The democratisation of internal party life is the main arena of the party's perestroika. Fundamental changes to the CPSU's statutes must be envisaged to accelerate this process. They are aimed at democratising the formation of leading elected organs, staffing all components of the party apparatus on a multiple candidate basis, utilising an efficient mechanism for recalling members of party committees at any level, and reviving the Leninist idea of protecting the rights of a minority in the party.[102]

This was intrinsic to the discussion about changes in the party Rules which was getting under way late in 1989.

The course of democratisation seemed to receive a boost in early 1990 with the replacement of party leaders in some areas as a result of popular pressure. In a number of party organisations including Tiumen,[103] Voroshilovgrad and Donetsk,[104] Kostroma,[105] Cheboksary,[106] Sverdlovsk,[107] Ufa,[108] Chernigov,[109] Tomsk[110] and Volgograd[111] popular dissatisfaction with the leadership led to the overthrow of local leaders, often through the splitting of the leading group and the resignation of the first secretary. According to one correspondent, 'In Ukraine, for example, almost one third of obkom first secretaries have been ousted as a result of stormy rallies and demonstrations . . . '[112] These were important because they represented the real danger posed by the democratisation process to entrenched power in the party, but they were also evidence of the limited strength of that process at this time: the total number of such overturns was relatively small.

### The party in society

The pluralisation of society reflected in the emergence of parties to challenge the CPSU and the party's evident loss of position as a result of the establishment of the new state legislative and executive organs created pressures in the party for a multi-party system. These pressures were reinforced by the collapse of the communist regimes in Eastern Europe. During the second half of 1989 some spokesmen had discussed the need for and probability of the party dropping its constitutionally enshrined 'leading role' and thereby leaving the way open to a multi-party system,[113] but Gorbachev had consistently rejected the possibility of a multi-party system in the USSR;[114] at the meeting of the Supreme Soviet on 14 November 1989, Gorbachev had led the opposition to the proposal to place Article 6 of the Constitution (which enshrined the party's 'leading role') on the agenda of the forthcoming session of the Congress of People's Deputies. But under the impact of events in the Baltic republics, and with some mobilisation of opinion elsewhere in the country and party, the official position began to shift. On 7 December the Lithuanian Supreme Soviet amended the republican constitution to eliminate the article guaranteeing the party's 'leading role'.[115] The following day *Pravda* declared that Article 6 could be subject to re-evaluation, modernisation and even exclusion, but only in the course of a careful consideration of the Constitution, not under political pressure.[116] Gorbachev then repeated this position, and hinted that Article 6 might not be essential.[117] This position was then widely espoused by party figures.[118] The appeal to the people adopted at the 9 December CC plenum was significant in this regard.[119] After declaring that the party was freeing itself from irrelevant economic and administrative functions and was undergoing a process of self-cleansing to restore its ideological and moral quality, the appeal declared that the party was open to dialogue and partnership and to constructive collaboration with all social movements, cooperatives and groups acting on a socialist basis.

The culmination of this trend of development came at the February 1990 plenum. In his address Gorbachev declared:

> In a society that is renewing itself the party can exist and fulfil its vanguard role only as a democratically acknowledged force. This means that its position should not be enforced through being constitutionally legitimised. The CPSU naturally intends to fight for the position of being ruling party, but it intends to do this strictly within the framework of the democratic process, renouncing any and all legal and political advantages, putting forward its own programme, defending it in discussions, cooperating with other public and political forces, constantly working among the masses, living their interests and needs. The broad democratisation now under way in our society is being accompanied by a growth in political pluralism. Various public and political organisations and movements are emerging. This process can also lead at some stage to the creation of parties.[120]

Within a few short moments, Gorbachev had done away with the constitutional entrenchment of the party's 'leading role' and opened the way to the emergence of a multi-party system. This was ratified by the CC and, at the Congress of People's Deputies session in March, the Constitution was amended to eliminate reference to the party's 'leading role'.[121] Although the conception of the party's role contained in Gorbachev's speech, that it must earn its leadership position, was a logical extension of his initial position in 1985 that it should earn its position through deeds not words, there were few who had considered such a constitutional change possible in March 1985.

However, this shift in position in favour of abolishing the party's constitutionally-enshrined leading role had not gone unchallenged in party ranks. It was clear to all that the emergence of the nascent parties and a public arena of politics posed a real threat to the party's continued dominance of the society. This was seen principally in terms of the emergence of a multi-party system, and while some people in the party were not hostile to this,[122] others saw no need for it. According to Estonian first secretary Vialias, 'As far as the multi-party system is concerned, however, it should be said immediately that the present extent of democracy allows for fairly extensive political pluralism in the country of socialist democracy. Public movements here participate actively in political life, thus ensuring that all the main social forces are represented in politics.'[123] The malign implications of a multi-party system were clear. In the words of Politburo member Vadim Medvedev,

> Certain persistently repeated ideas about a multiparty system were objectively aimed against the party. Our fundamental position on this matter has been repeatedly made clear. The point is that in the specific situation prevailing in society an emphasis on a multiparty system would inevitably belittle the party's role, lead to a weakening of the potential of perestroika, and essentially push the country into a vague position from which it would be difficult to find a way out.[124]

According to Sokolov, a multiparty system would exacerbate destructive trends on national, social and other planes,[125] while in the view of a *Pravda* editorial note 'those who warn against the illusion that a multiparty system is, so to speak, the imperative of the time and will deliver society from all our ills are right. The reality is that it will lead to the exacerbation of the political situation, a struggle for power, for influence over people's minds', when what is needed is unity and consolidation.[126]

### Crisis of confidence

The debate over Article 6 and the multi-party system is symptomatic of a real crisis of confidence in the party. Increasingly

Table 5.1. *Membership changes 1985–1990 (figures as at 1 January)*

|      | Full       | Candidate | Total      | % increase |
|------|------------|-----------|------------|------------|
| 1985 | 18,041,881 | 701,730   | 18,743,611 |            |
| 1986 | 18,288,786 | 715,592   | 19,004,378 | 1.39       |
| 1987 | 18,566,787 | 700,928   | 19,267,715 | 1.38       |
| 1988 | 18,827,271 | 641,515   | 19,468,786 | 1.04       |
| 1989 | 18,975,725 | 512,097   | 19,487,822 | 0.09       |
| 1990 | 18,856,113 | 372,104   | 19,228,217 | −1.33      |

Sources: *Izvestiia Ts.K. KPSS* 2, 1989, p. 138 and 4, 1990, p. 113; *Partiinaia zhizn'* 21, November 1987, p. 6; and Ezhegodnik *Bol'shaia Sovetskaia Entsiklopediia* Moscow, 1985, p. 13

a sense of malaise had been setting in, with many feeling that the party had lost its way and its sense of purpose. This was reflected in the increasing loss of party members. In Krasnodar, 211 people had handed in their party cards in 1988, but in the first five months of 1989 the number had reached 610.[127] In Omsk, the corresponding figures were 129 and 339 (six months).[128] According to official figures in 1989, 136,600 party members and candidates handed in their party cards, 7.5 times more than in 1988 (18,000).[129] The overall picture on party membership is given in table 5.1. This table shows that during 1989, the size of the party fell, for the first time since 1954.

In Latvia at the end of April the CC Commission on Party Organisational and Cadre Work attributed the fall in party membership to 'the decline in the prestige of the republican party organisation, which to all intents and purposes has been passively sitting on the fence on a number of topical issues of the domestic political situation'.[130] A more sanguine view was expressed by Moscow first secretary Zaikov who noted a trend toward declining admissions and rising numbers expelled or resigning, but attributed this situation to 'the policy of forcibly swelling the party ranks which was pursued for years, the formalistic approach to the shaping of the party's qualitative composition'.[131] According to a participant in a roundtable discussion on party renewal in February 1990, those leaving the party in his region were those who found it difficult to work in the party because of their age or those who had joined by chance or as a result of past admission quotas.[132] *Pravda* sought to place the departures in context by arguing that

Some 18,000 people have indeed left the party of late. But here is another figure: in the same period more than 20,000 advocates of perestroika have joined the party. It is true that those who have left include not only 'parasites' and 'chameleons', but also honest, decent people. May their decisions remain on the conscience of those party workers who were indifferent to the fate of communists who failed to withstand the storm of moral ostracism.[133]

A more moderate tone was to be found in a discussion of changes in the party Rules in *Pravda* in late November.[134] This acknowledged the increasing numbers of withdrawals and fewer applications to join, and said that what was necessary was the creation of conditions in the party which would attract politically active people and enable them to blossom within party ranks. More specific were the comments of the CC Commission on Party Construction and Cadre Policy which recognised the role of the continued prevalence within the party of old ways of thinking and acting, of sentiments hostile to perestroika, in repelling those generally supportive of change.[135] Perhaps a more accurate guide to the reasons for the withdrawal of at least some members was a letter from one party member saying that he was resigning because the party had abandoned its principles.[136]

This crisis of confidence is also reflected in increased passivity. The party apparatus was declared to be inefficient and demoralised,[137] with many party members knowing little about the activities of their own party organisations.[138] Party members were accused of failing to support the party's positions, and even opposing them. In Estonia in the middle of 1989, a CC resolution accused some party organisations of directly opposing the line of the CPE while some party members participating in social movements adopted ideas incompatible with those of the party and did not seek to carry out party policy.[139] In Moldavia first secretaries were called upon to 'show more firmness in evaluating non-party actions of certain CPSU members and insulate the party organisation of the capital from the influence and infiltration of random, politically unstable elements'.[140] In Donetsk, some party members were accused of organising strikes[141] while *Pravda* accused some members of preaching 'a different path of development based on negation of our system'.[142] Other party members were accused of becoming confused and panicking in the face of the polemics surrounding the course of reform[143] and it was noted that people were reluctant to take on responsible positions in the party.[144] Other party members simply refused to pay their membership dues; the number of members who had not paid their dues by 1 July 1989 (181,000) was almost 2.5 times greater than it had been a year before,[145] a development which not only showed growing demoralisation within the party but was also having an effect on that organisation's capacity to function.[146] *Pravda* also asked, while people sought to blacken the party's name, where were the party members, including first secretaries, speaking up in defence of the party?[147]

Many also bewailed the decline in the party organisation's prestige and public standing. For Zaikov, the 'decline of some party organis-ations' prestige is a major cause of alarm',[148] while Ul'ianovsk obkom secretary Kazarov, bemoaning the poor recompense gained by holders of responsible positions and the consequent loss of good cadres, said that the 'prestige of party work is declining catastrophically in conditions where moral and material incentives are lacking'.[149] In a reply to Kazarov's article, one letter writer said that the party's prestige was 'the lowest it has been in all the 72 years of our state's existence', a result of the party's being out of step with society.[150] Another worker said the party had destroyed its own prestige by its laxness and lenience towards infringements of 'society's moral criteria' by party members.[151] With the decline in the party's prestige went the undermining of its authority.[152] Popular support was waning, and recognised to be so: participants in a conference of workers, peasants and engineering and technical workers held in January 1990 expressed concern that it was not clear whose interests the party represented and there had been a decline in trust in party policy.[153] In Estonia it was reported that a poll had shown that only 4 per cent of Estonians and 10 per cent of non-Estonians supported the CPE.[154] A survey conducted in February 1990 on the attitude to the CPSU held by different groups of the Soviet population elicited the returns shown in table 5.2. The decline in party prestige and support was also reflected in the reduced circulation of the party press: in the first six months of 1989, subscriptions to *Pravda* dropped by 4 per cent, *Kommunist* 4.2 per cent and *Partiinaia zhizn'* 3.4 per cent.[155] The party was recognised to be out of touch with the people.[156]

In the middle of 1989, Politburo member Medvedev aptly summarised the situation:

> Problems connected with the state of the party's authority, the prestige of the party apparatus and the party worker, and the title of communist are being raised and discussed with great alarm. Attacks on the party have arisen in direct or covert form . . . Some party committees and party workers have found themselves in a state of

virtual psychological shock in the new political situation and are quite
unable to lose the habit of the former methods of leadership of the yea
or nay kind . . . [157]

There was disagreement over the theoretical basis of the party, with the
traditional adherence to Marxism-Leninism beginning to be challenged
by Gorbachev's notion of 'human values', with some looking to the
forthcoming congress to elaborate a new concept of socialism.[158] The
prospect of suffering the same fate as the parties of Eastern Europe was
alive for some people.[159] Many foresaw a split in the party, [160] others
believed the party could survive only if it became a democratic,
parliamentary party.[161] It was argued that the party as an organisational
entity was doomed in its old form: it was becoming balkanised both
through the pressures of nationalism flowing through the republics and
the way in which increasingly local party organisations were retaining
party dues for their own purposes instead of passing them on to the
centre, as in the past.[162] This was not, it was recognised, a good state in
which to have to confront the elections to republican and local soviets
early in 1990.

During 1989 the party leadership offered little solution to these
problems. The Politburo's response to the disillusionment in party
ranks was to repeat the answers that had been applied in the past.[163] It
called for the unity of party ranks on the basis of Marxism-Leninism,
the conscious discipline of communists and the wide democratisation
and renewal of internal party life as a means of displacing the inertia
and patterns of the past.[164] It laid emphasis upon the need to ensure the
higher quality of party members through stricter supervision of more
regularised entrance procedures and the elimination of those who did
not measure up and who besmirched the party's noble ideals. The
independence and responsibility of PPOs were stressed. These types of
solutions were firmly within the traditional style of party statements[165]
and were seen widely as not offering any solution to the problems to
which they were addressed.

Party members looked to the plena of February and March 1990,
respectively designed to adopt the draft party Platform and Rules for
discussion prior to the XXVIII Congress later in the year, to restore a
sense of direction and of momentum to the party. The former plenum
was preceded by a mass public rally of some half million people in the
heart of Moscow on 4 February. Although officially sanctioned, this
was not a party rally and was designed to press the case for further
democratisation. The rally was addressed by radical figures like Yuri

*Table 5.2. Attitude to the CPSU.ª (in percentages)*

|  | Agree | Disagree/ Don't know/ No answer |
|---|---|---|
| The authority of the party has fallen in the last 2–3 years. | 80.7 | 19.3 |
| The party does not exercise great influence on the life of the country. | 34.3 | 65.7 |
| Party committees are unnecessary in enterprises, institutions and organisations. | 42.8 | 57.2 |
| The party has lost the initiative and allowed the uncontrolled development of events. | 49.1 | 50.9 |

ª Vsesoiuznoi tsentr izucheniia obshchestvennogo mneniia po sotsial'no-ekonomicheskim voprosam pri VTsSPS i Goskomtrude SSSR, 'Obshchest-vennoe mnenie v tsifrakh', Vyp.10 (17) (Moscow, April 1990).

Afanas'ev and Boris Yel'tsin, with the latter attacking four years of 'half-measures' and 'compromises' and declaring that this was 'the last chance for the democratisation of the Communist Party'.[166] A *Pravda* editorial on the day the plenum opened also noted the need for party renewal, for getting rid of official time servers, and for meeting the challenges confronting it.[167] The opening of the plenum occurred amidst numerous rumours about the struggle between radicals and conservatives in the party, about the way the party was going to move decisively in the direction of democratisation, and how it was willing to share power with other political forces.

Gorbachev's address to the plenum[168] opened with a proposal to advance the date of the forthcoming congress (which had already been advanced from 1991) from October to June–July 1990. He then went on to discuss the draft Platform. On the party's place in the political system and society, as indicated above, he advocated the abandonment of the constitutional entrenchment of the party's leading and guiding role, acknowledged the possibility of the emergence of other parties and declared that the communist party would cooperate and maintain dialogue with organisations that based themselves on the Constitution and the social system inherent in it. He supported the clear delimitation of functions of party, state and economic organs and the development of a real federation. He also supported the establishment of a presidency with wide executive powers. He called for further democratisation of the party, including a rethinking of the meaning of democratic centralism, increased rank-and-file activism and power, and a streamlining of the CC. Reflecting the recent Lithuanian events, he acknowledged that party bodies could have their own platforms, and he rejected dogmatic interpretations of socialism.

The draft Platform[169] covered much of the ground Gorbachev had traversed in his speech. It renounced a simplistic class approach counterposed to international human values while reaffirming the 'commitment to the socialist choice and the ideas of October', but all of what it purported to stand for was expressed in the form of principles with little real detail. It advocated legal guarantees of rights and freedoms, radical economic reform leading to a 'planned market economy' and the democratisation of society, including political parties. It also emphasised the need for a mechanism for the implementation of state laws, seen in terms of a presidency with executive powers, and for a strengthening of legality and law and order. National self-determination within a renewed federation to be brought about by a union treaty also featured.

On the party, the Platform acknowledged that the party could retain its vanguard role only if it 'radically restructures itself', and that it could continue as the ruling party only by gaining mass voter support. The abolition of Article 6 and the stripping of state authority from the party were seen as necessary. The party was seen to be based on Marxism-Leninism and humanist values. The Platform advocated increased democratisation of the party. This was to include a rethinking of democratic centralism; collegiality in work; pluralism of opinions; freedom of criticism; diversity of approaches and platforms; referenda; the minority's right to uphold its views subject to mandatory fulfilment of decisions made by the majority (but no fractions with their own internal organisation and discipline); expanded rights of PPOs; direct contested election by all communists of conference and congress delegates; contested election of first secretaries at meetings, conferences and congresses; elected organs not to be filled on an *ex officio* basis; real autonomy for union republican communist parties, which could have their own programmatic documents independently to tackle organis-ational, cadre, financial and publishing questions; republican parties should have direct representation in leading party organs. The Platform reaffirmed the territorial-production basis of party organisation (thereby rejecting the view that the party should become primarily a parliamentary party), advocated the election of a party Chairman by the congress and a Presidium by the CC, and declared that all party activity should be funded solely from party income. It also called for discussion of the question of a republican party organisation for Russia prior to the congress.

If it had been hoped that the draft Platform would rally the party around its leadership and unite ranks, that hope was not realised. While one speaker, a drilling foreman from Turkmenistan,[170] declared that the Platform met the demands of the time and contained 'quite constructive proposals and conclusions, effective measures', the overwhelming impression from the plenum speeches is that many were disappointed with the document. The Platform was accused of giving inadequate leadership, of being unclear, of lacking any sense of practicality or concern for how its goals might be achieved, of being superficial and omitting much, of being trite and offering few answers. It was declared to be confusing, an obvious compromise document designed to patch over the differences that existed within the party's leading ranks. For some it showed the isolation, and even excessive passivity, of the party leadership in the face of the serious challenges currently threatening the party's position. When a decisive demonstration of leadership was needed to quell the panic that was appearing in some party ranks and to encourage party members to regain the popular trust that had ebbed from the party in recent times, the Platform that was produced was highly inadequate. Some conservative speakers, such as Brovikov and Gidaspov, used the occasion to attack many aspects of the reform programme, while many others showed through their critical comments the reservations, doubts and concerns that the current situation engendered.

One line of criticism of the Platform was that it did not sufficiently clearly and unambiguously reaffirm the party's commitment to Marxism-Leninism as the guide to its activities. In its specific form, this complaint from the conservatives had more general application. What the Platform failed to do was to enunciate a clearly-defined vision of the future (in which the party had a prominent place) that would seem to have any currency in contemporary conditions. It did not seem to make much sense to talk of the party winning back popular trust when all of the available evidence seemed to suggest that the party's position among the populace was being even further eroded. If the Platform had suggested some ways in which the party could have recovered its position, it might have helped to rally party forces. But by simply repeating the formulae of the past, which in the eyes of some party members was the real cause of the problem in the first place, the Platform seemed to offer no way out of the impasse. It was a compromise, and as a source of direction, it was sadly deficient.

The plenum of March 1990 was organised into three sessions: the 11 March session discussed, and accepted, the abolition from the Constitution of the party's leading and guiding role, the 14 March session nominated Gorbachev as President of the USSR (a post to which he was elected by the Congress of People's Deputies on 15 March), and the 16 March session discussed the draft party Rules. Gorbachev's opening speech[171] was unremarkable. He rejected calls to eliminate the word 'communist' from the party's name, saying this would be a blow to the party's ideological foundation and would lead to disillusionment, he supported the elimination of Article 6 from the Constitution and the creation of a state of equality for other political and social organisations to take part in political life, and he supported genuine democratisation in the party. He highlighted a number of aspects of the new draft Rules: PPOs should be given the power to decide questions of party membership; candidate membership should be abolished; provision should be made for members leaving the party; in the election of conference and congress delegates there should be choice of candidates, nomination from below and direct election; first secretaries should be elected by congresses and conferences, not plena; the territorial-production principle should be maintained as the basis of party organisation; there should be greater autonomy for lower levels of the party; republican communist parties should be given a direct and influential part to play in central decision-making; standing commissions of the CC should be established, differing from their predecessors by possessing the power to make decisions within their areas of competence; a party chairman and deputy should be elected by the congress; a combined Central Control and Auditing Commission should be established; 50 per cent of party subscriptions should be left in the hands of the PPOs; and the party's budget should be made much more open to scrutiny. Turning to the forthcoming congress, Gorbachev supported the principle of party organisations determining for themselves the procedure for electing delegates and said that he favoured the conduct of report and election meetings before the congress.

Because of the intermittent nature of the sessions of this plenum, the debate does not seem to have gained the same momentum as that which had characterised its predecessor in February. Nevertheless, as well as the universal acceptance of the removal of the constitutional provision enshrining the party's leading and guiding role, the support for Gorbachev's nomination as president, and the discussion of individual articles of the draft Rules, this plenum too registered profound uncertainty and concern about the party's health.[172] A number of speakers bemoaned the party's loss of ideological and organisational unity (Nazarbaev accused the 'militant radicals' of using intra-party debate to negate constructive action and weaken the party from within)[173] and the apparent relegation of Marxism-Leninism to the sidelines. A sense of drift, of lack of clear leadership and ambiguity about goals was said to prevail; for some there was even a crisis of identity, reflected in the absence from the draft Rules of the words 'communist' and 'democratic centralism'. Like the Platform, for some the draft Rules were inadequate because they gave no sense of guidance for the future. The charge of lack of leadership is reflected in the fact that the central party leaders left it up to the central committees of the republican parties, obkoms and kraikoms to decide how delegates were to be elected to the congress[174] and whether report and election meetings would be held before or after the congress. This apparent vacuum at the top was sure to stimulate the sense of demoralisation at lower levels.

It is clear, in retrospect, that the radicalisation of the political agenda at the XIX Conference and the effects of the implementation of that agenda in 1989 accelerated the processes of decomposition at work in the party. During 1989 major challenges emerged to the party's leading role in Soviet society. As the national question began to spin out of control, nationality-based public organisations in some republics applied increasing pressure to the party and its continued hold on power. New proto-parties seeking to challenge the CPSU's dominance of the political agenda emerged to offer alternative vehicles of political action for both the population at large and disgruntled party members. New state legislative organs threatened to displace the party from the decision-making arena, while the establishment of a new presidential post (Chairman of the Supreme Soviet) and its transformation into a powerful executive presidency in February 1990, potentially edged the party out of its accustomed role of leadership in the system.[175] Fears of this can only have been heightened by Gorbachev's comment in his first speech as President when he declared that he would be the 'representative of the whole nation', not of 'some separate layer and political tendency'.[176] But when faced with these challenges, instead of responding in a coherent and forthright fashion, the party erupted into a cacophany of competing and discordant voices. The organisational basis of the party was challenged vertically, in territorial/national terms, and horizontally in terms of the beginning of the emergence of organised fractions. The organisational basis of unity thus came under severe strain. In addition, the rhetoric about the withdrawal of the party from a direct administrative role called into question the party's basic role and raison d'etre. Furthermore for the first time on a wide scale, the party leadership and its priorities came under bitter and open attack. At successive CC plena, at less formal meetings like that of July 1989, in the parliamentary organs and in the press, the party leadership was abused for the mistakes it made and its failure to give satisfactory guidance. The disunity in the party was more extensive than it had been before and more open to public view. The image of a party uncertain of what it was, what its role should be, and unclear about how to stop the process of disintegration was apparent.

Paradoxically this image of a disintegrating party accompanied that of the increasing power of the pro-reform tendency focused on Gorbachev. Through his election to the Chairmanship of the Supreme Soviet in May 1989, a position to be filled through election by the Supreme Soviet, Gorbachev rendered himself more secure against removal as national leader by the CC in the way Khrushchev had been displaced. With the introduction of the Presidency, he gained even more executive power. Personnel changes in the leading party organs also appeared to strengthen the reformist position. At the September 1989 plenum, two new full members Kriuchkov and Masliukov (the latter promoted from candidate status) replaced Shcherbitskii, Chebrikov and Nikonov, while Primakov and Pugo replaced Talyzin, Solov'ev and the promoted Masliukov as candidate members of the Politburo. Four new CC secretaries were named, Stroev, Manaenkov, Usmanov and Girenko, to replace Chebrikov and Nikonov. With Shcherbitskii's departure, the entire composition of the Politburo and all CC secretaries had been appointed under Gorbachev.[177] But this did not bring about the sort of agreement within the leadership that might have led to a clear definition of a solution to the party's growing identity problem. The rapid shift of events in a radical direction increased tensions within the leadership. Gorbachev, seeking to carry his more conservative colleagues with him, did not seek the sort of open break that might have liberated the reformists from the search for compromise. Their opponents were not sufficiently powerful to act against the reformist course except in a negative, blocking fashion. With such a disposition of forces, it is little wonder that the party leadership was unable to develop a coherent response to the challenges confronting the party as an organisation. All sides looked to the XXVIII Congress scheduled for mid-1990 to provide a way out of the impasse.

# 6    The lead-up to the Congress

The plena of February and March 1990 set the scene for the preparations for the XXVIII Congress of the party and for continuing debate about the party's identity. The February plenum had adopted the draft Platform for discussion prior to and at the Congress. The March plenum had brought the date of the congress forward to 2 July, adopted a draft agenda, set out the provisions for the election of delegates, and adopted the draft party Rules and a draft decision on the Central Control and Auditing Commission (CCC) for discussion both before and at the congress. In addition, the former plenum accepted the elimination of the party's constitutionally entrenched monopoly position, and the latter plenum made provision for the convening of a conference of the party organisations of Russia before the party congress. The decisions of these plena provided the formal basis for debate within the party in the months leading up to the congress.

The critical nature of the party's situation was again made clear by its performance in the elections to local and republican soviets in early 1990. Although in numerical terms it was able to dominate the newly elected soviets in many parts of the country,[1] Uzbekistan was a case in point, the party suffered clear defeats in the two most important city soviets in the country, Moscow[2] and Leningrad. In both cities a loose radical reform alliance entitled Democratic Russia gained a majority and was able to install administrations led by people who had clearly distanced themselves from the party even though they both remained at that time party members, Gavriil Popov in Moscow and Anatoly Sobchak in Leningrad. In both cities the new relationship between party and state organs was an uneasy one. It did not get off to a promising start when, prior to the newly elected soviet meeting, the local party organisation moved to establish its sole control over both premises and newspapers (*Moskovskaia Pravda* became the organ solely of the gorkom while *Vecherniaia Moskva* remained shared; in Leningrad *Leningradskaia*

*Pravda* was unilaterally taken over by the obkom) formerly shared by both bodies.[3] Both party first secretaries declared that they were willing to pass power over to the soviets.[4] However, in practice it was not that easy. Although Popov and his supporters in particular were active in Moscow, their ability to act independently was constrained by shortages of funds. The resources available to the soviets were limited, while despite much talk, little immediate attempt was made to divest the party of much of the property and income-generating enterprises which had been significant in sustaining its position and were essential for the soviets. Furthermore, there was open obstruction to the effective transfer of power. In Sobchak's words:

> For a month already I have occupied the post of Chairman of the Leningrad City Soviet, but the daily reports on what is happening in the city are put on the table of Boris Gidaspov, First Secretary of the Leningrad Regional Party Committee. The heads of the administrative bodies do not consider it to be necessary to supply me, the Chairman of the Leningrad City Soviet, with corresponding information. I informed these comrades that the City Soviet will confirm them in their posts and, therefore, they need to make a choice about who governs them – the state or the CPSU.[5]

Sobchak's words reflect the real difficulty that arose: if the party could not control the soviet through the numbers it had on the floor of the assembly, what sort of relationship was to exist between these two bodies?

The party's difficulty in adjusting to the need to share power with the newly elected state organs was exacerbated by one aspect of that erosion of party discipline noted in the last chapter, the independent positions taken by many party members in the new bodies. This undermined the party's capacity to dominate local organs even where numerically it constituted a majority. The independent stance taken by some of the delegates to the First Congress of People's Deputies, has been noted. Significant too was the ability of Popov and Sobchak (and those who supported them) to pursue an independent policy and to openly criticise the party while remaining within its ranks and suffering only the criticism of more conservative party elements. It was reflected too in the proceedings of the Congress of People's Deputies of the RSFSR which opened in May. In this assembly, party members were openly split over the question of who should be the president of the Russian Federation. The final two candidates, Boris Yel'tsin and A. Vlasov, were both formally members of the CC and the final victory of Yel'tsin came only after an attempt by Gorbachev to sway the delegates in support of Vlasov. This open split between party members shows the party's inability to exercise the sort of discipline that formerly had been a feature of its internal life: the ability to reach a decision and have all party members support it in open fora. This was, in part, a function of the conflict that was going on in the party at this time and of the widespread disillusionment within the party among the rank-and-file.

Both of these issues, the relationship with state organs and the inability to exercise discipline over soviet delegates, were crucial to the broader question of how the party was to survive in a multi-party environment. This issue, central to the party's future following the abolition of Article 6 and its constitutionally-enshrined leadership role, was not a major focus of debate during this period, but it did receive some attention in party discussion. Recognition of the problem of the relationship with other political forces is reflected in the establishment of a new CC Department for Work with Socio-Political Organisations.[6] But despite the existence of this body, no clear answer was forthcoming. In a competitive electoral situation, with the level of its support palpably eroding, the party had to decide what its attitude would be towards the newly-emergent political forces. Should it seek to cooperate with all organisations regardless of ideological outlook, or should it restrict itself to those of a 'socialist orientation'? What form should such cooperation take? – an electoral alliance?, a round table along East European lines?, or a coalition government? These issues rebounded through party debates without clearly defined answers emerging. To the extent that a general position did emerge during the course of this debate, it was one which favoured cooperation with 'all progressive parties and public movements'.[7]

### Party identity

The increasingly parlous position of the party was for many reflected in its perceived declining base. Formally it was described as a party of all the people, able to reflect and represent all those interests because of the non-antagonistic nature of them.[8] However, in the months leading up to the XXVIII Congress a frequent theme in party discussions concerned the way in which the party was unable to cater for the vast diversity of interests that had emerged in Soviet society.[9] Moreover, and in the eyes of many of those making this complaint, in the attempt to represent all sections of society, the party had forsaken its working class base and become cut off from that class. Instead of looking after the interests of the class in whose name it ruled, some critics charged, the party had introduced policies which actually harmed those interests. Why, asked a worker from Magadan, was economic reform begun with changes that hurt the workers?[10] Instead of pursuing such policies, the party should implement policies which defended and promoted the interests of the workers, ensuring that their living standards did not fall and that their interests were protected.[11] Its failure to do this was blamed for the departure from the party of large numbers of working class members.[12]

The other side to this charge of failing to defend the interests of its class base was the argument that too few workers were represented in the party's leading organs. With the approach of the national congress and the corresponding party meetings at all levels, this charge was most often made with reference to the under-representation of workers among the delegates to these bodies. At the Moscow city conference, only 7.2 per cent of the delegates were categorised as workers,[13] while at the Russian conference the corresponding figure was 9.5 per cent;[14] at the national congress the proportion of workers was about 11 per cent. From the industrial oblast of Yaroslavl not one industrial worker was sent as a delegate to the national congress, while from Omsk it was claimed that the apparatus had squeezed out workers from the selection process.[15] An open letter addressed to Gorbachev, reportedly signed by more than 2000 workers and citing Lenin for authority, called for workers to be represented at higher party meetings and on the party's leading bodies in the same proportion as they constituted party membership.[16]

The accuracy of this charge was acknowledged, with the result that 200 workers and kolkhozniks were invited with a 'consultative vote' to the Russian conference and 350 to the national congress to boost the representation of these groups. But this move was little more than symbolic, and caused some resentment among both elected delegates and many of those coopted workers and peasants; the former, because many of the coopted people had stood for election as delegates and been defeated, and the latter because they now saw themselves as second-class delegates. Furthermore, this recognition of worker under-representation did not change the way many leading party figures viewed the party and its future social base. The Moscow gorkom first secretary well illustrated this attitude when he declared that although the party would continue to express the interests of the working class, the potential base for the party's renewal is that widest rank of the population who links their fate with the fate of socialism, supports socialist equality and the fundamental rights of man, and the growing role of moral and spiritual values.[17] Or, as the draft Rules declared, 'The CPSU rests on the working class, the peasantry, the intelligentsia and other social strata adhering to the socialist choice'.[18] But for many, in this diversification of its social base, the party was losing its class essence.

Such a non-class approach was also linked with the perceived spiritual crisis in the party. Although there had been widespread concern for some time about the ideological ramifications of the reform programme, two factors seem to have combined to project this issue into a prominent place in the party debate at this time. The first was the increased levels of haemorrhage of party membership in the first half of 1990. Throughout this period speakers at all levels of the party continually bemoaned the exodus of members from the party, particularly those of working class origin. In June Razumovskii gave some substance to these concerns by acknowledging that in the first five months of 1990 some 130,000 people had left the party, a figure close to that for all of 1989.[19] The second factor was the strengthening of the push for marketisation in the economic sphere. As economic performance continued to disappoint, the urgency with which market solutions were openly pressed increased. This stimulated the fears among many of a return to capitalism, a concern heightened by the measures announced by Ryzhkov in May involving substantial price rises on basic food items. This seemed to reinforce the perception that the reform programme was designed to achieve a market economy at the cost of the party's basic constituency, the working class. Declining membership and policies which seemed to overthrow much of the established orthodoxy with regard to the structuring of economic relations suggested a spiritual crisis of major dimensions to many within the party.

A conservative speaker at the conference of Russian communists gave voice to some of these concerns. He declared that while some claimed that the party had been carried away by a superfluity of theorising and that it did not give an analysis of the changing situation, only the second part of this statement was accurate. Theoretical work was in oblivion, and therefore not having resolved the general questions, the party tended to flop around when faced with tactical issues. No alternatives to 'perestroika dogmatism' have been aired. Instead, there has been a dogmatic interpretation of the slogan of the priority of general human values over class values and a move away from a class approach, from class analysis, from class as an instrument of policy.[20] Picking up on this theme, future first secretary of the new Russian party Ivan Polozkov criticised the ideological disorder in the party (which he referred to in terms attributed to Yakovlev as 'definite indefiniteness') and the failure of the current party leadership to give a decisive rebuff to the subverters of Marxist-Leninist theory and the practice of socialist construction.[21] The reaffirmation of faith in Marxism-Leninism accompanied by the charge that the ideals of the party had been turned upside down was a common line of complaint and criticism of the party leadership at this time;[22] the emergence of the Marxist Platform in the party (see below) was attributed directly to the failure on the part of the leadership and of the party to give guidance on the basis of Marxist principles in the crisis situation.[23]

Those reformist elements in the party who were blamed for the ideological erosion of Marxism-Leninism remained unbowed by this criticism. Their line was not that Marxism was irrelevant, as some outside the party were arguing, but that it was not a dogma and needed to be supplemented by other sources. This theme was prominent at the conference of the Moscow city party organisation in June. First Secretary Prokof'ev argued that the ideological legacy of Marx and Lenin was the basic but not the only theoretical source of the contemporary ideology of the party. What was required, in his view, was a new conception of socialism, communist perspectives, not ideological models but a fully defined orientation, which the classics of Marxism did not give.[24] For the Democratic Platform (see below), the theoretical basis of the party was to be the richness of democratic thought, including Marx, Engels, Lenin, Gramsci and other theoreticians of Marxism.[25] In the words of the draft Rules, the party was based upon 'the creative development of the ideas of Marx, Engels, Lenin and the communist perspective, on the achievements of progressive social science, independent internationalism and general human goals.'[26] In all of these formulations the orthodox ideological basis of the party, at least as seen by the critics, was being downgraded. Marxism-Leninism was no longer the unchallenged lodestar of the party, to the chagrin of many. Before a hostile audience, Gorbachev himself justified this when, in welcoming intellectual rivalry in the CPSU, he declared 'We believe that the clash and struggle of opinions is fully normal, even necessary for a political party'.[27]

Challenge to the established ideological orthodoxy was not new in the party. But previously such challenges had gone largely unspoken. While some of the central tenets may have been modified or even overthrown, this usually was hidden behind a language which, by emphasising continuity, tended to obscure the nature of the intellectual break. But this time such an appearance of continuity could not be sustained. One reason for this was the existence among many leading reformers of the conviction that one of the main impediments to reform was precisely that continuity which had previously been so valued. As a result, instead of obscuring the rejection of the former orthodoxy, this group sought to emphasise it. Furthermore, it is difficult to envisage a language of reform that would be more directly opposed to the established orthodoxy: market, private property, pluralism, multi-party system were all concepts prominent in the debate which clearly affronted the central aspects of Marxist orthodoxy. Such a direct challenge to that orthodoxy was bound to engender a reaction. Opposition to the changes was one source of the charges of ideological heterodoxy. But another was deep-seated belief in the validity of the ideological principles. We should not assume that all in the USSR were motivated by purely personal interests and saw the ideology in an instrumental, cynical light. For those who were true believers, the impact of the reform programme was likely to be disillusionment. In the words of one correspondent to *Pravda* : 'My mother is a pensioner. She asks me: why was the October revolution necessary if after so many years the old comes back? I cannot answer this question.'[28]

### Party fractions

The spiritual crisis in the party and the rejection of Marxist orthodoxy which was at its root also had its organisational side. This is reflected in part in the crystallisation of organised fractions in the party. The erosion of the ethos of monolithic unity of views and the acceptance of the existence of a range of views inside the party opened up the question of the compatibility of this situation with the organisational principles structuring party life. Particularly important here were the linked issues of the right to organise in order to press views, how minority dissenting opinion was to be handled and the achievement of unity of action. The immediate context for this discussion was the new draft Rules and the emergence of two new fractional groupings in the party, the Democratic Platform and the Marxist Platform.

There was little objection to the presence in the party of a diversity of opinions on issues, but the more conservative elements tended to interpret this strictly in terms of the traditional understanding of the decisions of the X party Congress in 1921. This involved recognition of the right of free discussion along with the demand that this not be conducted through the activities of organised fractions and that once a decision had been reached, all were to eschew their opinions and fall in behind that decision. The difficulty in maintaining this position was that all were agreed, at least publicly, on the need to reject the command-administrative structure and methods of the Stalin era, and yet this position was intrinsically part of that legacy. Moreover, the party had officially adopted competitive elections for party positions as officially desirable, and this seemed to imply greater fluidity and freedom than the established interpretation permitted. These difficulties meant that the more conservative side of this debate rarely spoke openly about monolithic unity in the party.[29] Instead, they spoke in broad, general terms. Ligachev referred to the need for the consolidation of party ranks on a principled basis and declared that he had no complaint against those with different opinions, only those whose actions weakened the party.[30] There were frequent calls for the continued prohibition of organised fractions and for the maintenance of organisational unity.[31] This sentiment became stronger in the published record the closer the congress approached because of the widely perceived possibility that the party would split at that congress.

A lead in this emphasis upon unity came from the central leadership in April 1990. Following a meeting of the Politburo the report of which expressed concern at how 'some members of the CPSU are making persistent attempts to divert the debate from a constructive channel onto the road of fractional struggle and to provoke a split in the party', the CC issued a letter entitled 'For Consolidation on a Principled Basis'.[32] The letter began by referring to the wide process of debate that was unrolling in the party and society on the basis of the draft Platform and Rules issued by the CC. It acknowledged the wide diversity of views that had been expressed and declared that the party 'comes out for open and honest competition of ideas'. However, the CC 'considers it impossible to pass over the attempts being made by certain people to lead the party away from the strategic course it has adopted and if this does not succeed then to provoke a split in it. This is being done both from the right and from the left', by those who see perestroika as a 'liberal-bourgeois degeneration' of society and the party and by those who declare October to have been a tragic mistake (the letter seems to have these two groups reversed). Furthermore many in the party have not yet broken with the legacy of Stalinism and stagnation. The letter continued:

No less concern is evoked by the fact that a number of members of the CPSU have unfurled a struggle against the party from pseudo-radical positions under the flag of perestroika. Declaring themselves to be 'consistent democrats', virtually the only champions of radical changes, they have carried out an attack upon the ideological and organisational foundations of the CPSU, and some of them have taken up arms directly against Lenin and Leninism. In this connection attention is drawn to the activity of individuals who have united around the so-called Democratic Platform.

While these people have the right to express their views, they seek to 'turn our party into some kind of shapeless association with complete freedom for fractions and groups'. They seek to split the party from within, and have begun organising the better to pursue their ends. The letter opposed splitting the party and called for consolidation of its ranks based upon acceptance of the party's ideological-theoretical and organisational foundations. It then continued:

The time has come when, while not giving up freedom of discussion and while strengthening its constructive basis, it is essential to get to the bottom of the question of what is to be done with those members of the party who insistently and purposefully lead matters toward a split, who create fractions with organisational structures within the ranks of the CPSU, who deny the socialist choice of the Soviet people, and who by their views and conduct have in effect placed themselves outside the party. Is it possible for such people to remain within the ranks of the CPSU? . . . Drawing the line between those who have entered upon the path of struggle against the party is not a purge and not a repression of dissent. It should be directed against those who organise fractional groups . . .

Not, that is, those who have simply been carried away by pseudo-revolutionary phrases and are unable to understand properly the processes taking place in society; for these people, explanation will suffice.

The argument contained in this letter was taken up in a *Pravda* editorial five days later.[33] The editorial was directed against those who disrupted the party's ideological and organisational unity by, among other things, 'creating within it organisationally formalised fractions with their own group discipline'. This did not mean, and the CC's letter should not be taken as encouraging, reprisals against independent-minded communists or an excuse for 'revenge' by conservative forces, it meant neither a purge nor a split, but a unifi-cation of the party on the basis of adherence to the principles of perestroika. The message contained in the CC's letter and the *Pravda* editorial was clear: the unity of party ranks was essential, and it may be that the only way this could be achieved was through the expulsion of Democratic Platform supporters from party ranks.

The other side of the debate emphasised democratisation inside the party, again a theme which all viewed publicly in a positive light. While the most forceful proponents of the need for democratisation agreed on the need for unity, they believed this could come about only through the clash of views and the open resolution of issues rather than what they saw to be a crude, organisationally-engendered unity. Appealing to traditional party symbols and the prevailing ethos, many called for democratic centralism rather than bureaucratic centralism.[34] Although some called for the legalisation of fractions in the party,[35] the more moderate position was the call for full freedom of views and tendencies.[36] The formal position had been set out in the draft CC Platform adopted at the February plenum. This called for 'pluralism of opinions, freedom of criticism, diversity of approaches and platforms . . . and the minority's right to uphold its views subject to mandatory fulfilment of decisions made by the majority' along with a prohibition on 'the formation of fractions with their own internal organisation and discipline'.[37] This was clearly a compromise between reformers and conservatives: while maintaining the ban on fractions and unity of action, it provided some scope for freedom of discussion and opinion. In effect, much of the debate during these months constituted an elaboration of the essence of this position.[38]

In one sense, the most crucial issue in this discussion, that of the formation of fractions, was obscured by a conscious ambiguity. This was the use of the term 'platform'. This was something which was consistent with pleas for democratisation, with the open exchange of views and with competitive elections, but it avoided the sort of direct organisational implications embodied in the notion of 'fractions'. Some attempts were made to distinguish between these. One prominent party leader declared that the distinction was not one of the presence or absence of organisational linkages between adherents. He argued that when there were millions of party members spread over a wide area, the combining of people together in definite ideological positions would generate a system of organisational ties. Fractionalism existed, therefore, only when the activities of a particular group opposed the activities of the whole party, were directed at the breakaway of its supporters, or when they became ideologically separated from the party.[39] This distinction reflects the use of the notion of 'fractionalism' as a political weapon and little else; it provided no clear criteria for distinguishing between acceptable and unacceptable activity. In practice, of course, this was impossible. Freedom to design and project a policy or ideological platform presupposed the sort of organisation and perhaps discipline which the CC Draft Platform had abjured. However, by talking about this question in terms of platforms, the party was able, at least for the time being, to slip over the hard question of organisation.

This issue was given a concrete form by the crystallisation within the party of two fractions, or as they preferred to call themselves, platforms, the Democratic Platform and the Marxist Platform. Both possessed an organisational structure, but the main concerns which motivated their emergence were different: the main focus of the Democratic Platform was the internal structure and operating procedures of the party itself, while the Marxist Platform sought to offer a Marxist solution to the crisis facing the country as an alternative to what it perceived to be the inadequate response of the party leadership. The main focus of one was organisational, the other policy. The Democratic Platform was the first to emerge.

The immediate roots of the Democratic Platform are to be found in the Moscow Party Club 'Communists for Perestroika' organised in April 1989.[40] This body tried to mobilise support for the early convocation of a party congress, but was unable to get the support of the 33 per cent of members necessary for such a development. They thus decided to create their own left democratic association inside the party. The first All-Union Conference was convened on 20–21 January 1990. Overwhelmingly dominated by white-collar workers and professional people,[41] this formally constituted the new association and set in train the registration of supporters. By mid-April democratic associations and party clubs existed in all republics and more than one hundred cities, regional coordinators had been elected, a fifty-seven-person All-Union Coordination Council had been formed, and a newspaper called 'Democratic Platform' had been established with a circulation of 50,000.[42]

The II All-Union Conference was scheduled for 16–17 June, some two weeks before the party congress. This was preceded by a series of regional conferences at which positions for the national conference were worked out.[43] At the national conference there were almost 900 delegates from 12 union republics and 65 oblasts, krais and autonomous regions of the RSFSR. The conference discussed both the policies that should be adopted and the future of the Democratic Platform itself. On the latter question, a questionnaire administered to the delegates elicited the following breakdown: 20.3 per cent favoured staying in the party and working for democratisation regardless of the outcome of the party congress, 56.4 per cent favoured remaining in the party only if the congress adopted the positions of the Democratic Platform, and 15.3 per cent favoured leaving the party before the congress.[44] The position adopted was that favoured by the majority of delegates, staying in the party to see what would come from the congress.[45]

The policy position of the Democratic Platform was outlined on a number of occasions.[46] In essence, the Platform supported the transformation of the party into a social democratic, parliamentary party which, instead of being characterised by a monopoly of one ideology, was open to a variety of influences. It was to give up its monopoly on power, instead competing in the multi-party electoral arena for popular support. The official status of party committees in enterprises and other organisations should be liquidated and the coercive arms of the state depoliticised. The principle of democratic centralism should be replaced by general democratic principles, the nomenklatura system and apparat privileges abolished, and the monopoly of the production-territorial principle in party construction eliminated. The unitary nature of the party should be replaced by the federal principle. The party's responsibility for the state of the country should be acknowledged, discredited leaders should be replaced through election, and party members should undergo reregistration on the basis of the platforms they support. As one critic pointed out, this was not a platform in the same sense as that of the CC was a platform; this was much narrower, focusing on the party and its problems rather than general issues of policy.[47] It did not address itself to the general problems of the society and was in this sense entirely about party structure and processes.

The level of support achieved by the Democratic Platform within the party is unclear. Reports appeared in the press supporting the Platform and its aspirations[48] and there were calls for an emphasis upon the common aspects of the positions of the Democratic Platform and other elements of the party in order to facilitate the emergence of a common programme.[49] But there were also frequent invocations against the Platform and the perceived damage it was doing to the cause of party unity; Yuri Afanas'ev in particular came in for severe criticism.[50] Although some argued that claims of the level of support for the Platform were exaggerated,[51] the application of organisational measures against it reflects the concern by some about its possible strength. The CC Open Letter noted above[52] was important in this regard because it seemed to legitimise both opposition to the Platform and the use of organisational measures against it. Complaints were publicly aired by Platform supporters about the use of such measures.[53] Some membership figures are available. In April, the Democratic Platform was reported to have 100,000 members in the CPSU.[54] In the election of delegates to the party Congress, Gorbachev was opposed by a supporter of the Platform, Valerian Nikolaev.[55] In the election, Gorbachev received an approval vote of 61.1 per cent, with 38.1 per cent voting against.[56] A proportion of that 38.1 per cent would have been Platform supporters, but it is unlikely that all would have been so; Gorbachev's candidacy provided a perfect opportunity for both a general protest vote and for conservatives to enter their opposition to the changes. Among delegates to the party Congress, only some 100 of the almost 5,000 delegates were affiliated with the Democratic Platform. But this is likely grossly to understate Platform support because of a possible lack of geographical concentration of its members in the electoral okrugs and local manipulation to ensure apparat representation.[57] One study of deputies in the Russian Congress of People's Deputies suggests that support for the Democratic Platform was more likely among junior members of the apparatus than senior members, who tended more towards the Marxist Platform.[58] But while the precise level of support is unclear, it is probable that that level increased following the conservative-dominated founding conference/congress of the Communist Party of the RSFSR in late June (see below). In any case, during this period the Democratic Platform was a more prominent feature in the course of intra-party life than the other fraction which emerged at this time, the Marxist Platform.

The Marxist Platform began as a group of people who left the Moscow Party Club (which supported the Democratic Platform) because they believed that neither the Democratic Platform nor the party offered a Marxist analysis of the current crisis. Around this nucleus was formed a federation of Marxist party clubs with an aktiv of nearly 40. The first conference was held in April with nearly 300 people attending, of whom 97 were delegated by party organisations. The II All-Union Conference was held in Moscow on 16–17 June and was attended by 91 delegates and 147 guests from eight union republics and 64 cities.[59] The intellectual nucleus of the Marxist Platform was to be found primarily in the social science departments of Moscow State University, while its membership consisted mainly of scientific, pedagogical and creative intelligentsia and representatives of the lower levels of party work. Workers were a small component, reportedly having increased from 4 per cent to 7.7 per cent of the membership between April and mid-June.[60]

Like the Democratic Platform, the Marxist Platform was able to publish its theses in *Pravda*[61] and these were discussed during the course of the intra-party debate.[62] The Platform favoured the transition to a market economy, but this had both to benefit the workers and to be under popular rather than bureaucratic control; consumers' unions were cited as an example of how this might work. Workers were to take more control and responsibility in the workplace while soviets were to exercise real responsibility in the conduct of public affairs. They opposed parliamentarism as the style of work of the party, believing that power should lie in the hands of a democratic bloc of social mass organisations rather than an elite parliamentary body. The party should work in the democratic movements in order to win support and a dominant position. Within the party, widescale democratisation should replace the bureaucratic centralism that had formerly prevailed. Restrictions upon lower level-activism and initiative should be removed, minorities should be accorded specific guarantees including the right to criticise decisions and form platforms, but there was to be no freedom for fractions. Power was to lie with party meetings, congresses and conferences, with committees and bureaux only to coordinate the work of party organisations in realising adopted decisions.[63]

The strength of the Marxist Platform is even more difficult to estimate than that of the Democratic Platform. It is not really clear what the Platform had to offer. Although its programme was wider than that of the Democratic Platform, it had no logical constituency. For that element which was looking to the traditional corpus of Marxism for an answer to existing difficulties, the Marxist Platform's endorsement of the market is unlikely to have struck a responsive chord. For many of those reformists who saw the market mechanism as being part of the solution, Marxism as it had traditionally been understood was part of the problem, with the result that any grouping professing its Marxist credentials would be unlikely to win favour with them. It thus appeared to sit uneasily between the reformist and conservative sides. Furthermore, given its commitment to remain within the party and to press its views through party fora regardless of the outcome of the XXVIII Congress,[64] it did not present the same threat of organisational split as the Democratic Platform and was not as prominent in the course of party debate.

## A Russian party

If the pressures for making provision for a degree of political pluralism within party ranks were manifested in the emergence of these two platforms alongside the official CC platform, those pressures making for greater recognition of national diversity which had been so powerful towards the end of 1989 and early 1990 continued to play themselves out. But this time the chief issue inside the party was not the Baltic republics, but Russia itself. The official position opposing the federalisation of the party was maintained and was ritually uttered on formal occasions.[65] However at the same time the pressures favouring the development of an independent party for the RSFSR within the CPSU strengthened.[66] This sentiment was manifested by the appearance in the central press of articles discussing the unique nature of Russia and its problems, an image clearly designed to project Russia as an entity different from the USSR as a whole and therefore in need of its own party organs.[67] A poll of citizens of Russia taken in early May added substance to this by showing that the overwhelming majority favoured an expansion of the independence of Russia and a corresponding reduction in central controls.[68]

While this popular campaign was an important element in the build up of momentum leading to the establishment of a Russian party, the crucial organisational impetus stemmed from Leningrad.[69] The March plenum had authorised the Russian Bureau to convene a Russian party conference prior to the XXVIII Congress. This was to consist of the delegates elected to the Congress by Russian party organisations.[70] The Russian Bureau was also instructed to form an organising committee from representatives of krai, oblast, okrug and the Moscow city party organisations. This committee decided that the conference would open in Moscow on 19 June.[71] The 3 April joint meeting between the organising committee and the Russian Bureau established a commission and four working groups to prepare documents for the conference. However there were early difficulties in the functioning of these groups, with the result that they really only began their work in the middle of May. The main reason for this seems to have been a lack of leadership on the part of the Russian Bureau,[72] a situation which was interpreted (correctly) by conservative elements in the Russian Republic as reflecting the national leadership's reluctance to see a Russian party established.[73]

In part in reaction to the perceived tardiness of the national leadership and in part in order to force the pace of developments, a number of so-called initiative groups were established in various parts of the republic to proceed with the organisation of the conference.[74] These came together in Leningrad on 21–22 April in the first stage initiative congress of communists of Russia, entitled the Initiative Congress for Reviving the Russian Communist Party. The congress established an organisational bureau to proceed with the work of organising the conference and resolved that a Russian party should formally be established prior to the XXVIII Congress.[75] The organising committee of the working groups for the XXVIII Congress invited members of the organisational bureau established by the Leningrad congress, along with representatives of the Democratic and Marxist Platforms, to participate in the preparation of the draft documents for the forthcoming All-Union congress, thereby giving some official standing to the bureau. The second stage of the initiative congress met in Leningrad on 10 June. It claimed to represent some 1,764,000 communists, called for more work to be done on the programmatic documents and nominated candidates for a CC for the proposed Russian party. And in a scarcely veiled threat, it declared that if the Russian Communist Party was not created at the forthcoming Russian conference, the organising committee and the CC nominees would take on the responsibility of the CC RCP. On the day before, the Russian Bureau and the organising committee had met. They supported the call for the establishment of an independent Russian party, acknowledged the pressures to transform the forthcoming conference into the constituent congress of the party but said that this had to be decided by the delegates, and declared that because there were too few representatives of the working class and peasantry among the delegates, an extra 200 would be invited to the conference.[76]

It is clear that there was a major change in attitude toward the establishment of a Russian party on the part of the national leadership and the popular campaign stemming from Leningrad may have been part of the reason for this. However, other factors were also important. Arguments about the way in which the Russians did not have equal rights with other nationalities because they lacked a party organisation of their own were valid. There may also have been some truth in the view that Russian interests were often not well served under the existing arrangement because they were always being subordinated to perceived national interests. But what gave this argument increased potency was the changed political situation. Particularly important here was the growing momentum for a reworking of the state federal arrangements and, especially, for an assertion of Russian state sovereignty. Buttressed by the First Congress of People's Deputies of the RSFSR which opened on 17 May and which formally established a new state governmental structure for Russia, the sentiment favouring a Russian party was strengthened: if a new political system was to emerge in the RSFSR, the communist party would be handicapped if it were represented by the all-union party rather than one whose sole concern was Russian affairs. This was particularly evident, many argued, in the electoral arena where the absence of a Russian communist party was a large part of their explanation for the poor performance of party candidates in the recent elections. An additional factor generating support for a Russian party in some circles was the political complexion it was believed such a party would have. The opinion was widespread that the delegates coming from the Russian hinterland would be overwhelmingly conservative in their views. This perception was reinforced by the Leningrad initiative congress[77] and by the support given to the enterprise by people like Ligachev.[78] Such a party was seen by more conservative elements in the leadership and the party at large as a potential counter to the pro-reform leadership group in the all-union party around Gorbachev. After the election of Yel'tsin as Chairman of the Supreme Soviet of the Russian Republic and his vigorous espousal of Russian national interests and state sovereignty, this view of the need for a conservative counter-weight would have been strengthened.

The fears that the Russian party would be a conservative-dominated body were realised when the conference met;[79] 42.3 per cent of the delegates were full-time party workers.[80] Although Gorbachev gave a vigorous defence of the changes he had sponsored, most speakers generally adopted a critical line when discussing the current situation, responsibility for it and the performance of the party leadership; the early days of the conference in particular were marked by vigorous criticism of the leadership and its failure to give a clear theoretical orientation to guide both party and society.[81] The election of Ivan Polozkov, the conservative party chief from Krasnodar who had been defeated by Yel'tsin in the ballot for presidency of the Russian Republic,[82] as first secretary of the new party is a further indication of the nature of the assembly. Indeed, the fact that he defeated a candidate (Politburo member A.V. Vlasov) openly promoted by those supportive of Gorbachev is reflective of the general orientation of the gathering. Despite some opposition,[83] the conference transformed itself into a congress and proceeded formally to create the Communist Party of the RSFSR. This was to be a body within the CPSU: there would be one membership card while the Rules and Programme of the Russian party were to be consistent with those of the CPSU. The congress adopted a series of resolutions and decided to postpone the election of a CC and the adoption of a programme until after the XXVIII Congress.

The establishment of the new party and its conservative nature had an almost immediate impact: a number of party organisations in Russia wrote to the party leadership rejecting the authority of the conference to turn itself into a congress and establish the new party and declared their desire not to become part of the new party but to remain constituent elements of the CPSU.[84] The Russian party was important at two levels. Firstly, in terms of practical politics in the party, it increased the disillusionment among the liberal intelligentsia, especially in Moscow (many of the party organisations making these protests were the homes of this intelligentsia), and thereby stimulated the exodus from the party among this group that was already underway; it also gave increased force to the similar feelings among those who had decided to wait and see about the outcome of the party congress. Secondly, in terms of the party structure, it raised the question of the relationship between the all-union party organs and those of the Russian Republic. Of course the emergence of a Russian party only raised once again the more general question applying to all of the republican parties, but in a more acute form. While the central party organs had responsibility for developments within the Russian Republic, they had a valid reason for retaining a capacity to become involved in all aspects of domestic policy. Once that capacity was no longer necessary at the centre, there was no reason not to either dismantle it or transfer it to the Russian party. In either event, the capacity of the centre to interfere in the domestic affairs of the con-stituent republics would be reduced, the power of the central apparatus rolled back, and the independence of the republican parties enhanced. But this also raised the question of what the central party apparatus was now going to do. If the republican parties, including the Russian, sought to expand their independence, the role of the central organs would diminish; it would be little more than a clearing house for those common issues which concerned the republican parties. As such, it would be transformed into a mere office-keeping appendage of the republican parties. This problem of the consequences of the establish-ment of a powerful Russian party was recognised in the lead-up to the Russian conference, but it tended to be publicly presented in terms of the possibility of the creation of two centres of power within the party, the central and Russian organs.[85] People were very conscious of the power that would rest with the new Russian party given that more than half of the membership of the CPSU would formally belong to it. The fear was that the Russian party would use this power to dominate its sister parties.

### Pre-Congress debate

The criticism that the party leadership came under at the Russian conference/congress echoed a prominent theme in party discussions during this period. The lack of activity and of leadership provided by the CC and Politburo was reported to be a common complaint in the PPOs.[86] They were accused of being cut off from and ignoring rank-and-file sentiment, out of touch with reality, of introducing policies which discredited the party and led to the loss of popular faith in it, and of being in need of radical renewal.[87] In a decision adopted by the Moscow city party conference, it was said that the leadership in the CC and Politburo 'lagged behind the development of events, most of all in the democratisation of the party, and often took decisions only under pressure of public opinion.'[88] A hostile speaker at the Russian conference declared:

> Instead of strengthening all links of the party, of defining its strategy and tactics in answer to the given political moment, the leadership of the CPSU devoted itself to a position of defencelessly sitting in the entrenchments under the massed fire of quickly organising anti-socialist forces, in the consolidation of which a large role was played by some means of mass information and the exceedingly contradictory, occasionally unpredictable policy of the party leadership. (Stormy applause).[89]

This sort of criticism should not have been unexpected: the Politburo's leading role had not been very prominent and the Secretariat had worked very weakly,[90] and although major decisions about the party had been taken in the CC in February and March, major policy questions for the country had not been discussed in this body. Ligachev directly criticised this; he criticised the lack of collectivism in the leadership, called on the party leader to devote all his time to the party, and declared that there was a need for self-criticism on the part of the leadership which had allowed anti-socialist forces to increase their activity.[91] But it was Kemerovo obkom first secretary Mel'nikov who drew the logical conclusion from this sort of complaint: that decisions were being made elsewhere than in the leading party organs. He argued that political forces had split the General Secretary off from the Politburo and CC, and that the efforts of circles close to the General Secretary were leading to the development of a cult of the individual personality. This was characterised by the gradual separation of the CC and the party itself from the taking of decisions on the most important issues, the monopoly on decision-making by a narrow circle of people, the pretensions of the leadership to ultimate truth, the joint occupation of many posts,[92] and the threat to abandon work in the Politburo and CC if subjected to criticism. Although extreme in its language, this charge that the party was becoming irrelevant to the decision-making process doubtless hit a responsive nerve among many party members.

Proposed solutions to this problem of a lack of leadership on the part of the party's leading organs were not very imaginative. No one really came to grips with the basic issue: that the structural changes underway in the political system were designed to reduce the role played by party organs in the decision-making process. Some accorded blame to communists at lower levels for exercising insufficient supervision over leading figures, with the implication that greater supervision would overcome the problem.[93] Others called for the radical renewal of these bodies,[94] reflecting the belief that the problem lay in the personnel rather than the processes of change currently under way. Furthermore this was a solution which lower levels of the party could hope to impose when these bodies came up for re-election at the party congress.[95] But many also argued that, given the work of these organs was deemed to be unsatisfactory, responsibility for this needed to be laid at the door of those who had made the mistakes. Consequently, it was argued, individual leaders should give personal accounts of their own activities over the period since the last congress. Indeed, declared one speaker at the Moscow party conference, it was unacceptable that at a time when people were calling for reports on individual members of the Politburo, the published information that had earlier appeared on Politburo sessions should no longer appear.[96] In an apparent attempt to blunt this criticism, beginning on 21 June individual Politburo members began giving interviews which were effectively reports on what they had done and how they thought.[97] It is clear that there was substantial discontent with the way the leadership had performed, and especially its apparent unwillingness to give due regard to the views of the lower levels of the party. This was to reach a climax at the XXVIII Congress.

Dissatisfaction with the performance of leading elected organs was also evident in the concern about the role played by the party apparatus. During this period speakers confirmed the view that the apparatus must facilitate the work of the elected organ and that its size and specific functions must depend upon immediate circumstances.[98] More directly, some spoke of the party as already comprising two parties, the party of the apparat and the party of the workers,[99] while there were also complaints about the arrogant and abrasive attitude of some responsible office-holders.[100] One correspondent even referred to the 'apparatus without honour'.[101] Surprisingly there was little discussion at the national level of the wage rises responsible party officials had received at the end of 1989, although one correspondent did argue that work was being hindered by the popular perception of the privileges of the party worker. However, he added, even after the pay rise, the party worker averaged only 110 roubles per month for each family member.[102]

The complaint that work was being hindered by popular perceptions was part of the more general disquiet about the work and standing of the apparatus. One correspondent argued that one reason for the negative attitude toward the party apparatus was its inability honestly to sum up a situation and to take bold measures to meet it.[103] Another complained that frequently the apparatus had insufficient funds to sustain its operations, a situation which would become worse as a result of the new financial instructions to be adopted at the party congress;[104] a former member of the Krasnoyarsk kraikom apparatus said that the demands of paper work left little time for apparatus workers to go among the workers despite their desire to do so. He also acknowledged that there were some unworthy workers in the apparatus, but that most were of high quality.[105] These sorts of claims may be seen as an attempt to justify the performance of the apparatus against the charges of inadequate leadership levelled against leading organs. They also constitute in themselves a complaint against the measures to reduce the party apparatus taken after the XIX Conference.

Surprisingly there was little discussion of the proposals for the restructuring of the party's upper echelons made in the draft Rules adopted at the March plenum.[106] However, there was considerable attention devoted to the primary organisations of the party. The general theme that party committees and organisations should be independent in their own organisational matters, reflected most clearly in the quest for greater independence on the part of the national parties, was also applied to the PPOs. There were calls for the PPOs to enjoy organisational and financial autonomy, to be able to structure their own operations in accord with the prevailing circumstances and to fund those operations from their own resources.[107] With this in mind, there were proposals that the PPOs should retain 50 per cent of the membership dues they collected, a measure which would have given many of them the financial autonomy they sought. The PPOs were called upon to be more active in party life and in the discussion and resolution of issues. Instead of waiting for initiative from above, they should present their own ideas and proposals and be directly involved in the working out of party policy. Some even argued that the formation of policy should begin at the lower levels and work its way through the structure to the top rather than the reverse.[108] One means of achieving greater activity on the part of PPOs was believed to be the creation of horizontal associations which would unite the PPOs of a given area and thereby provide them with a channel for discussing local problems and working out relevant solutions. Such councils of PPO secretaries began to spring up in various parts of the country.[109] The greater activity of the PPOs was seen as one means of overcoming the passivity of many party members.[110]

Two other issues concerning the PPOs were prominent at this time. The first related to the basis upon which they should rest: should they retain the dual production-territorial principle whereby primary units were formed in places of work as well as of habitation, or should they switch exclusively to the territorial principle and be based solely on place of habitation? This issue was bound up with the more general question of whether the party should seek to be a vanguard party or a parliamentary party. As Moscow gorkom first secretary Prokof'ev argued, there was much scholasticism in this debate,[111] but to the protagonists the implications were real. Those who favoured the vanguard role argued that such a party reflected the interests and views of the working class and that it did this by remaining in touch with that class through organisation in the workplace, while a parliamentary party sought only to gain votes in order to gain power and therefore constituted a means of alienating people from power. Some even argued that the consequences of the liquidation of production cells could be seen in the dissolution of communist power in Eastern Europe.[112] Those who argued for the transformation of the party into a parliamentary party[113] argued that with the transfer of power to the soviets, competition in the electoral arena and the organisation of activity in the parliamentary arena would become the crucial concerns of the party. It had, therefore, to clearly orient its activities to these concerns.

Although in principle the distinction between vanguard and parliamentary party was clear, in practice this was less so: a vanguard party would still have to organise in such a way as to maximise its chances of success in the parliamentary arena, while a parliamentary party would need extra-parliamentary organisations if it was to have a stable political existence. However the different types of party did have direct implications for the organisational basis of the party's primary units. Those favouring the vanguard model supported the strengthening of the production basis of PPOs while acknowledging the need to increase the level of activity in places of habitation, while those favouring the parliamentary model were content to see the production basis eliminated and PPOs being formed solely on the basis of place of habitation, because this was to be the basis of the electorates. This issue was one of the few occasions on which there was direct debate about the implications for the party of the new political structure and of the emergence of a multi-party system.

This issue of the vanguard party was also relevant to the debate over whether the party should have organised units in the coercive arms of the state, the military, KGB and MVD forces. On one side was the argument that if the party was to maintain its position of primacy, it had to retain the capacity to influence developments in these bodies through party organisations within their structures. This was bolstered by the argument that the coercive arms of the state were politicised in all political systems and that the Soviet should be no different in this regard.[114] The other side of the debate called for the depoliticisation of the coercive arms of the state through the dissolution of formal party organs inside these institutions; individual members were to belong to PPOs based on their place of habitation rather than their place of work. Primary organisations of the party must not be elements of the administrative-productive structure.[115] The basic principle adhered to by this group was the separation of party from state, a principle formally accepted by the party in mid-1988. But the withdrawal of party organs from these institutions was vigorously opposed not only because it would have deprived the party of control over these bodies, but because this would have undercut part of the argument for maintaining PPOs in the enterprises and for the retention of a vanguard role.

The concerns about the state of the PPOs reflected a deeper concern that was percolating into the party consciousness at this time, the dimensions of the widespread popular disillusionment with the party. One source of this was the growing conviction that, as the economy spiralled down, leading party members were using their positions to line their own pockets.[116] The party's performance in the elections earlier in the year and the continuing exodus from party ranks gave substance to this fear.[117] Now this became a point of open discussion, with references to a strengthening of an anti-communist or anti-party mood in the country.[118] According to one speaker, the party was so discredited that in the soviet elections, some candidates 'forget' to mention that they are party members.[119] This disillusionment was now also presented in statistical terms, even if the form in which the statistics were presented leaves many issues (including the representative nature of them) uncertain. According to a questionnaire distributed among party members and reported in mid-May, only 17 per cent of respondents believed that the party could regain its authority through perestroika and the achievement of its ends.[120] Another survey taken at the end of May showed that while there had been some improvement in the evaluation of the work of party organs since November 1989, only 27 per cent believed that there had been positive changes in the activities of the CC.[121] Furthermore, 53 per cent no longer saw the party as the leading political force in the country, a result that elicited the comment that 'the authority of the party is continuing to fall'.[122] Perhaps more telling was the report that only 12 per cent unambiguously believed that the present government could extricate the country from the economic crisis (with 20 per cent saying the government could not and a further 18 per cent 'rather yes than no' and 29 per cent 'rather no than yes'). To a question about the extent to which they trusted the country's leadership, 13 per cent said 'completely', 44 per cent 'in the main' and 30 per cent 'not at all'.[123] The publication of these sorts of figures enhanced the sense of crisis which was evident in the party at this time. The concerns about the erosion of the party's position and authority were real.

It was in this sort of atmosphere, with concerns about the future reflected in the increasingly open clash of ideas between radicals and conservatives in the society, that the elections took place for congress delegates. The CC instructions on the conduct of the delegate election process prescribed secret ballot but made the existence of competitive candidates optional.[124] The result of this process was a delegate body of which 45 per cent were officials of the party apparatus and a further 20 per cent managers in the economy;[125] barely 11 per cent were workers. This heavy representation of the apparatus may be explained in three ways. Firstly, it may be that most party members believed that these people were the best suited to represent their interests and views at the congress. However, given the extent of criticism of such leaders during this period, this explanation is unlikely. Secondly, although there was an emphasis upon democratic procedures and a broader cross section of the party standing for election, those leaders who were generally most prominent in local affairs and who were better known by the electorate stood a better chance of gaining election than a little known worker or peasant. The election of local notables simply because they were familiar is an argument with considerable weight. Thirdly, what one correspondent described as 'apparat games'.[126] Clearly there were cases when the selection process was manipulated. It was claimed that in Omsk the apparatus had squeezed workers out as candidates. In another okrug a complainant declared that there had been no meeting to discuss candidates, only the programme of the raikom first secretary had been prepared for the voters, and there was no opportunity to discuss alternatives; an editorial note to this article reported that there had been many letters complaining of this sort of thing. In a number of okrugs, the voting turn-out had been very low, a development attributed by the writers to apparat machinations.[127] The extent of such manipulation cannot be measured.

The results of the election of congress delegates from among members and candidate members of the Politburo and members of the Secretariat provides an interesting insight into the process (neither Vorotnikov nor Sliun'kov took part in the elections),[128]

|  | No.of positions | No.of candidates | Votes % for | Votes % against |
|---|---|---|---|---|
| Gorbachev, M. S. | 1 | 2 | 61.1 | 38.1 |
| Zaikov, L. N. | 1 | 3 | 61.3 | 38.5 |
| Ivashko, V. A. | 1 | 2 | 96.0 | 3.9 |
| Kriuchkov, V. A. | 12 | 20 | 77.7 | 21.2 |
| Ligachev, E. K. | 1 | 3 | 79.8 | 19.8 |
| Masliukov, Iu. D. | 1 | 3 | 65.0 | 34.0 |
| Medvedev, V. A. | 1 | 1 | 90.0 | 9.9 |
| Ryzhkov, N. I. | 1 | 10 | 61.3 | 36.0 |
| Shevardnadze E. A. | 1 | 2 | 74.4 | 24.4 |
| Yakovlev, A. N. | 6 | 65 | 63.4 | 35.9 |
| Biriukova. A. P. | 37 | 37 | 92.5 | 7.5 |
| Vlasov, A. V. | 3 | 3 | 74.6 | 25.3 |
| Luk'ianov, A. I. | 1 | 1 | 96.1 | 3.9 |
| Primakov, E. M. | 10 | 10 | 98.7 | 1.3 |
| Pugo, B. K. | 6 | 6 | 94.6 | 5.2 |
| Razumovskii, G. P. | 16 | 29 | 85.9 | 14.1 |
| Yazov, D. T. | 10 | 13 | 93.4 | 6.0 |
| Baklanov, O. D. | 1 | 2 | 80.0 | 18.9 |

| Girenko, A. N. | 1 | 2 | 86.3 | 13.7 |
| Manaenkov, Iu. A. | 1 | 1 | 96.6 | 3.4 |
| Stroev, E. S. | 1 | 1 | 98.8 | 1.2 |
| Usmanov, G. I. | 1 | 2 | 76.8 | 22.8 |
| Frolov, I. T. | 16 | 16 | 99.0 | 1.0 |

A number of aspects of these data are interesting. All leaders appear to have been elected easily, with Gorbachev having the closest squeeze with the lowest positive vote and the second highest negative vote. However according to a report in *Argumenty i fakty*, before standing in Belgorod okrug where he received the above result, Egor Ligachev had stood in another okrug where only 48 people had voted for him and 3,096 against.[129] More than a third of these leaders stood uncontested, including Gorbachev supporters Medvedev, Luk'ianov, Primakov and Frolov. Furthermore, a number of these leaders stood in unusual constituencies: Ligachev in Belgorod, Medvedev in Vitebsk, Biriukova in Kirgiziia, Primakov in Severno-Ossetiia, Pugo in Dushanbe, Razumovskii in Latvia, and Frolov in Chimkent.

In the week preceding the scheduled opening of the congress, concern among reformers about the way in which the congress which founded the Communist Party of the RSFSR was dominated by conservatives allied to the widespread view that the congress would be the scene of the final showdown between the pro-reform elements and those who wished to moderate this course led to the circulation of rumours that the all-union congress would be postponed. However, a CC meeting on 29 June confirmed that the congress would go ahead and finalised preparations for it. The fears about a conservative congress were borne out following the congress opening on 2 July.

### The XXVIII Congress

Gorbachev opened the Congress by delivering the CC Report[130] in which he reaffirmed the commitment to perestroika. He argued against a dogmatic and blind obedience to Marxist tenets rooted in the nineteenth and early twentieth centuries. He sketched in general terms what an updated CPSU might look like, and although this retained the view of the party as one 'of the socialist option and communist perspective', it seemed devoid both of clear ideological commitment and of the traditional organisational principles which had characterised the CPSU in the past. He declared that the party would seek to remain the ruling party through winning majority support at the ballot box, and he reaffirmed strong support for the maintenance of the production principle in the structuring of party organisations, continued party organisation in the military (although he also acknowledged that other parties could organise here), the impermissibility of fractions, and the widening of the rights of PPOs. Gorbachev's speech was greeted coolly, and he was followed by a string of bitter, even disillusioned, speeches by party figures. Almost all of these speeches reflected profound unease about the challenges to and loss of the party's position, both practically and ideologically, and many placed the blame for this directly on the party leadership.[131] The depth of this feeling is reflected in the demands that the whole of the Politburo resign and be disqualified from holding office at the congress, and that individual leaders present personal accountability reports outlining their role in reducing the party to its present state

When leading reformers like Medvedev, Yakovlev[132] and Ryzhkov attempted to deliver such personal reports, they were vigorously attacked, heckled and interrupted from the floor. Only Yakovlev emerged relatively unbowed from this process. In contrast to this sort of treatment, those who, like Ligachev, qualified their support for perestroika by serious criticism of recent mistakes received a warm reception from the overwhelmingly conservative delegate body. However, the conservative dominance of the initial days of the Congress did not last. Through a combination of skillful chairmanship (which enabled Gorbachev to ensure that the Politburo was judged on a collective rather than an individual basis), the exercise of his persuasive powers, a number of deals which appear to have been made off the floor of the congress, and with help from Yel'tsin[133] and Yakovlev, Gorbachev was able to blunt the conservative push. In his speech at the end of the debate on the CC Report,[134] Gorbachev was much more aggressive than he had been in his opening remarks. He vigorously defended the course of perestroika, declaring that there was no alternative to continuing with it and that the 'only accusations that can be made against perestroika are that it is not being implemented resolutely and consistently enough'. He acknowledged that some mistakes had been made, but that the problem was that in the new situation many in the party tried to continue to act in the old way. He accepted as 'largely justified' the attribution of blame to the CC and some of its leaders for the way in which 'the party is losing authority, its position is becoming weaker. It is being crowded out by other political forces, and in some places communists have been forced into becoming the opposition.' But he also attributed the blame for this to party committees at all levels. Gorbachev was greatly helped in his rebuff of the conservative thrust by the disunity among conservative forces, by the absence of a credible alternative party leader[135] or coherent conservative programme, and by the way in which the whole course of the debate was now structured in reformist terms – for example, the discussion of the economic solution was cast in terms not of whether a market was desirable or not, but what type of market.[136] The absence of viable alternative leadership candidates was shown by the way in which Gorbachev was re-elected General Secretary (although some 25 per cent of delegates voted against him)[137] and his nominee Vladimir Ivashko defeated Egor Ligachev (3,109 to 776) for the new post of Deputy General Secretary.

Although some of the changes to the party's leading organs proposed at the March plenum were significantly modified at the Congress, the changes introduced to the leading organs were the most extensive in the party's history. Furthermore they constituted a major defeat for the more conservative elements who sought to continue to maximise the party's role.[138] The proposal that the General Secretary be replaced by a Chairman of the party, originally advocated by Gorbachev, was discarded and the Politburo was retained, although largely in the form of the projected Presidium. The Politburo became much more representative of the republican parties as a result of its new composition; it consisted *ex officio* of the General Secretary and his deputy and the fifteen leaders of the union republican parties, plus seven other members elected by the CC.[139] The implications of this were significant. With a majority of Politburo members republican leaders, it was impossible for the full Politburo to meet frequently. Furthermore by ensuring that five non-ex officio members of the Politburo were also part of an expanded Secretariat (a body to be chaired by the Deputy General Secretary), the status and potential power of that body was enhanced. But perhaps most importantly, the General Secretary was the only member of the Politburo who was also on what was seen as the leading executive body of the state, the Presidential Council; the separation between party and state at the top was thus almost fully realised and the ability of the Politburo to become involved in high level policy-making was restricted.[140] The withdrawal of the party from policy-making was now made a reality, at least at the top of the hierarchy. The capacity of the Politburo to play a prominent role in party affairs, already handicapped by its membership, was further hampered by a new provision that gave republican parties the right to demand review by the CC of any Politburo decision that affected them.

It is difficult to conceive of any decision that would not be subject to such a review process. It is clear that the changes introduced at the Congress removed the capacity of the Politburo to play an active part in party life.

The Congress also introduced a new secretarial structure. Most importantly, the General Secretary and the new post of Deputy General Secretary were now to be elected directly by the congress rather than the CC, a change which significantly strengthened the position of party leader *vis-à-vis* his immediate leadership colleagues. A new Secretariat was created, consisting of eighteen people: the General Secretary and Deputy General Secretary, eleven other secretaries (of whom five were also in the Politburo), and five members of the rank-and-file membership.[141] The latter group seem to have been included purely for symbolic effect. The Secretariat was to be headed by the Deputy General Secretary, a move which should in principle have enabled Gorbachev to maintain close supervision over this body while remaining active as President, and was to organise the fulfilment of party decisions and direct the work of the CC apparatus. Reflecting the generally acknowledged unsatisfactory performance of the existing CC commissions,[142] it was left to the CC to form new commissions.

The Congress also significantly changed the way the CC was composed. Membership was now based on a quota system; General Secretary and Deputy General Secretary were elected in their own right, each republican communist party/security sector had a quota of representatives,[143] while the remainder of the 412 members were representatives of public bodies and sectors of life;[144] candidate membership was abolished. The CC was clearly being turned into a representative parliament of the party. In accord with this change in purpose of the CC, the profile of leading state figures was dramatically reduced (from 24.7 per cent in 1986 to 6.6 per cent), while the proportion of central party figures also fell (from 9 per cent in 1986 to 5.1 per cent).[145] The biggest increase in representation occurred among 'mass representatives' (9.2 per cent to 31.6 per cent) and local party representatives (1.5 per cent to 10 per cent),[146] reflecting the reduced importance of the CC. In the election to the CC, the turnover level was higher than at any time in Soviet history, with only 14.1 per cent of those elected in 1990 being members in 1986, and only 4 per cent were there in 1981.[147] The election to the CC also saw a significant delegate backlash against many prominent pro-reform candidates. High profile figures who had been associated with perestroika and who had significant votes cast against them in the CC election included (of a possible total of 4,459 votes) Shatalin (1,100), Abalkin (1,681), Bunich (1,088), Latsis (1,139), Falin (1,110), Vlasov (1,418), Roy Medvedev (1,875), Mikhail Ul'ianov (1,768), Shevardnadze (872) and Yazov (1,010). The symbolic effect of this was probably offset by the announcement of Ligachev's retirement from politics. But in a practical sense this mattered little; the proposed future role of the CC was not to be one of an active and energetic participant in party affairs.

The new Rules ushered in a number of other significant changes to the way the party was meant to function. The principle of democratic centralism, which had been excluded from the March draft, was retained, party members were given increased rights of access to information about the party and its affairs, and the rights of PPOs were enlarged by according to them the right to discuss important issues before they were passed on to the CC and to retain up to half of the income they collected from membership dues. However, the level of membership dues was reduced from a maximum of 3 per cent of income to 2 per cent, thereby making returns to PPOs smaller than they might have expected. Fractions remained forbidden, although the right to form 'platforms' and 'horizontal structures' (such as clubs and seminars) was acknowledged, as was greater respect for minority rights. For the first time, the Rules also provided for voluntary withdrawal from the party. Provision was made for competitive ballots in party elections but this was still not mandatory, while two consecutive terms in elected office was made the maximum. Candidate membership was abolished. Republican communist parties were given the right to work out their own programmes and normative documents and to resolve a range of issues without reference to the centre; all party organisations were declared independent in disposing of their budgets and in resolving questions that arose. Provision was also made for a conference between congresses, with the power to renew the membership of the CC by up to 33 per cent, and for a new Central Control Committee.[148] The push for depoliticisation of the coercive arms of the state failed, with party organisation being retained in these institutions. So too did the move to switch the basis of the PPOs solely onto the territorial principle,[149] although the congress did approve a strengthening of attention to this. Many of these changes were consistent with the reduction in importance of central party organs, the withdrawal of the party from administration, and the direction of its attention towards readying itself to exercise political influence rather than administrative power. But if it was to do this, it had to have a coherent programme to give it a sense of unity and commitment.

The Congress adopted a much revised version of the CC Platform presented to the February plenum.[150] This document was adopted not as the new party programme much heralded in preceding months, but as a 'policy statement' of the congress, to remain in force until a commission could produce a new programme. The fact that after six months of debate this document could not be adopted as an official programme shows the degree of disagreement that rent party ranks. Like its predecessor, this document was a compromise. The main themes of debate earlier in the year were reflected in the document. Marxism-Leninism was significantly downgraded as a source of ideological guidance, there was a commitment to a renewed federation, to independent republican communist parties within the CPSU, to intra-party democratisation, to the renunciation of the nomenklatura approach to personnel work, to the free competition of socio-political organisations rather than a single party monopoly, and to continuing reform in all areas. There was acknowledgement that leadership organs had lagged behind developments in society and had therefore failed to provide effective leadership, that party activity and influence had declined, and that there was opposition inside the party. But the document gave no hint of the sorts of practical measures that might lead the party and the country out of the impasse into which they had entered. The vague generalisations were unlikely to stimulate the sort of enthusiasm that was necessary to unite and revive the party.

Many had seen the congress as the possible arena in which the party might split. There was no major organisational split at the Congress, but there were some notable departures from the party's ranks. As expected, Boris Yel'tsin announced his withdrawal from the party, declaring that he could not fulfil the responsibilities he owed to the Russian people as Chairman of the Supreme Soviet if he was subject to party discipline. In addition, the leader of the Democratic Platform Viacheslav Shostakovskii announced that the fraction would withdraw from the party later in the year (twenty-four members of the Platform announced they were leaving at the congress).[151] In the meantime supporters were encouraged to register in the party as members of the fraction with a view to establishing the extent of support for the Platform to facilitate the making of claims to a share in the party's assets when the Platform did leave. The mayors of Moscow and Leningrad, Gavriil Popov and Anatoly Sobchak, and prominent historian Yuri Afanas'ev also announced their departure from the party, citing the party's inability to come to grips with the problems facing the society as the reason for this.

The charge by Popov and Sobchak had considerable weight. The party congress had been almost wholly bound up with its own internal affairs, with the struggle between supporters of different tendencies. Little attention had been devoted to the major policy questions facing the society. But in a sense this was understandable. Given the inability of the different views in the party to be reconciled on specifics regarding policy alternatives, there was no way that the congress decisions were going to change the policy adopted by the government. The crucial question for many in the party was what the future held for it. The answer in the eyes of many was bleak. Its popular support was eroding. Internal unity was elusive. It seemed unable to generate a coherent view of the future which could unite party members around it. And increasingly severe financial problems were hindering its capacity to continue to function even at a rudimentary level.[152] The sense of demoralisation and crisis had become palpable. The Congress and its decisions had gone no way towards combatting these problems. For many of the ardent reformers, the conservative mood of the delegates convinced them that the party was no longer capable of reform and could not act as the mid-wife of a new society. For conservatives, there was alarm at the changes in the party's leading organs, particularly the Politburo, because these had now been rendered useless in the day-to-day conduct of state affairs. Gorbachev had effectively shifted power to the state, principally in the form of the presidency, and those with their political bases in the party realised that, in an institutional sense, their future was limited. With its position steadily eroding and unable to achieve internal coherence, stability or peace, the party's future did not look bright.

# 7    The party imploding

In the twelve months following the XXVIII Congress the problems which had afflicted the party were substantially exacerbated. It soon became clear that the Congress had neither resolved the growing differences within party ranks nor generated sufficient commitment and enthusiasm to dispel the malaise which had permeated the party.[1] The organisational fracturing of the party, which had become manifest with the Democratic Platform's announcement at the Congress that it would leave the party, proceeded apace during the following year; according to one report, in March 1991 there were up to ten 'platforms, avenues and movements' operating in the party.[2]

### Organisational splintering

The concerns about the implications of the party splitting were publicly reflected in an attack upon the Democratic Platform (and Popov and Sobchak) for leaving the party shortly after the congress ended.[3] The Democratic Platform was accused of plotting this well in advance and of being determined to carry it through regardless of anything that the party did; they were unwilling to recognise 'the congress' evolution toward democratisation'. But the Democratic Platform was itself not a united body. The announcement of the projected departure from the party at the Congress crystallised the split that had been emerging within the organisation from the June conference of the group. When that section around Shostakovskii announced its intention to depart, another section organised itself into the Working Group of Communist Reformers Section of the Democratic Platform in the CPSU. This body sought to achieve a solution to the country's and the party's problems by remaining within the ranks of the latter and working through it.[4] This group saw the party as being reformable and as having a positive role to play in resolution of the mounting problems; what was needed was a strengthening of the party's position and further democratisation of its work, the creation of a 'renewed party "from within" '.[5] In contrast that section of the Democratic Platform which was leaving the party argued for cancellation of the principle of democratic centralism, greater protection of the rights of minorities within the party, departisation of the military and security apparatus, and a party of democratic socialism rather than communism which would allow for extensive pluralism and factions.[6]

The Democratic Platform set about creating itself as a new political party. It sought to attract members and define more clearly its policy stances.[7] In some areas this led to the expulsion of party members who were known to belong to the Platform,[8] but it also occurred against a background of charges that in the face of such organisational activity, the CC and the party remained passive.[9] A constituent conference of the Platform was convened on 17–18 November to examine and adopt a statute and programme of the new party and to elect the leadership. The new party, called the Republican Party of Russia, saw itself as a social democratic parliamentary party (and therefore favoured the eventual merger with the Social Democratic Party) favouring a market system and free enterprise with a variety of forms of property ownership.[10] By December it was estimated that the party had around 1,000 members in Moscow.[11]

The departure of the Democratic Platform and its establishment as an independent party was an important development; it was the first time there had been a group exodus from the party with the intention of forming a new party grouping. However despite the fears of many, this did not lead to the substantial splitting of the CPSU. This may have been due in part to the fact that no first rank leaders of the party threw in their lot with the breakaway group, thereby denying it the sort of leading figure which could have catalysed support and given it a much greater support base from within party ranks. Although Yel'tsin resigned at the XXVIII Congress, he sought no association with the breakaway grouping. Nor did other leading figures Shevardnadze and Yakovlev when they quit the party in July 1991.[12]

Although the party did not formally split with the departure of the Democratic Platform, it continued to haemorrhage internally. Despite the continuing ban on fractions, organisational splinters continued to appear in its ranks. A conference of such groups as the Democratic Platform within the CPSU, the Marxist Platform, Democratic Unity, Left Centre and Young Communists was held in November 1990 to try to bring about some unity between them, but without any success.[13] More conservative groups also organised within party ranks. A Bolshevik Platform headed by Nina Andreeva was established in July 1991, and sought a restoration of Leninism and communist ideals in party policy and a rejection of Gorbachev.[14] The Initiative Congress of the Communists of Russia, which had played a significant role in the establishment of the Russian Communist Party, held its second congress in two stages, in April and June 1991 with respectively 752 and 820 delegates present. It adopted conservative positions, criticising social democratic tendencies within the party and the course of recent policy and harking back to the workers' movement as the lodestar for policy direction. The Initiative movement saw its task to be continually to pressure the party to ensure that it did not succumb to the social democratic line supported by some of its leading figures.[15]

Also remaining in existence throughout this period and continuing the pressure for a more conservative orientation was the Marxist Platform. In November 1990 the Platform sought, through the establishment of a movement called Marxists 21, to assert a leading role over a range of these organisational groupings with a view to achieving transformation within the party.[16] Little seems to have come of this organisational effort. Nevertheless the Marxist Platform retained its own form, although this was distinctly ambiguous in organisational terms: according to member of the coordinating council Aleksei Prigarin, the Platform did not have its own rules, dues or register of supporters, and its decisions were not binding on anyone.[17] However it did have sufficient organisation to plan conferences for January, May and August 1991.[18] Throughout this period it continued to press for a return to the ideals of communism and opposition to the sort of ideological erosion that was constituted by social democratic trends and by bureaucratism within the party. Although critical of Polozkov and those like him, the Platform did constitute a major element in the organised conservative ballast of the party.

An important source of further fragmentation within the party was the establishment of fractions of deputies within the soviets. With the disappearance of the party's dominance in the soviets following the state elections of 1989 and 1990, increased emphasis was placed upon the need for communist deputies to organise in order to maximise their impact within the legislative arena.[19] Despite frequent complaints that deputies were not doing this, and thereby leaving control over the soviets to anti-communist elements, when such organisation was engineered, potentially it constituted a basis upon which autonomous bodies could develop inside the party. This potential was most clearly realised in the Russian parliamentary institutions. In the Congress of People's Deputies and the Supreme Soviet, communist deputies formed themselves into the Communists of Russia parliamentary faction. This was established with some 400 members during the first RSFSR Congress of People's Deputies on 19 May 1990. Its activity in the legislative chamber was charted by a leadership group composed of eleven co-chairmen.[20] This group adopted a consistently conservative stance, although its unity was not solid; a split among the communists enabled Yel'tsin to be elected Chairman of the Supreme Soviet at the end of May 1990. By the end of 1990 they were being criticised for what was seen as a consistently conservative and obstructionist stance. In March 1991 they were instrumental in the unsuccessful attempt to persuade the Congress of People's Deputies to remove Yel'tsin.[21]

The faction split in early 1991. A new body, called Communists for Democracy and headed by CC RCP member (and future Vice-President of Russia) Alexander Rutskoi, was established as a counter-balance to Communists of Russia, and by early April some 179 deputies were reported to have agreed to join this legislative grouping.[22] The immediate stimulus for the formation of this body was the attacks upon Yel'tsin at the Third Congress of People's Deputies, attacks which clearly had the RCP and its leadership in the vanguard. While the new grouping was seen as a means of balancing the Communists of Russia, it was also envisaged as the basis for a broader public movement which could counter-balance the partocratic, nomenklatura domination of the communist party in Russia, which was seen to be giving no leadership to the republic and to be ruling only in its own interests.[23] To this end organisational committees were established in many towns and oblasts of Russia.[24] While some in the party welcomed this move,[25] many saw it as a real threat to continuing party unity.[26] The accuracy of this view was shown in July when the Communists for Democracy group announced that it would form a Democratic Party of Communists of Russia to provide an alternative to the RCP.[27] Legal registration of the split was to occur at a congress in August, and a claim was to be made for a share of the party's property.[28] When the founding conference was held on 2–3 August 1991, the new party was declared to be a constituent part of the CPSU while at the same time renouncing the RCP.[29] The response was swift; on 7 August the CC RCP announced the expulsion from its ranks of Rutskoi and his co-founder Vasilii Lipitskii.[30] According to one report, soon after the party's foundation it had 7,000 members.[31] Although the potential significance of the emergence of

Communists for Democracy and its transformation into the Democratic Party of Free Russia was overshadowed by the coup and its effects, the creation of the party, led by a war hero whose communist credentials were unchallenged, could have been critical for the CPSU's capacity to maintain members. Particularly if the new party had cut all of its ties with the communist party following the expulsion of its leaders and appealed to party members to join it, it could have split the conservative camp within the party and considerably hastened the forces for disintegration that were already at work within its structures.

The demolition of central control in the party that is clearly reflected in the fracturing noted above was also evident in the position of the republican parties. As republican governments adopted courses that in many cases were becoming increasingly divergent from those of the centre, republican parties usually found that they had to fall into line with this development if they hoped to retain any influence upon local events.[32] One case where a republican party did not fall into line with a nationalist government, and which was to have important ramifications upon developments at the centre of Soviet politics, was in Russia.

The first session of the founding congress of the Communist Party of the RSFSR had been held prior to the national congress in July and had resulted in the election of Ivan Polozkov as first secretary. The election of Polozkov and the harsh tenor of the speeches generally convinced many that the party was of a distinctly conservative hue. The result of this was that many individual party members and party organisations within Russia openly dissociated themselves from the new organisation. A lead was taken here by a number of RSFSR people's deputies. In a statement they declared that the constituent congress of the RCP projected 'the line of counterreform, protection of the slipping authority of the more aggressive and conservative forces of the party and state apparatus' and that Polozkov was 'known for his aggressive conservative views'. Declaring that these were in sharp contrast to the programme upon which they were elected, they said: 'We state that we do not consider ourselves to be members of the Communist Party of the RSFSR, for whose creation we, like millions of other communists, gave neither our authority nor our agreement. We will not be bound by the decisions of this constituent congress and we call for communists who share our convictions to do the same thing.'[33] Many party organisations in Russia adopted this position; some refused to send dues to the Russian party, instead either sending them direct to the CPSU or retaining them for their own use;[34] according to Moscow gorkom first secretary Prokof'ev, 112 party organisations in the capital (out of a total of 10,000) announced that they would not enter the RCP.[35] According to Polozkov, 162,750 people left the party in the RSFSR during July alone,[36] and although not all were reacting to the congress, the size of this exodus reflects the extent of disillusion within party ranks.

The conservative orientation of the RCP was shown in the convocation of the second stage of its founding congress in September 1990. In July, following the national congress, preparations were begun for the second stage of this congress with an attempt to work out the party's action programme.[37] The party was clearly associated with what it termed the protection of the working class' interests and commitment to the 'socialist choice'[38] and this was reflected in the draft programme when it was published towards the end of August.[39] However the absence of a clear line within the party leadership is reflected in the fact that at a number of points the draft presented alternative proposals; the drafting group clearly could not agree.[40] Despite disagreement about the timetable and procedure for consolidating the party, the congress was called for 4 September.[41]

When the congress opened, Polozkov gave the report on the party's action programme.[42] His report was uninspiring and offered nothing new. He criticised mistakes in the leadership of perestroika, confirmed that the RCP would operate within the CPSU on the basis of a single Programme and Rules although with its own action programme for immediate policy priorities, affirmed the rejection of the formal nomenklatura approach to cadre policy and the importance of platforms and debate within the party, and supported the development of horizontal structures within the party. Polozkov's report stimulated criticism from the delegates. Leningrad party boss Boris Gidaspov criticised the report for its superficiality and failure to provide clear cut solutions to the problems,[43] while for others the action programme he was espousing ran counter to the positions of the CPSU and the spirit of the times and was destructive.[44] The result of the widespread opposition to the draft was that the congress decided not to proceed with it. Instead it declared that the RCP was guided by the CC CPSU programmatic statement 'Toward a Humane, Democratic Socialism' and the CPSU Rules, and that a new action programme reflecting the views of wide party circles be drawn up, published by mid-October and adopted by a joint expanded sitting of the CC and CCC RCP no later than December.

The inability of the congress to adopt the action programme reflects the absence of unity of outlook among members of the party.

Discontent with both the course of events and the direction in which the party was heading resulted in calls for Polozkov's removal from the party leadership, but these were dismissed at the congress. The congress did elect a CC and a CCC, and the former then elected a Politburo (reportedly on a 'contested basis'), thereby providing the party with the sort of leadership structure which it had formerly lacked.[45] While this seemed to give the party an appearance of institutional solidity, the health of the organisation was clearly not robust. The general financial difficulties being experienced by the CPSU throughout the country affected its Russian constituent. According to Polozkov, the budgeted income of the RCP would fall by R227 million, which could only be compensated by an increased subsidy from central party coffers, something which would bring that subsidy to 24.5 per cent of the total spending of the republic's party bodies. In 1991 income was projected to fall by R410–430 million, leading to a deficit of R900 million. This had to lead to reductions in spending, particularly on established party personnel.[46] As the leadership took on a more established form, the party structure beneath it was thereby coming under increasing pressure. In addition, the wide policy and ideological differences remained unbridged. As an *Izvestiia* article declared, the congress delegates were unable to decide what the republican party should be like, what the specific nature of its activity should be, and why it was being established.[47] At the end of the congress, the RCP was no further advanced towards finding a meaning for its existence that would satisfy large sections of the rank-and-file than it had been at the time of the first session of its founding congress.

This was basically an issue of identity and of purpose, and was to remain unresolved throughout the life of the party prior to the coup. According to two participants in the party's affairs, those who were unhappy about the course of the congress and what emanated from it could be divided into supporters of three different courses of action: those who sought to split from the RCP and create an alternative Communist Party of Russia on the CPSU platform, those who sought to maintain direct membership of the CPSU and to by-pass the RCP, and those who sought to form a platform of democratic forces within the RCP and work for change within its structures.[48] Typical of the attitude to the RCP was the view advanced by Moscow gorkom first secretary Prokof'ev when he said 'what is needed is a party capable not of lagging behind reality but being a step ahead of life and responding to its democratic aspirations. What is needed is not a new party of apparatus officialdom but a party of working people.'[49]

The new draft of the RCP's action programme was published on 19 October.[50] Although in appearance it was less conservative than its predecessor (for example, it acknowledged a multi-party system, no longer talked about the vanguard role and it acknowledged the need for a public stocktaking of party property instead of the open rejection of claims on party property in the earlier document), it maintained the commitment to Lenin and the socialist future and still offered little by way of concrete guidance for the resolution of society's (or the party's) problems. The continuing confusion in the leading ranks of the party is reflected in the issuing of a statement by the CC RCP on 19 October expressing its desire for cooperation with the forces making up Democratic Russia[51] followed five days later by a statement from the CC RCP Secretariat vigorously attacking Democratic Russia.[52] It seemed that not only did the party leadership not have a clear idea about its own nature and goals, but it also had little understanding of the nature of political forces within Soviet society.

In mid-November a joint CC–CCC RCP plenum was held. As well as establishing seven CC standing commissions,[53] it issued a resolution reflecting alarm at the course of developments in the republic.[54] The resolution, which was more conservative than the draft programme published in October, pointed to the growing crisis in the social, economic and political spheres and warned that the forced transition to the market could have disastrous consequences for society. Inside the party it attacked the 'inconsistency and opportunism, an unprincipled attitude in the ideological struggle, and timidity in defending political and moral positions', which all caused confusion among communist ranks in the face of intolerable attacks from without. It declared that the RCP opposed the policies leading to ruin and called upon the General Secretary/President to fulfil the decisions of the XXVIII Congress 'which confirmed our socialist choice'. The resolution also affirmed the need for a strong Soviet centre. The conservative nature of the Russian party leadership reflected in this document was confirmed by an interview with CC Secretary Il'in published at the same time.[55] Il'in criticised those outside the party who continually attacked it and hinted at the need for the expulsion of those 'forces undermining the party from within'. He affirmed the need for restoration of the Leninist understanding of democratic centralism, which he interpreted as meaning freedom of debate when discussing questions and unity of action after adopting decisions. The transition to market relations was to occur 'within the framework of the socialist choice', with collective ownership being given priority; he opposed private ownership of land.

He also deplored the way in which, in the face of media attacks on the RCP, many communists had been disarmed ideologically.

Polozkov provided one political answer to the crisis: the consolidation of organisational unity within the party, the adoption of a clear class analysis of events, and alliance with 'patriotic and democratic forces' in order to save the Fatherland.[56] Firm commitment to the 'socialist choice' plus rejection of 'vague phrases about the common good and the supremacy of common human interests' can overcome the confusion and demoralisation evident among the ranks of the communists.[57] This sort of call for a tightening of organisational and ideological unity and the rejection of vague non-class positions was associated with continuing emphasis upon the protection of working class interests and attacks upon those who sought to erode and question the dominance of traditional party values.[58] The party needed, in this view, to take up a firm and unambiguous stance of opposition to destructive forces and commitment to the 'socialist choice', something which the leadership of the CPSU was not doing. Gorbachev in particular was accused of 'insufficient resoluteness in upholding the ideals of socialism',[59] a charge which was the basis upon which the RCP leadership pushed for his removal as General Secretary at the April 1991 plenum (see below).

The position adopted by the RCP, and its emergence as the leader of the more conservative forces, should have provided a fillip for those forces because it offered an organisational vehicle through which the conservative message could be projected. However, the effect of this was ameliorated by the inability of the RCP leadership to design a programme that could command both agreement and support. In this way, rather than offering a dynamic leadership which could unite conservatives on the basis of a popular programme and give them the means to compete in the new marketplace of ideas, the RCP leadership headed an organisation which seemed plodding and out of step with the times. Certainly those who were not wedded to conservative positions inside the party viewed the RCP in this way; it was an organisation that was hindering the party's capacity to respond purposefully to the challenges facing it and raised the real possibility of a split within party ranks.[60] By satisfying no one, the RCP leadership isolated itself and left itself vulnerable to calls for its removal.[61] Almost constantly under attack from both outside and inside the party,[62] the leadership finally succumbed, and at the CC RCP plenum in early August 1991, Polozkov was replaced as first secretary by Valentin A. Kuptsov. Despite Kuptsov's less conservative reputation, the leadership change brought no discernible change in orientation on the part of the party leadership as a whole. The plenum heard and endorsed a conservative speech by the outgoing Polozkov in which he vigorously attacked the new CC CPSU Draft Programme,[63] it expelled Lipitskii and Rutskoi from the party, and the resolutions it adopted differed little in tone or sentiment from any adopted at earlier such gatherings.[64] There is little evidence that Kuptsov's election could have reversed the trajectory of development of the RCP and made it a more effective political force. It remained riven by organisational and ideological differences and unable to devise a programme that was likely to generate widespread support. As the leadership struggled with these issues, the structure of the party was disintegrating beneath it. But this was characteristic of the CPSU as a whole.

### Organisational disarray

An important indication of the continuing haemorrhage of the party was the escalating membership loss. According to CCC Chairman Pugo, in the first six months of 1990 a total of 770,000 ceased party activity: 370,000 left the party, 250,000 were expelled and 150,000 stopped paying dues.[65] In Moscow 27,000 left during the first six months and a further 19,000 in July,[66] presumably under the impact of political events of the summer; in the party as a whole, 311,000 left in July and August.[67] By October in Moscow, some 90,000 people had surrendered their party cards, more than half in the last two months.[68] Similar reductions occurred in other parts of the country. In Moldova (as Moldavia was now known) the membership loss, 3,000 in six months, was attributed to a number of factors: 'They became disenchanted with the ideas and aims that we proclaimed, others simply lost their heads and do not want to 'get involved' in this politically complicated and unpredictable life, and still others pursue speculative aims.'[69] A party official from Yaroslavl attributed the membership loss in his oblast in part to the disillusion felt by many communists who, having believed in certain ideals for all of their party life, cannot now understand what is happening in Soviet society and cannot see why they should be the object of 'moral oppression'.[70] For others, the answer was that the exodus represented the departure of careerists and that their absence thereby made the party stronger.[71] By mid-October 1990 according to CC Secretary Shenin, 800,000 had left the party and only 200,000 had joined.[72] The general trend is reflected in the party's annual growth rate shown in table 7.1.

The membership loss was clearly of major concern to party leaders, but there was little they could do to stem the flow.[73] According to Gidaspov, 110,000 people, or almost 18 per cent of the membership, had left the Leningrad party organisation, and although this reflected the departure of careerists, he also attributed it to a loss of faith in the party leadership at both the central and obkom levels.[74] The disillusionment of many leaving was also pointed to by the chairman of the CCC RCP, N. S. Stoliarov when he said that as well as those leaving for opportunist motives, there were

> those who have lost their faith, the conscientious, and those who have heaped on their own shoulders the entire burden of responsibility for the miscalculations and mistakes in party policy and the immodesty of party functionaries disgracing the title of communist. This is a heavy burden, and it is no wonder that many honest people have faltered. Such people will, I am sure, return to our ranks. They are already returning, incidentally.[75]

But this view was too sanguine. One party member of forty years standing announced that he was quitting the party, declaring in part that it was a criminal organisation and 'an instrument of the party nomenklatura, which is defending its power, interests, and the so-called party property that it has acquired over many decades of lording it over the country in an uncontrolled manner. Today there stands before us a party that is prepared to protect those interests and this property from the people even with bullets.'[76] The numbers in the party continued to drop alarmingly.[77] In 1990 membership was reported to have fallen by some 14 per cent,[78] with disillusionment with the results of the party Congress being a significant element here;[79] in the Russian Republic, 1,280,000 were said to have left the party organisation.[80] According to a report from the CC Secretariat in May 1991, 1,800,000 people had left the party in 1990, whereas in the first quarter of 1991 587,000 had left.[81] Even gloomier figures were given by Gorbachev at the July 1991 plenum: he said that the party had fallen by 4.2 million people in the eighteen months from the beginning of January 1990,[82] a reduction of 21.8 per cent. Although these figures are not mathematically always consistent, they do suggest a substantial membership loss which, despite calls for the organisational strengthening and ideological revitalisation of the party,[83] could not be stemmed. The loss had a particularly erosive effect on party morale, especially given that such membership loss was particularly severe among blue collar workers.[84] But it also had more evident

Table 7.1. *Annual Growth Rate of the CPSU*[a]

| 1981–83 | 2.0% | 1987–88 | 1.0% |
|---------|------|---------|------|
| 1983–86 | 1.6% | 1988–89 | 0.1% |
| 1986–87 | 1.4% | 1989–90 | −1.3% |

[a] Bohdan Harasymiw, 'Changes in the Party's Composition: The 'Destroyka of the CPSU', *The Journal of Communist Studies* 7, 2, June 1991, p. 140.

organisational consequences. One of the most important of these was budgetary.

An immediate and inevitable consequence of lower membership numbers was decreased collection of membership dues. Combined with the loss of the state subsidy and decreasing circulation levels for party publications, this created a major financial crisis for the party. For many party organisations, this was to be exacerbated by the entry into force on 1 January 1991 of the new regulations permitting PPOs to retain 50 per cent of their income from membership dues for their own purposes and the lower membership dues mandated at the XXVIII Congress. In mid-1990 according to Ivashko, only 11 party organisations were able to continue functioning without a subsidy from the centre.[85] Some, incomplete, details of the party budget were presented to delegates to the XXVIII Congress. This reported an annual income for 1990 (projected) of R2.6 billion and an expenditure of R2.1 billion.[86] But this apparent satisfactory situation was belied by the real situation on the ground. Many party organisations found it difficult to make ends meet.[87] Moreover the financial situation was about to deteriorate catastrophically. Deputy administrator of affairs of the CC CPSU N. Kapanets reported on the situation in mid-September. He reported that as a result of the new, lower membership dues, income from this source would decrease by 40 per cent, not counting the effect of the loss of members and the income accordingly forgone. With 50 per cent of this income going towards financing the PPOs, there would be substantially less to sustain party committees and institutions, including at the centre. Moreover as a result of changing tax laws (he did not mention decreased circulation),[88] income from publications would drop to 20–25 per cent of its 1989 figure. The overall income loss would be up to 60 per cent of the 1989 income level. Furthermore as a result of increases in prices, rates and state social security contributions, expenditure on existing structures and staffs of party bodies would increase by R450–550 million. Kapanets projected a budget deficit of up to R1.5 billion, with a corresponding need to reduce staff numbers and review party structures.[89] In October Shenin was forecasting a budget deficit of R1 billion and reported that the only party organisations that did not need a subsidy from the centre were those of Moscow and Leningrad. He acknowledged that the party would need to use its reserves to cover the deficit;[90] it was projected that the 1991 income would be reduced by two times compared with 1990.[91]

But the problem was not just one of the future. In the first half of 1990, income was only 48.9 per cent of that planned, a shortfall that was attributed to a lack of concern by party organisations for ensuring prompt and full payment of dues, the wilful setting of levels of dues by individual party organisations and arbitrariness in their expenditure, under-payment of dues and of the amounts forwarded to higher bodies, and reduced profits from publishing.[92] According to official figures, the party's expenditure exceeded its income by 9.2 per cent, or R209,269,700.[93] By the end of 1990, no oblast party organisation was able to survive on the income it was getting;[94] in the party budget for 1991 adopted at the joint CC–CCC plenum in January of that year, it was projected that the income of the republican parties would be exceeded by expenditure by a sum of R1.060 million, a deficit which was to be covered from the CPSU budget.[95] Some party organisations needed subsidies to cover 70–80 per cent of their expenses.[96] This situation of heavy reliance on the centre for subsidies clearly undermined the prevailing sentiment, also reflected in the rules adopted to structure the party's financial arrangements, that party organisations should be independent in solving their financial problems.[97] Despite attempts to increase party income through greater involvement in commercial activity and the transfer of funds from the Ministries of Defence and Foreign Affairs into party coffers,[98] it was clear that the party was rapidly going bankrupt; by mid-1991, party income was only half the level of expenditure.[99] A succession of deficits over income could only eat away the party's accumulated reserves, and with a declining resource base, the pace of this was likely to quicken.

There were also attacks upon party property. In the public eye the more sensational aspects of this were the attacks on statues of Lenin that occurred in various parts of the Soviet Union, and although the party did not own these, such action was a direct attack upon the main symbol of the party and its message. But perhaps of more fundamental importance to the party's continuing capacity to function were the attacks upon its property. The XXVIII Congress had declared that party property could be disposed of only with the consent of communists and in accordance with state laws. Such a statement had been deemed necessary because of the growing conviction that much of the party's property had been transferred without charge from state to party ownership, and that this should now be passed back to the people.[100] According to the budget statement given to the XXVIII Congress, as of 1 January 1990, some 5,254 buildings (valued at R1.9 million) were used for the activity of republican CCs, kraikoms, obkoms, gorkoms, raikoms and party establishments. Some 935 buildings were built with other organisations using some party resources, 216 had been handed over to party organisations for accommodation of their apparatus, while 337 belonged to other organisations and were leased by party authorities. The party had 3583 newspapers. There were 114 publishing houses (111 belonged to republican CCs, kraikoms and obkoms) and 23 sanatoria and recreation centres.[101] This list does not include buildings used by the central party structure. In addition, the party had fleets of cars and dachas at its disposal. Defence of this position was not easy for the party, because the legal right to property throughout the Soviet Union was increasingly brought under question as the legitimacy of the regime itself was called into dispute, and the circumstances under which the party had gained the property were in many cases highly questionnable. Furthermore there was not a long-established legal basis of property rights upon which disputes over ownership could be settled to everyone's satisfaction. Party speakers frequently rejected popular calls for nationalisation, but were unable to mount any effective defence of the party's right of ownership.[102] It was to try to shore up the party's property that a presidential decree entitled 'On Measures to Protect the Inviolability of the Right of Ownership in the USSR' was adopted on 12 October 1990.[103]

Throughout this period there were calls for the party to 'return to the people its "illegally" received assets', while soviets moved to examine the circumstances under which party property was held and acquired with a view to establishing their control over it.[104] In Ternopol in response to such calls, the party committee had transferred part of its administrative building to city authorities, but on 8 October the city soviet nationalised all property belonging to the party (and Komsomol) within its jurisdiction.[105] A raikom in Moldova lost part of its building and had its office ransacked and employees abused.[106] In Estonia, some party property was nationalised and the government launched an investigation into the circumstances whereby the party had acquired the rest of its property,[107] and in a number of other republics including

Armenia, Georgia and Latvia, party property was nationalised.[108] In Moscow too municipal authorities laid claim to party premises, with disputes occurring between party bodies and local soviets throughout the city.[109] In the lead-up to the presidential elections in Russia in June 1991, Democratic Russia sought to collect sufficient signatures to have the question of nationalisation of the party's property put to popular referendum,[110] but failed. The party press too was an object of takeover by municipal authorities throughout the country.[111] The wave of moves against party property in this way, added to the decline in the party's financial resources, severely hampered the party's ability to act effectively to defend itself in a hostile environment.

This was exacerbated by, *inter alia*, the widespread reduction of the apparatus forced on the party by financial pressures. In September 1990 it was declared that the staff of the CC apparatus would be reduced by 40 per cent compared with pre-XXVIII Congress levels.[112] Reductions were also occurring at lower levels. By mid-1990 the apparatus of Moscow gorkom had been reduced by 50 per cent compared with its size two years earlier.[113] In Ukraine in September 1990 it was announced that there would be a 40 per cent reduction in the staff of the party apparatus, with cuts occurring at all levels,[114] while in Moldova the cut was to be 50 per cent.[115] In addition, the reduction of full-time party workers was associated with a decrease in the size of the nomenklatura. According to CC Secretary Shenin, the sphere of cadre decisions falling within the competence of the CC was being drastically reduced, with the former figure of 15,000 positions falling under the CC now being only about 2,000.[116] In some places, the whole nomenklatura was eliminated.[117] However that this reduction was not always what it seemed is suggested by the complaints emanating from Minsk. A letter from a party member asked why there was no discussion among the rank-and-file and in the PPOs about these reductions, why 'in an overwhelming majority of cases are the reductions affecting primarily rank-and-file workers in the party apparatus but not the higher echelon of party functionaries', and why are decisions being taken according to plans made from above by a small group of party members?[118]

Declining resources and shrinkage of the party's full-time staff reflects an organisation under severe pressure. This picture was confirmed by the way in which across the country large numbers of party organs effectively ceased to operate. In some areas raikoms were dissolved and the staff transferred into the PPOs in an attempt to improve links with the working people;[119] elsewhere gorkoms were abolished.[120] In some cases, party organs ceased to operate because of a catastrophic fall in membership, or at least attendance at meetings; the second stage of the Donetsk City Party Conference was inquorate, a development attributed to the declining confidence of party members in the area.[121] The party organisation in the newspaper of the Baikal-Amur Railway ceased to exist when all of its members applied to leave the CPSU.[122] Other party organisations seem to have gone into a state of paralysis, afraid to act without instructions from above. Communists in Dnepropetrovsk oblast were told that

> it is inadmissible for the oblast's communists to bide their time, confine themselves to stating the facts, underestimate the acuteness of the situation, and manifest lack of organisation and confidence . . . the plenum's participants adopted an appeal to M.S. Gorbachev, demanding that the Politburo and the CPSU Central Committee give clear indications as to how they should act in conditions of the approaching market. The desire to carry out orders and not think and choose for themselves revealed for the umpteenth time their habit of working in the old way without enterprise and creative quest.[123]

Waiting for orders from above instead of working out their own programmes of action as they were supposed to do was a frequent criticism directed at lower party bodies.[124] Such inaction undermined the party's ability to exercise any influence within society.[125] According to a speaker at the October CC plenum, 'many primary organs are inactive and some have ceased to exist, while confusion reigns in a significant proportion of them', a situation attributed in part to lack of leadership from above.[126] According to Shenin, many party organis-ations were characterised by passivity and paralysis, with meetings not being held, the organisation failing to exercise influence in its region, and individual communists losing touch with one another. Some party organisations were declared to be on the brink of disintegration and self-liquidation.[127] In February 1991, it was reported that in Moldova some 812 PPOs had ceased to exist,[128] a phenomenon common through-out the country as a whole. Other party organisations which remained in existence had simply lost their influence in the collective.[129]

Party organs at all levels were accused of lagging behind events, adopting superficial analyses of what was happening and of main-taining only weak links with other levels in the party structure.[130] Some adopted a weak, conciliatory, defensive stance against what were euphemistically called 'negative phenomena';[131] passivity during election campaigns was an instance of this.[132] Greater initiative and activism on the part of lower party organs were declared to be necessary.[133] Furthermore there had been a breakdown in linkages between the centre and local party organisations, with many lower organs refusing to abide by party Rules[134] and others refusing to transfer membership dues to higher levels in the party structure.[135] What was needed was greater discipline in the party, with lower level organs not going their own ways but obeying the instructions and directives sent out from the centre;[136] in some cases, it was argued, lower level organs were not even aware of the decisions taken at higher levels.[137] In March 1991, the Secretariat adopted a decision calling for the wholesale renewal of the activity of PPOs in an attempt to improve their all-round performance.[138] Despite the formal establishment of Councils of PPO Secretaries[139] and the holding of zonal conferences of PPO secretaries,[140] little seems to have changed as a result of this decision.[141]

The demoralisation of party members was an acute problem at this time. In the words of a report of the deputy head of the CC CPSU Department for Work with Public and Political Organisations, I. Zaramenskii, 'Apathy and desire to abandon the cause and become wrapped up in one's own personal concerns is becoming apparent. Not only "rank-and-file" party members are doing this but also some functionaries and apparatchiks who have yielded to moral pressure or have just changed their "stripes" to something more advantageous at this point.'[142] For Shenin, many party members (and PPOs and party committees) have lost their combat fighting spirit, their initiative, their ability to influence the situation and their political confidence; they have become dismayed by the attacks upon the party.[143] Democratisation had been slow to take effect in many party meetings, with the result that few party members became involved in party work, and many became disillusioned.[144]

### Displacement of the party

An important element in this failure of party bodies to function effectively was the failure of communist deputies in the soviets to organise themselves into viable factions that would both remain united and obey central party directives;[145] in the words of a discussion of the situation in Kremenchug, 'The gorkom and party committees are still exerting only a weak influence on the activity of communists who are people's deputies. While they make up a majority in the city soviet, the communists sometimes act in isolation and do not always succeed in directing the work of the soviet into a constructive channel.'[146] Increasingly party members wore their membership lightly as the more radical compositions of many elected bodies adopted programmes and positions at odds with party views. Disputes over party property were a particularly acute instance of this. Communist deputies increasingly were confronted with the choice of maintaining their party positions or acting in ways which might enable them to retain some relevance to the course of legislative life;[147] some found that they had to come out into open criticism of the party[148] and splits within communist groups were common. In any event, the inability of the communists to act as a firm cadre of party forces in the soviets was a frequent cause of party complaint.[149]

The inability of party organs to operate effectively was also linked to the moves for depoliticisation of leading organisations in Soviet society. There were two aspects of this. The more extreme, which was to become more prominent following the coup, was the call for the removal of all party members from positions of responsibility. The more usual form in which depoliticisation occurred was the removal of party organisations from work places. In some areas communist organs were simply excluded from places of work by decision of local work councils, with the party organs either having to find alternative premises or simply disintegrating.[150] In other cases party meetings simply voted the party organisation out of existence as an organised entity.[151] As the period wore on, pressures for the expulsion of party organisations from enterprises and organisations increased.[152] While such action often found its roots in the enterprises themselves, there was also a signifi-cant stimulus coming from above as republican governments adopted decrees on state power which abolished PPOs in enterprises, organis-ations and institutions,[153] or more specific decrees abolishing party organisation in the armed forces and security apparatus;[154] an important case was the Soviet President's decree transferring control of political organs in the military from the party to the state.[155]

But the most important of these was the decree issued by Russian President Yel'tsin on 20 July 1991 and due to come into force fourteen days later entitled 'Decree on Ending the Activity of Organisational Structures of Political Parties and Mass Public Movements in State Bodies, Establishments and Organisations of the RSFSR'.[156] This decree, while guaranteeing the right of individuals in responsible positions to maintain membership of political organisations, forbade the existence of primary organisations, committees and other organisational structures of political parties and social movements in all bodies of state administration. He also called on the Russian legislature to recommend to the USSR Supreme Soviet that it ban party activity in government institutions and the armed forces. While party organs protested this decree,[157] the CC formally requested that it be examined for its legality by the Committee for the Supervision of the Constitution and by Soviet President Gorbachev.[158] However, Gorbachev took no action to countermand the decree, a stance which evoked criticism from some within the party.[159] Rumours began that at least one party organisation, in response to the decree, was preparing to adopt underground work, in the form of the illegal party prior to 1917.[160] When the decree came into effect on 4 August, party organisations reacted in a variety of ways. Some dutifully began to dissolve themselves in accordance with its demands,[161] while others sought to ignore its import and carry on as though it had not been introduced; indeed the CC RCP called on all party organisations to do just this, explaining that they should assume that the Committee for Supervision of the Constitution was reviewing the constitutionality of the decree and they should continue to act normally until that review was completed.[162] Even near the top, opinions were divided: on the same day that he criticised Gorbachev's inaction with regard to the decree, Gidaspov was reported to have acknowledged that the decree would have to be fulfilled.[163]

The party sought to argue against the wave of demands for and subsequent legislation bringing about depoliticisation, but not very effectively. Party speakers claimed that in all countries members of political parties headed major structures in society and that this should also be the case in the Soviet Union. Furthermore they claimed that moves for depoliticisation were directed specifically against the CPSU and that such demands infringed principles of freedom and democracy and were a denial of the human and legal rights of party members who should be able to retain their preferred party membership while performing their employment functions. The continued presence of party organs was also justified on the grounds that their presence ensured a plurality of views in the workplace. [164] Such arguments did not carry much weight in the course of public debate, particularly when they were patently not accepted by large sections of the party itself.[165]

The disintegration of many lower level party organs and the open moves against the party through the depoliticisation measures reflects the continuing erosion of the party's position among the populace as a whole over this period. One indication of this is the party's declining support and trust as registered in opinion polls. While care must be taken because of the primitive nature of Soviet opinion polling methodology, the consistency of the results over time suggests that they were registering a real fall in the party's prestige. A poll conducted by sociologists at the Academy of Social Sciences attached to the CC CPSU in June 1990 showed that 37 per cent of respondents placed their hopes in the CPSU, 29 per cent believed there to be no alternative, and 32 per cent gave no definite answer.[166] In a poll taken during the XXVIII Congress, 64 per cent disagreed with the proposition that the CPSU was the only force capable of extricating society from the crisis, and 31 per cent believed the party should be disbanded (with a further 28 per cent answering it was 'difficult to say').[167] Another poll published in November 1990[168] reported that the number 'for' the CPSU had fallen as follows: December 1989 27 per cent, March 1990 16 per cent, June 1990 14 per cent. A poll published in March 1991 showed that only 12 per cent of Muscovites were more inclined to trust the party than Democratic Russia.[169] Another poll published about the same time suggested that, across the country, 60 per cent of men and 44 per cent of women had abandoned communism.[170]

But the decline in the party's support was evident in other ways as well. Popular demonstrations against the party continued to occur, even if they did not all have the same impact as the anti-communist demonstration on May Day 1990.[171] Party spokesmen acknowledged the erosion of the party's popular base; Moscow gorkom first secretary Prokof'ev openly recognised that 'many people have lost their trust in the party'.[172] Also opposing political forces, particularly from within the democratic movement, continued to mount major public criticisms of the party.[173] In the words of second secretary of the CC of the Belorussian party A. S. Kamay, 'subversive forces are under the guise of perestroika [sic] managing step by step to inflict well-aimed blows against the party of communists'.[174] The seizure of party property noted above was one aspect of such attacks. In some areas local authorities cut off services, including telephones, to party offices.[175] Claims of persecution and victimisation of communists were frequently heard.[176] There were even calls for a public trial of the CPSU,[177] calls which were realised by the holding of a symbolic mock trial in Moscow beginning on 30 October.[178] The sense of being under attack, and of being able to do little to prevent this from happening, pervaded all party meetings at this time.[179] It was more acute in areas like the Baltic republics,[180] where events had long been outside party control, than in Central Asia where the old command structures remained substantially intact. In Russia this feeling was strengthened by the overwhelming victories achieved by Yel'tsin, Popov and Sobchak in the elections on 12 June 1991.[181]

The party's position was clearly being eroded at the lower levels over the twelve months following the congress. Registration as a public association, which was achieved at the all-union level on 11 April 1991,[182] could not prevent this from occurring, despite the view that such registration would provide legal protection for the party against encroachments on its prestige and property.[183] One of the party's problems was that increasingly it appeared irrelevant as the soviets and republican governments moved into a more central position in the political process.

In many parts of the country in the year following the XXVIII Congress, the party had an uneasy relationship with the soviets. Although formally emphasis was laid upon the party cooperating with the soviets and working in the soviets through organisations of communist deputies, the relationship tended to be much more conflictual. This was so for two main reasons. First, the soviets had an expansive view of their own rights, prerogatives and powers, the exercise of which was bound to come into conflict with the more established, party, centres of power. Second, the traditional centre of power had been in the party apparatus. Even if the party had been able to maintain control in the soviets through communist fractions within them, there would have been tension between the established bureau-cratic power of the political machine and the newer legislative-based power of the soviets.[184] The conflictual nature of this relationship was evident even when party speakers described their relationship with the soviet as cooperative and collaborative.[185] A more candid, if perhaps still understated, evaluation came from Donetsk: 'the leaders of the new soviet of people's deputies and the party gorkom . . . have formed no relations. Representatives of the soviet believe the party gorkom is constantly putting spokes in their wheels while the party leaders have accused the soviet of underestimating the political force that the city party organisation represents in Donetsk.'[186]

It is clear that despite the official line that the party should allow the soviets to operate as governing bodies,[187] many party organisations sought to undermine the growing power and authority of the soviets, seeking to retain for themselves the capacity to control develop-ments.[188] In the words of a resolution of the XXVIII Congress of the Ukrainian Communist Party in December 1990,

> individual party committees, in their organisational work, are contributing insufficiently to the establishment of the soviets as organs of real power, are trying to reserve to themselves the right to act in their stead and oversee them excessively, and are not offering

an appropriate evaluation on the position of communists who demonstrate passivity and indifference in the execution of their duties as deputies.[189]

In some cases the party sought, successfully, to take control of news-papers formerly shared with the soviet.[190] But despite such successes, throughout most of the USSR the party was losing the struggle with the organs of state power.

The erosion of the party's position was most clearly seen at the all-union level and in Moscow. The year following the congress witnessed the party increasingly being pushed to the political sidelines, princi-pally as a result of the expansion of the competence of state organs. Both the All-Union and Russian parliamentary organs continued to meet regularly throughout this period. Their deliberations, while sometimes issuing forth in the form of legislation, were more important because of the locus of authority which they projected. Despite growing concern that the membership of these bodies (particularly at the All-Union level) reflected an earlier stage of the reform process and should perhaps therefore be renewed, the vigorous debates in these assemblies projected them as the appropriate fora for national decision-making.

But of greater importance for the place of the party was the growth of presidential power. At the all-union level, an executive presidency had been established in March 1990 and Gorbachev had been elected to it. The extensive powers of this office were expanded in September 1990 by the granting to Gorbachev of the right to institute emergency measures to 'stabilise the country's socio-political life' for a period of eighteen months and, three months later, by the shift to a fully presidential system through the replacement of the Council of Ministers by a presidentially-appointed Cabinet. This shoring up of presidential power (which included provision to the president of executive advisory bodies but no means of ensuring that decisions were implemented), reflected most clearly in the number of decrees that flowed from Gorbachev's office, created an activist head of state who formally possessed the power to rule almost as he wished. The fact that this position was occupied by the party's General Secretary should have been a positive factor for the party, but because of the way Gorbachev chose to play out his role (see below) this was not the case. An even less positive development for the party occurred with the emergence of the Russian presidency. The election of Boris Yel'tsin to the position of Chairman of the Russian Supreme Soviet in May 1990 catapulted him into the position of leader of the Russian republic. His position was immeasurably strengthened by the creation of a full presidential system and his popular election to this post in June 1991. In this election Yel'tsin soundly defeated his opponents from the party, including former prime minister Ryzhkov and acknowledged moderate Bakatin.[191] Yel'tsin's victory was significant because it gave him a broad popular mandate which included popular rejection of party candidates through the ballot box. For the party this was a disastrous outcome; it brought to power someone who had osten-tatiously left the party and who had been very critical of it. His attitude was soon shown by the decree noted above on removing party organ-isations from state structures in the RSFSR.

As well as the challenge posed by an expansive state sector, there was the continuing challenge emanating from the streets in the form of the myriad of new political parties that were exploding onto the Soviet scene. These forces had been emerging for some time, but this process was stimulated by the Law on Public Associations adopted in October 1990.[192] This provided the mechanism for the registration of political parties and effectively laid the basis for a multi-party system. Although the proto-parties that emerged were numerous, they were small in size. But their importance was two-fold: they provided an alternative organisational vehicle to the CPSU for those who wished to be involved in politics, and through their vigorous participation in public debate they played a significant role in both structuring and radicalising that debate. They made it easier for those who wished to leave the party by providing an ideological and organisational home for them to go to. But they also posed a dilemma for the party: what should be its attitude to them? The party recognised that this was a problem.[193] The official position was that the party should enter into relations with all of those parties, groups and social movements which accepted the Constitution and agreed to abide by the laws and had 'chosen the socialist option'.[194] Some within the party sought to emphasise the 'socialist choice' as a means of anchoring the party in its traditional positions, while others sought to ally with those who thought like them regardless of their attitude to socialism.[195] So the emergence of these proto-parties had an effect on the party not just within the broad political arena,[196] but also inside the party through the debate on how it should respond to such a development.

In the face of such an expansion of state activity at all levels and of the growth of political competitors, what the CPSU needed was a clear sense of direction and leadership. This is precisely what many at lower levels of the party believed was lacking. According to Uzbek leader I. A. Karimov, following the XXVIII Congress the party had 'no clear stance, purposeful work or unified ideology'.[197] The Congress had produced no answers to the party's plight.[198] The party leadership was accused of being isolated from the masses.[199] In the words of the Belorussian Politburo, 'In our view, those who captain the flagship and plot its course also bear a considerable share of the blame for the fact that "our ship is rudderless" and that "everyone is little by little getting sick". Expertise has been displayed more in acts of demolition than creation.'[200] The leadership had to take the lead in elaborating the party's strategy and tactics rather than allowing it to drift along;[201] it had to provide a clear political line.[202] In the words of CCC chief Boris Pugo: the party masses 'are displeased with the state of organisational and ideological work in the CPSU and criticise the Central Committee Politburo and Secretariat for tardiness and indecisiveness in defining positions on particular questions'.[203] The lack of direction and action meant that the party had 'been transformed from a leading party into a talking party'.[204] The Politburo and CC were accused of being passive, with key questions of state policy not being discussed in leading party organs and those organs lacking a clear understanding of the current situation and what needed to be done.[205] Leading party organs were being by-passed,[206] while in the view of one CC member, there had been many mistakes, but no one admitted any responsibility.[207] The party's leading organs were losing positions in the course of the continuing debate in the country,[208] and the party was declared to be bankrupt in terms both of realising its aims and gaining popular support.[209] Much of the blame for this was directed at Gorbachev, and is reflected in calls for his removal.[210] There was also an unsuccessful attempt to force his resignation at the April 1991 CC plenum;[211] some called for the resignation of the entire party leadership.[212] One speaker, Russian CCC chairman Stoliarov even blamed democratisation in the party for the absence of effective leadership over lower party organs by those higher in the structure.[213]

Much of this criticism of the centre seems exaggerated and excessive,[214] but there was some justice in the general charge of a lack of clear leadership. In noting the lack of leadership from the centre and the central organs' reluctance to take firm decisions, Prokof'ev declared 'Central Committee plena are not held for months on end, Central Committee Politburo sessions are held only occasionally, and the meetings of its Secretariat fail to examine problems of paramount importance'.[215] But how accurate was such criticism?

In the twelve months following the congress, there were five CC plena. The plenum of 8–9 October 1990 established the new CC commissions and discussed current affairs, while that of 10–11 December discussed the draft union treaty that had been published in November, coming out in support of a renewed and preserved unitary Soviet Union that was socialist in character.[216] The plenum of 31 January 1991 discussed the current situation in the light of the military activity that had occurred in the Baltic republics earlier that month, issuing a statement 'On the Current Situation and the Tasks of the Party'.[217] The 24–25 April joint CC–CCC plenum which followed the surprise Novo-Ogarevo agreement between Gorbachev and nine republican leaders and which witnessed the attempt to remove Gorbachev, critically discussed the crisis programme that had been introduced into the Supreme Soviet some days before by Prime Minister Pavlov.[218] The 25–26 July plenum examined the new draft party programme and discussed Yel'tsin's decree banning party organisation in Russian institutions.[219] All plena witnessed vigorous attacks on the Gorbachev leadership and the course it was pursuing, thereby highlighting the disunity at the apex of the party.

The Politburo reaped the consequences of the changed membership profile adopted at the XXVIII Congress. Despite the view of at least one new member, Estonian first secretary Sillari, that the Politburo would be the forum for resolving union-wide problems,[220] as a body it did not function as an effective decision-maker. The Politburo did not meet until 13 September, a full two months after the congress,[221] and then its main task was to prepare for the forthcoming CC plenum. The public rationale for the more irregular and infrequent meetings of the Politburo was seen to lie in the tasks attributed to that body: according to CC Secretary Shenin, the Politburo was concerned with the 'Elaboration of large-scale issues and decisions on implementation of the strategic orientation of party policy . . . '[222] The gaze of the Politburo appears to have shifted to strategy and longer-term planning rather than the handling of more immediate matters. But such an idea was overrun by events; the idea of a long-term plan was replaced by the struggle for survival, and in this the Politburo seems to have played no positive part.

The Secretariat, and once established the CC commissions, seem to have been more active than the Politburo. The task of the Secretariat was said to be 'to ensure effective everyday operation of the Central Committee's organisational-political activity. In other words, it must deal with matters of current policy, operational activity with republic and local party organisations, and communication and coordination of activities with the soviets and other state organs, with party and social organisations.'[223] The Secretariat met on a weekly basis[224] and, according to Gorbachev, was to throw itself open to the influence of the populace rather than remaining isolated behind closed doors.[225] There is no evidence that such an exhortation had much effect on the way the Secetariat conducted its business. Reports suggest that in its meetings, the Secretariat discussed the whole range of issues confronting the party and society, in much the sort of way that the Politburo had done when it had been the true central decision-making organ of the party. The range of the Secretariat's concerns is reflected in the formal responsibility of its secretaries noted above (see chapter 6, n. 141). However, it is not clear that the deliberations of the Secretariat were always as soundly based as they might have been. According to one secretary 'There is an understanding of the need to scrutinise the essence of the issues under examination comprehensively and thoroughly. Although quite frankly, we don't always succeed in doing this.'[226]

The Secretariat's work was supplemented by that of the commissions of the CC. At its meeting on 12 September, the Secretariat decided, in line with the decision of the XXVIII Congress, to establish standing commissions for the main areas of CC activity: ideology, work in the socio-political sphere, socio-economic questions, agrarian policy, questions relating to women and the family, nationalities policy, problems of the party's international activity, and renewal of the PPOs' activity. Also to be created were commissions for culture, education and science, youth policy, military policy, privileges and the new party programme.[227] They were formally established at the October plenum.[228] The commissions were designed to ensure the wider participation of party members in the work of the party by including in their membership CC members and other members of the party. The standing commissions were to be headed by CC secretaries, the others by members of the Politburo or Secretariat. The standing commissions were to be concerned with the continuing areas of CC concern; the other commissions were to cover issues reflected in the resolutions of the XXVIII Congress.[229] Reports of the meetings of commissions occurred in the press, with discussions occurring on the full range of issues and their deliberations feeding into the continuing party debate, but there is no sense of them exercising a significant policy-guidance or formulation role.[230]

The complaints about the lack of leadership emanating from central organs do not reflect an absence of institutional opportunity to provide such leadership: even if the Politburo rarely met as an institutional entity, the CC met on five occasions over the year and the Secretariat seems to have met on a regular basis. Institutional irregularity is therefore not a sufficient reason for the absence of central direction. The causes of this lay much deeper.

It is clear that the weakness of central direction does not reflect a lack of appreciation of the dangers facing the party. Both the speeches of leading figures and the calls for guidance from below reflect an acute sense of awareness about the problems. The party press carried long analyses of the difficulties being experienced by the party and suggestions about how these difficulties could be overcome.[231] So ignorance was not the problem. Certainly events moved fast in the twelve months following the congress. Continuing debates over economic reform and a new union treaty, the restructuring of executive power late in 1990, the further fraying of Soviet power on the Russian periphery, the crackdown in the Baltic republics in January 1991, the replacement of Ryzhkov by Pavlov as prime minister, the growing assertiveness of the Yel'tsin-led Russian government, the March referendum on a renewed union, the Novo-Ogarevo agreement, the miners' strike, the popular election of Yel'tsin shortly followed by his depoliticisation decree and the proposed signature of the draft union treaty, were all significant developments in a domestic political agenda that was both outside party control and clearly accelerating. The speed with which events were unrolling made it difficult for any organisation to keep pace and to chart a consistent policy line. Certainly the communist party was not the only organisation that lagged behind events in the public positions it adopted. But this too is inadequate as an explanation for the failures of leadership. The most basic cause lay in the differences within the upper levels of the party itself.

The XXVIII Congress had resolved none of the difficulties within the party. The result of the congress had been a stalemate with the vigorous verbal attacks on the Gorbachev leadership being balanced by acceptance of the major institutional changes championed by that leadership.[232] But the impasse was most clearly reflected in the inability of the congress to agree on a programmatic document for the party. This impasse was not resolved during this period, with the July 1991 plenum adopting the draft programme presented to it only for further party-wide discussion. During the discussion that preceded the plenum, it was apparent how wide the differences were that remained among groups in the party. From the Bolshevik Platform on the conservative side through to those of a more liberal disposition like Gorbachev allies Yakovlev and Vol'skii, the differences in outlook were stark. While the former called for the party to return to much more traditional stances,[233] it was the latter, through an informal working group, which by-passed the official programme commission and produced the social democratic draft that was presented to the plenum.[234]

The draft programme, entitled 'Socialism, Democracy, Progress'[235] consisted mainly of vague statements of principle with little indication of how those principles might be realised. It condemned the crimes of the Stalin era, and committed the party to, *inter alia*, conversion of the USSR into a democratic federation of sovereign republics, a democratic multi-party state based on the rule of law, separation of powers, assurance of the rights and liberties of citizens and alignment of human rights legislation with international standards, legality and law and order, a controlled market economy, and an extensive range of social welfare measures. It emphasised the party's commitment to internal democratisation and to operating by legal political methods within the framework of parliamentary democracy. The draft programme avoided any tying of the party solely to the working class, instead committing it to defending the interests of workers, peasants, those working in public service (eg. physicians, the military and police), women, the youth, older people and veterans. The rejection of a class basis for the party was accompanied by the failure to affirm Marxism-Leninism as the ideological basis of the party's life, instead declaring that the ideological value upon which the party was built was 'humane democratic socialism', which emerged not only from Marxism but from 'other concepts from domestic and world humanistic thinking'.

The generality of the draft and its failure to present Marxism-Leninism as the ideological basis of the party shows the party's theoretical disarray; the established ideology had been rejected but nothing was put in its place. The rejection of Marxism-Leninism was criticised at the plenum.[236] This was foreseen by Gorbachev, who tried to meet it in his opening speech:

> The main objective in the draft is to break away decisively from the outmoded ideological dogmas and stereotypes and to aspire to bring our philosophy and politics into accord with all the experience of the development and the vital requirements of the country and the people. A description of the CPSU's ideological basis ends the draft programme. We were and remain adherents of the socialist organisation of public life. In the past, the party recognised only Marxism-Leninism as the source of its inspiration, while this doctrine itself was distorted to the extreme to suit the pragmatic purposes of the day and

was turned into a kind of collection of canonical texts. It is now necessary to include in our ideological arsenal the riches of our and the world's socialist and democratic thought. Such an approach is dictated by the fact that the realisation of the socialist idea and movement along the path of economic, social and spiritual progress can be successfully implemented only in the channel of the common development of civilisation . . . I have no doubts that comrades paid attention to the fact that communism is merely mentioned in the programme. It should be recognised that our experience, and not only ours, provides no grounds for thinking that this aim is realistically attainable in the foreseeable future, but the communist idea – the free development of each person is the condition for the free development of all – has been and remains an attractive guideline for mankind.

Such explanations did not satisfy those who deplored the party's loss of the ideological banner which, in their eyes, had given it its past direction and was its chief defining characteristic. This reflected the fact that there was no unanimity and very little agreement among those debating the party's future about the course it should follow. Another congress, scheduled for late in 1991, was seen by many as the only way out.[237]

The problem for those seeking unanimity at the top is that as the course of public debate became more radical, the split within party leading circles became wider: those like Yakovlev who sought to remain broadly in step with the flow of events were driven further away from the tenets of party orthodoxy, while those who opposed this trend were forced back even more heavily onto the positions of the past.[238] This situation of an increasing gulf inside the party was complicated by the ambiguity of Gorbachev's own activity. His initial support for the radical 500 Days economic programme was followed by his dropping of this in favour of the more moderate Ryzhkov programme. This was followed by his failure to censure those involved in the military action in the Baltics, his appointment of the conservative Pavlov as the prime ministerial replacement for Ryzhkov and his promotion of Pugo (in place of the moderate Bakatin), Kriuchkov and Yazov, and his support for a conservative turn in economic policy. In April he reached secret agreement with the leaders of nine republics to construct a constitutional structure which would provide for the right of republics to leave the USSR and for significant decentralisation of power away from Moscow. The prospect of more radical economic reform again appeared on his personal agenda. This oscillation between conservative and radical positions created uncertainty among all sides in the continuing intra-party debate. It also hamstrung Gorbachev in any attempt he might have made to stamp his authority on the party by exercising consistent policy leadership. His position as state President and his clear preference to work through this organ rather than the party also limited his ability to provide dynamic leadership for the party and served further to sideline the party from the main arenas of state decision-making.

Ultimately it was the divisions within the party which prevented it from reaching a clearly considered position on the challenges confronting it. The divisions at the top were mirrored at all levels, as republican parties increasingly aligned themselves with their own governmental authorities and against the centre, and the variety of differing tendencies inside the party squabbled over points of theory and policy. In such a situation, without a single dominant leader who could stamp his authority on this disputatious structure, and increasingly irrelevant to the course of politics focused in the state institutions, the cycle of demoralisation and institutional decay could only continue apace. What prevented the party from unravelling completely was the coup.

# 8 The end

The attempted coup of August 1991 ended the long drawn out haemorrhaging of the party that had been evident over the preceding twelve months. While some of the circumstances of the coup attempt remain uncertain, it seems that as an organisational entity, the party was not a prime mover in it. Certainly the leaders of the coup were all members of the party, but none were in the Politburo although Yanaev and Kriuchkov had been full members and Yazov, Pugo and Luk'ianov had been candidate members. Party members publicly had called for decisive action to prevent further disintegration.[1] But preparations for the coup do not seem to have taken place within the organisational structures of the party. Yanaev said that no consultation had taken place between the party leadership and the State Committee for the State of Emergency.[2] In the name of the CC the Secretariat, through the person of Ivashko, on 21 August demanded a meeting with Gorbachev and said it could give no assessment of the events of 19 August without such a meeting.[3] This sort of reaction certainly represents an attempt to sit on the fence, an unwillingness either to condemn or support the coup; it is also consistent with surprise and a lack of complicity.

But despite the apparent lack of organisational involvement, the attempt by the coup leaders to put a brake on the reform process was undoubtedly welcomed by significant sections of the party leadership. Party leaders in some republics came out in open support of the coup and the Emergency Committee: the party leaderships in Russia, Kirgizia, Uzbekistan, Azerbaijan, Ukraine, and Latvia adopted such a stance, while some others like those in Moldova and Belorussia sought to adopt a neutral, non-committal position. Once the coup had failed, all party leaders condemned it.

Although the party does not appear to have been a major institutional player in the coup attempt, the coup was the mechanism for the destruction of the party's remaining standing in Soviet society. By the time the Soviet Union was transformed into the Commonwealth of Independent States at the end of 1991, a combination of the hardening of popular opinion toward the party, the departure of many leading party figures and positive action against the party had reduced it to a fringe group on the political spectrum. The popular perception, ably espoused by Moscow mayor Popov,[4] was that the coup 'was an attempt to return power to the CPSU apparatus'. But even those who were convinced neither of this nor of party involvement were appalled by the party's inaction during the coup attempt, by its failure unambiguously to come out in opposition to the coup and in support of a restoration of constitutional order.[5] The result was the loss of much of the remaining support for the party among both the ordinary populace and party members. This disillusionment was reflected most starkly in the resignation from the party of leading figures including Gorbachev and Kazakh leader Nazarbaev. In this context of increased disillusionment, punitive action against the party was popularly accepted with equanimity.

When he resigned as General Secretary, Gorbachev called on the CC to dissolve itself,[6] banned the activity of political parties and political movements in the military and coercive arms of the Soviet state (including the KGB)[7] and instructed the soviets to take party property under their protection until its future use was decided in accordance with the law.[8] On 29 August, the USSR Supreme Soviet decided 'to suspend the activity of the CPSU all over the territory of the Soviet Union.'[9] In Russia, on 23 August President Yel'tsin suspended the activities of the RSFSR Communist Party,[10] and two days later he nationalised party property (including bank accounts) within the RSFSR;[11] he had earlier (22 August) provisionally suspended party newspapers.[12] On 6 November, a Yel'tsin decree banned the CPSU and the RCP on Russian territory.[13] Throughout the country, similar action was taken by authorities at all levels, from the municipal to the republican. The party was suspended, banned or declared illegal, and leading party figures resigned from its ranks. Republican parties declared their independence of the CPSU, while some sections of the party, like Rutskoi's Democratic Party of Russian Communists formally quit party ranks. Party property was seized and in some cases offices were ransacked. The party press, led by *Pravda*, declared their independence of the party and appeared as independent non-party publications, sometimes but not always with a reshaped editorial team. Party organisations in institutions and bodies of all sorts were dissolved. Despite the fact that, in a strict sense, the suspension of the party was illegal,[14] apart from complaints from party spokesmen, there was little public opposition to such action.[15]

The effect on the party in many parts of the country was devastating. Although many recent former party leaders were able to hold onto power, including Nazarbaev in Kazakhstan, Karimov in Uzbekistan and Mutalibov in Azerbaijan and many more at lower levels, the party structure in large parts of the country effectively melted away. In some areas, including at the republican level in Uzbekistan and Tajikistan, the party was simply renamed and continued to act in much the same way as it had acted prior to the coup. In many of the local areas, the formal party structure disappeared, but many of the previously most powerful individuals continued to exercise power through the informal political machines which formerly had underpinned communist power in the region, the family groups.[16] This situation, of former communists remaining in positions of responsibility,[17] was evident throughout much of the former Soviet Union. But the party as a coherent structure was broken; the weaknesses that had been evident in the preceding twelve months were exacerbated, and the structure collapsed.

In the succeeding twelve months, the fortunes of the party did not improve. Towards the middle of 1992, the Russian Constitutional Court began to hold hearings on the status of the CPSU. It originally had been called upon to consider the legality of Yel'tsin's decree banning the party, but its brief was extended to examine whether the party had acted constitutionally during its period in power. The outcome of such an investigation hardly seemed in doubt given the flurry of reports about the party using non-party, usually state, funds to finance its activities and those of its supporters abroad, and of placing large amounts in foreign bank accounts for private use.[18] However the court took no decision on the unconstitutionality of the CPSU, arguing that the party had gone out of existence a year earlier, and upheld Yel'tsin's action with regard to the central organs but not to those at the local level (thereby in effect re-legalising the Russian party). With the party rendered effectively illegal until this ruling, groups of communists in parts of the country had gathered in attempts to organise new political groupings.[19] There were also proposals to convene the XXIX Congress of the party,[20] some members of the CC convened a meeting in mid-June 1992 at which they planned the future convocation of a party conference and expelled Gorbachev from the party,[21] and on 10 October 1992 the so-called XX All-Union Conference of the party was held in Moscow.[22] Communists also organised popular demonstrations, most of which were smaller than had been expected given the hardship following the price rises of early 1992.[23] But the likelihood of such groups being able to resurrect the party as a powerful organisation in the short term was small. Popular opinion remained unfavourably disposed toward the party. A poll conducted in twenty-four regions of the Russian Federation and published in March 1992 showed that 46 per cent of respondents believed that the party should be forbidden while 32 per cent believed that the party was necessary, while 51 per cent believed that the party should be put on trial with 29 per cent believing that this was not necessary.[24] These results, following the difficult times resulting from the economic reform programme of the Yel'tsin government, were not heartening for those wishing to see the resurgence of the party, although the former communists' electoral success in Lithuania would have been a cause of encouragement for these people.[25]

Despite the former communists' success in Lithuania, in Russia the communist movement remained fragmented during 1993. Nominally the largest group was the Communist Party of the Russian Federation, which was the former Russian Communist Party reconstituted at a 'revival-unification' conference in February 1993. Headed by former RCP Ideology Secretary Gennadii Ziuganov, this party claimed by May to have 600,000 members and to have re-established local organisations in all regions of Russia.[26] Smaller and more shadowy were the Socialist Party of Working People (established October 1991) headed by Roy Medvedev, and the Russian Party of Communists (founded December 1991), both of which grew out of the Marxist Platform. The conservative Initiative Group in the RCP was the progenitor (in November 1991) of the Russian Communist Workers' Party headed by Albert Makashov, Viktor Anpilov and Viktor Tiul'kin, while the Bolshevik Platform produced the All-Union Communist Party of Bolsheviks (founded November 1991) headed by Nina Andreeva. There were also a number of other small bodies claiming the parentage of the CPSU in one form or another. These bodies did not play a prominent role in 1992–3, being most evident in street demonstrations, often organised in conjunction with extreme nationalist forces like the National Salvation Front. Such demonstrations usually attracted comparatively few demonstrators. However members of the Communist Party of the Russian Federation, through the parliamentary fraction Communists of Russia, were instrumental in the hostile stance taken by the legislature towards Yel'tsin at this time. When the president-legislature dispute came to a head in September–October 1993, these groups supported the parliament. Accordingly it was no surprise that among the groups and newspapers banned by Yel'tsin on 4 October 1993 were the Communist Party of the Russian Federation, the All-Union Communist Party of Bolsheviks, the Russian Communist Workers Party, the Russian Communist Youth League, the former party and now nominally independent newspapers *Pravda*, *Sovetskaia Rossiia*, *Glasnost'*, and the newspaper edited by Anpilov *Molniia*.[27] These bodies were but the pale and pathetic remnants of the once all-dominant CPSU.

## Why did the party collapse?

The coup was not the reason for the collapse of the party; it was only the final trigger. The causes of the collapse were evident in the party's performance over the preceding six years, and in particular in its inability to respond to the changing nature of the challenges confronting it. A significant part of the party's problem was the way in which the major arena of political activity shifted from one in which the party was organisationally dominant to one in which the party became only one among a number of players. It was the move from bureaucratic politics to the politics of the streets that outflanked the party. The opening up of the public sphere of politics, first through the principles of glasnost and the emergence of public policy debate, then through the emergence of electoral politics, the organisation of independent political activity and the development of vigorous state organs, projected the party into a realm in which it was not accustomed to act. For the first time since 1918 it had to compete for popular support against rivals whose main plank was opposition to the communists. It had to transform itself from an administrative party into one which could appeal successfully for popular support. Yet in this endeavour it was fatally handicapped by the legacy the Gorbachev-led party inherited.

The problem for the party was that it had to run on the basis of offering improved benefits in the future, a promise which to have any credibility required the populace to forget about the past. In an immediate sense, what the party had to live down was the responsibility for presiding over the drift into societal crisis that in the second half of the 1980s it sought to remedy. With the party in control of the country over the preceding seventy years, there was no way that they could avoid responsibility for the vast gap between promise and fulfilment that the ordinary Soviet citizen lived in everyday life. Furthermore as the promised economic improvement in the late 1980s did not occur, the regime's failure to produce the socio-economic goods became even more manifest. The past policy of mismanagement could not be evaded; it was reflected in the conditions in which society wallowed.

But the legacy was not only one that had a direct impact on standards of living. One of the problems for the party posed by the policy of glasnost is that it catapulted into the public eye many of the nastier aspects of Soviet history. The opening up of discussion of such issues as the number of casualties of agricultural collectivisation, casualty rates resulting from the application of terror throughout the regime's life, the famine of the 1930s, the role of the security apparatus and the use of such things as psychiatric hospitals for the incarceration of dissidents ate away at the moral authority of the regime. Furthermore the search for the roots of such phenomena, which soon embraced not only Stalin but also Lenin and the very foundation of the regime, undercut the moral legitimacy which the post-Stalin regime had sought to create. This legacy was one which the party could not shake off, particularly since every family in the Soviet Union would have had direct, negative, experience of these policies in the past.

But glasnost also applied to the contemporary party. Many aspects of contemporary party life received a public hearing, and many of these further repelled public opinion away from the party. The issue of privileges, which Yel'tsin had championed in 1987, remained an issue into the last year of the party's existence despite attempts to remove it from the public scene by the adoption of measures to restrict its excesses, including passing some of the facilities (such as sanatoria and dachas) over to public authorities.[28] The party's involvement in corruption, long recognised but unpublicised, was given the full glare of publicity. 'Personal considerations' had always been known to apply in cadre policy, but bribery, favouritism and clannishness were still being raised in discussions of personnel issues at the end of 1990.[29] The diversion of state funds into party purposes, and in particular to the financing of adventures abroad, although long suspected became public knowledge during the party's last days. None of these sorts of revelations added lustre to the party's name, but only served further to discredit it in the eyes of the populace. As the party's image became more tarnished and alternative vehicles of political activity emerged, popular sentiment shifted in favour of these newer bodies increasingly decisively. The traditional bases of legitimation of the party, teleology, Marxism-Leninism and the old form of popular mandate could not sustain the party when the populace was given a real choice.

Glasnost was significant in another way: it shifted disputes in the party into the public arena. This had a dual effect. First, it enabled non-party forces to intervene in party disputes, and by so doing radicalise those disputes. Instead of an issue being sorted out quietly between party actors, such disputes often now became tangled up with broader issues of controversy in society. As more actors became involved, issues became increasingly radicalised and party actors were forced into more extreme positions than they might otherwise have adopted simply to remain in the debate. Furthermore with the public airing of disputes, the party protagonists sought to use the public arena to garner support among other potential actors, both inside the party and outside. This reflects the changing rules of party conduct over this period (see below). Second, the publication of party disputes projected the image of a party continually at odds with itself. One effect of this was to increase the sense of disillusionment and demoralisation at lower levels of the party. With their leaders constantly arguing, the rank-and-file was bound to suffer an erosion of their enthusiasm as the period dragged on. This is linked to the changing rules of party life.

Part of the change in the rules governing party life stemmed from the attempt to shift the party from a direct administrative role in the economic life of the country into one in which it exercised purely political leadership. This was a fundamental change because it altered the job patterns of party leaders at all levels of the Soviet administrative structure. Their relationship with economic managers, bureaucrats and other types of administrative officialdom was no longer to be one in which they were part of a structural line of command, but instead they were to be sources of political guidance outside that formal command structure. But this replacement of administrative power by ideological influence thrust party leaders into a position which they did not know how to handle. They were used to being able to give orders, and to the extent that the new change was brought about, they were now reduced to giving advice. The practical problem was one of fitting into a new role in which the rules of operation were unclear. Many party leaders at all levels of the structure simply tried to ignore the injunctions to refrain from exercising administrative power and sought to continue as they had before. Others responded by trying to withdraw from an administrative role and to exercise ideological leadership, but struggled to come to grips with the demands of the new role they had taken on. Many others seem to have lapsed into a kind of paralysis, especially with the rise of public attacks on the party and on communists as the period wore on. In any case a common result of this was confusion and demoralisation as the old ways were publicly rejected and the new ones, characterised by a lack of clear definition, were much more difficult satisfactorily to fulfil than those they replaced. The newly assertive state sphere, symbolised by Yel'tsin, exemplified the new difficulties.

This shift of politics from the bureaucratic to the public realm, of which the elimination of podmena was a central aspect, combined with the general emphasis upon democratisation, which was crucial for the emergence of new non-party organised political forces, thrust new imperatives onto the party's operating regime. It demanded a more open, public discussion of the whole range of issues inside the party. If the party was to exercise ideological hegemony and its members were to be conscious and active fighters for the party's cause, they had to be convinced of the virtue of the party line. This clearly involved participation in the continuing public debate about the country's future and, within the party, about the role, tasks and future of the party. The burgeoning of debate within the party was the result. Yet the established rules, norms and channels of party life were inadequate to structure such debate. Debate could no longer be restricted to the closed party rooms or to the period before a decision was reached; such debate now raged the length and breadth of the party, in the whole range of party and non-party media, and both before and after party decisions were adopted. The party had, as many acknowledged, been reduced to a talking shop. The collapse of party procedures for structuring such discussion severely hindered the resolution of many issues, with matters continually being revived as recent decisions came under challenge. This was a source of significant levels of institutional demoralisation and erosion: as the party structures seemed less relevant for the conduct of internal party affairs, the party as a whole appeared less relevant to many people.

But also important in this process was the effect of the policy of democratisation. In the public sphere this had led to the destruction of the party's monopoly through the emergence of a range of political parties and movements to take advantage of the room created by the establishment of the new structure of state legislative organs. In the party this led to the fracturing of the traditional control mechanism whereby the centre had maintained its dominance over lower levels, the nomenklatura. By expanding the electoral principle at the expense of appointment, the centre removed from the higher levels of the party the capacity effectively to discipline the lower ranks and thereby to ensure obedience to central decisions. But more than eroding central control, what this did was to place responsible party leaders at all levels in positions with which they were wholly unfamiliar: they had to be responsive to those over whom traditionally they had exercised overbearing authority. Suddenly the positions of these main links in the party command structure were rendered much more problematic. Their future was now less dependent upon satisfying their superiors than upon keeping their electoral constituency happy. The rules of the game, as far as they were concerned, had changed, and their positions had become significantly less secure. The result among some officials was demoralisation. Some sought to overcome this by ignoring the new injunctions to greater democracy, but the result of this was the increased discontent, demoralisation, and disillusionment among rank-and-file party members. So once again the traditional norms and structures of party life were cast into question. Both the principle of central control through the nomenklatura and the traditional position of party leaders were undercut, but the system which was meant to replace these was, in the time available, unable to deliver an effective working structure to replace that which it was meant to displace. The command structure and lines of authority within the party thereby became confused and collapsed. Often what was left behind was the informal family groups, which had not been dependent on the party structure for their existence, and which continued to provide a form of structuring of local power.

The effect of intra-party democratisation was exacerbated by the way in which events outside the party increasingly had a substantial impact on affairs within the party. As public debate became more radical, local party figures and organisations were faced with a major dilemma: either they seek to maintain what they understand to be party positions and thereby get left behind by the sweep of events in the community, or they attempt to keep abreast of developments and thereby abandon the established party positions. If party organisations wished to remain relevant to the course of events, they had no choice but to adopt the latter tactic. This they did in increasing numbers as time wore on; the clearest example of this is the way republican parties fell in with the increasingly nationalist mood from 1989 onward. As a result, the unitary nature of the party disintegrated. Party organisations at all levels weakened and sometimes even cut the ties which had bound them to the centre in their search to retain local power. As an administrative and command structure, the party fractured under the pressure of the radicalisation of the public arena. Once again, then, confusion within party ranks and the fracturing of party structures was the result.

The confusion and uncertainty which pervaded party ranks through-out this period were stimulated by the constant disagreement and open conflict within the leadership. As the reform coalition which came to power in 1985 was fractured by the radicalisation of the reform programme, the intensity and scope of conflict within the party elite increased. Gorbachev sought to adopt a centrist course whereby he was able to keep both more conservative and more liberal elements of the leadership behind the reform programme, but this was at the expense ultimately of disappointing both. The effect of this tactic was certainly to prevent the emergence of a more coherent, and radical, programme from emerging, but it also prevented an earlier conservative backlash which might have destroyed the whole reform project. But another crucial effect of this constant disagreement and Gorbachev's inability to prevent it by stamping his authority unambiguously over the policy process was that it prevented the party from articulating any clear set of aims and objectives which could have given it a clear sense of direction and acted as a source of identification and commitment for party members. As the party as a whole looked for leadership out of the crisis into which the party, and country, had blundered, all it received from the party leadership was continued bickering over the whole range of policy and outlook. The leadership failed to give a clear sense of direction, so the party staggered on almost like a blind man.

The failure of the party was thus a failure of organisational adapt-ability, albeit in a very hostile environment. Under attack from a changing societal environment, the party was unable to generate the sorts of changes in its culture, structure and processes which would have enabled it to adapt readily to these challenges. The attempts that were made to alter the party's internal regime resulted in an under-mining of established ways of doing things without the replacement of them by new, effective processes and procedures. Without an effective leadership which could both impose its authority and generate rank-and-file commitment through the clear articulation of a set of party values which members would accept, the party could not gain any sense of coherence in the response required of it to meet the challenges it confronted. Lacking effective leadership, its internal processes hamstrung, irreparably divided on policy issues, and under vigorous attack from without, the party as an administrative structure could not survive. Unable to operate in the old way, it could not adjust to the new. What was paradoxical is that the changes to which the party had to respond were unleashed by the party leadership itself. At least until early 1989 those changes could have been halted, albeit at a price, but the prime mover of change, Mikhail Gorbachev, was convinced of its necessity and refused to abandon the reform programme. The result was the collapse of the party and of the USSR. The party's future in the individual Soviet successor states will be different, moulded by the diverse conditions in those states. But at least in Russia, despite gaining approximately 11% of the vote in the 12 December 1993 election, the party is unlikely to be able to regain the position of administratively-based dominance it once enjoyed.

This explanation of the collapse of the communist party is not unique to the Soviet Union. The process of disintegration that destroyed the CPSU was also occurring in the ruling parties of Eastern Europe, but it was prevented from running its full course by the rapid collapse experienced by these regimes. The process was essentially the same because it stemmed from the basic nature of the Leninist type of administrative party system. The key characteristic of the party which was at the heart of this type of system was organisational penetration of all sectors of society and strictly disciplined centralism. But when the party's basic task, direct administrative supervision, was removed, it found itself without a role that fitted its own organisational structures and culture or the new conditions. This was exacerbated by the emergence of new competitors challenging the party's power and position. In such circumstances, internal discipline collapsed and with it the party as a coherent organisation. The party could adjust neither its organisational structure nor its culture to cope with its changed environment. In Eastern Europe, it was pushed from power. In the Soviet Union it meandered into a dead end of indecision, ultimately becoming irrelevant to the course of political development. This suggests that the inflexibility of the administrative party system severely limited its capacity to cope with a changing environment, and was thereby the crucial factor in the collapse of communism.

# Notes

## 1 An administrative party system

1 For example, see the discussion of a typology of political parties in Giovanni Sartori, *Parties and party systems. A framework for analysis* (Cambridge, CUP, 1976), I, pp. 42–7.
2 *Vos'moi s'ezd RKP(b) Mart 1919 goda. Protokoly* (Moscow, 1959), pp. 428–9.
3 This is discussed in Graeme Gill, *The origins of the Stalinist political system* (Cambridge, CUP, 1990).
4 On the early funding, see Robert H. McNeal, 'The beginning of Communist party financial exactions from the Soviet State', in D. A. Loeber (ed.), *Ruling communist parties and their status under law* (The Hague, Nijnhoff, 1986).
5 See the discussion in Gill, *Origins*.

## 2 The personnel solution

1 For this argument, see Archie Brown, 'The Power of the General Secretary of the CPSU', in T. H. Rigby, Archie Brown and Peter Reddaway (eds.), *Authority, power and policy in the USSR. Essays dedicated to Leonard Schapiro* (London, Macmillan, 1980), pp. 135–57, esp. p. 136.
2 For one discussion of the changes at the apex of the party, see Ronald J. Hill and Peter Frank, 'Gorbachev's Cabinet-Building', *The Journal of Communist Studies* 2, 2, June 1986, pp. 168–81.
3 Reports of its meetings suggest a frequency of 8.2 days in 1985 and 9.3 in 1986.
4 See the discussions in Zhores Medvedev, *Gorbachev* (Oxford, Basil Blackwell, 1986), pp. 15–17 and Christian Schmidt-Hauer, *Gorbachev. The path to power* (London, Tauris, 1986), p. 113.
5 For the speeches by Yel'tsin and Ligachev, see *XXVII s'ezd kommunist-icheskoi partii sovetskogo soiuza 25 fevralia–6 marta 1986 goda. Stenograficheskii otchet* (Moscow, 1986), I, pp. 140–5 (esp. pp. 142–4) & 232–40 (esp. p. 236).
6 *Pravda* 3 July 1985.
7 For example, respectively, *Pravda* 14 July 1985, *Izvestiia* 5 January 1986, *Pravda* 20 January 1986, 27 January 1986, 2 February 1986, and 3 February

1986. A more extensive report on Uzbekistan will be found in *Pravda Vostoka* 1 & 2 February 1986. For a discussion in English, see James Critchlow, '"Corruption", nationalism and the native elites in Soviet Central Asia', *The Journal of Communist Studies* 4, 2, June 1988, pp. 142–61. Also see Peter Rutland, 'The search for stability: ideology, discipline, and the cohesion of the Soviet elite', *Studies in Comparative Communism* 24, 1, March 1991, pp. 47–50.

8 The origins of this phenomenon have been discussed in Graeme Gill, *The origins of the Stalinist political system* (Cambridge, CUP, 1990). Also see Graeme Gill, 'Ideology, organization and the patrimonial regime', *The Journal of Communist Studies* 5, 3, September 1989, pp. 285–302. Also see ch. 1.

9 See the report of the Ukrainian CC plenum, *Pravda* 26 March 1985.

10 'O sozyve ocherednogo XXVII s'ezda KPSS i zadachakh sviazannykh s ego podgotovkoi i provedeniem', *Pravda* 24 April 1985.

11 *Pravda* 20 April 1985. For references to the promotion of individuals on the basis of personal loyalty, acquaintance or local favouritism, see *Pravda* 27 July 1985.

12 *Pravda* 22 July 1986. Also see *Moskovskaia Pravda* 16 December 1986, FBIS Soviet Union 30 December 1986.

13 For example, *Moskovskaia Pravda* 19 March 1985, FBIS Soviet Union 2 April 1985.

14 *Pravda* 29 March 1985.

15 For example, *Pravda Ukrainy* 26 March 1985, FBIS Soviet Union 9 April 1985; *Sovetskaia Rossiia* 19 April 1985 FBIS Soviet Union 25 April 1985; and *Zaria Vostoka* 7 July 1985, FBIS Soviet Union 24 July 1985.

16 *Moskovskaia Pravda* 19 September 1985, FBIS Soviet Union 26 September 1985.

17 For example, see Grishin's speech to the Moscow aktiv, *Moskovskaia Pravda* 19 March 1985, FBIS Soviet Union 2 April 1985. Also see the report of the Kazakh CC plenum, *Pravda* 29 March 1985.

18 *Pravda* 2 April 1985.

19 *Pravda Ukrainy* 26 March 1985, FBIS Soviet Union 9 April 1985.

20 *Pravda* 5 September 1985. According to one editorial entitled 'Party conscience'

> There are still no pangs of conscience on the part of bureaucrats, 'window-dressers' and those who prefer to play safe, some of whom have broken all records for the number of words about the need to accelerate, but have done precisely nothing to put this into practice. They talk about quality, but are responsible for sub-standard work. They talk about efficiency, but generate mountains of paper. They talk about honesty and then produce false reports or encourage the production of false reports. (*Pravda* 29 May 1986)

21 'Iz besedy v Ts.K. KPSS s pervymi sekretariami nekotorykh oblastnykh komitetov partii', M.S. Gorbachev, *Izbrannye rechi i stat'i* (Moscow, 1987), III, pp. 16–25.

22 'O nedopustimosti iskazheniia fakticheskogo polozheniia del v soob-shcheniiakh i informatsiiakh, postupaiushchikh v Ts K KPSS i drugie rukovodiashchie organy', 26 November 1985. *Izvestiia Ts.K. KPSS* 2 February 1989, pp. 39–41.

23 *Pravda* 10 April 1985. On formalism, see *Pravda* 2 September 1985, 24 September 1985. Also *Sovetskaia Belorussiia* 30 July 1986, FBIS Soviet Union 10 September 1986, *Moskovskaia Pravda* 28 August 1986, FBIS Soviet Union 28 August 1986, and *Pravda Ukrainy* 4 November 1986 and 10 December 1986, FBIS Soviet Union 13 November and 22 December 1986.

24 *Pravda* 25 October 1985.

25 'O nedopustimosti . . . '.

26 'Politicheskii doklad Tsentral'nogo Komiteta KPSS', *Pravda* 26 February 1986.

27 *Moskovskaia Pravda* 19 September 1985, FBIS Soviet Union 26 September 1985.

28 *Pravda* 2 April 1985.

29 *Pravda* 5 September 1985.

30 *Leningradskaia Pravda* 23 March 1986, FBIS Soviet Union 6 May 1986.

31 M.S. Gorbachev, 'O piatiletnem plane ekonomicheskogo i sotsial'nogo razvitiia SSSR na 1986–1990 gody i zadachakh partiinykh organizatsii po ego realizatsii', *Pravda* 17 June 1986.

32 *Pravda* 22 July 1986. Also the report from Vilnius gorkom, *Pravda* 15 March 1985.

33 *Moskovskaia Pravda* 28 August 1986, FBIS Soviet Union 28 August 1986. For criticism of another Moscow raikom chief, Shakhmanov of Leningradskii raikom, see *Moskovskaia Pravda* 16 December 1986, FBIS Soviet Union 30 December 1986.

34 *Pravda* 7 July 1986.

35 *Pravda Vostoka* 31 January 1986. Also see *Pravda* 2 February 1986.

36 For example, *Pravda* 2 & 9 February 1986.

37 Gorbachev, 'O piatiletnem . . . '.

38 *Pravda* 29 May 1986. On excessive paper work to no effect, see *Pravda* 3 June 1985, 25 June 1986 and 22 July 1986.

39 Gorbachev, 'O sozyve ocherednogo . . . '. One side of this was also the failure to give concrete leadership to lower level organs. *Moskovskaia Pravda* 11 October 1986, FBIS Soviet Union 29 October 1986.

40 For example, see *Pravda* 6 April 1985 and *Moskovskaia Pravda* 19 September 1985, FBIS Soviet Union 26 September 1985.

41 More broadly, 46.1 per cent of full and candidate members of the CC and members of the Central Auditing Commission were newly elected in 1986. J. H. Miller, 'How much of a new elite?', in R. F. Miller, J. H. Miller and T. H. Rigby (eds), *Gorbachev at the helm. A new era in Soviet politics?* (London, Croom Helm, 1987), p. 70.

42 Thane Gustafson and Dawn Mann, 'Gorbachev's first year: building power and authority', *Problems of Communism* 35, 3, May–June 1986, p. 2. This article provides extensive figures on personnel changes.

43 Georgia (July 1985), Kirgizia (November 1985), Tajikistan (December 1985), Turkmenistan (December 1985) and Kazakhstan (December 1986).

44 At this time, many appointments into the regions were of people who had spent some time in the CC, usually as inspectors, rather than simple promotions within one region or cross-postings between regions. The former had been common before. In principle, such a practice should have given the centre more control and helped to break local ties. For a full discussion of promotion and personnel patterns, see Gustafson and Mann, 'Gorbachev's first year'. This pattern seems to have been moderated following the XXVII Congress. Thane Gustafson and Dawn Mann, 'Gorbachev's next gamble', *Problems of Communism* 36, 4, July–August 1987, p. 13.

45 For one discussion of personnel issues, see Rutland, 'Search for stability', pp. 25–57.

46 For example see reports of the plena of the Azeri, Turkmen, Kirgiz (*Pravda* 26 March 1985), Armenian, Latvian, Kazakh (*Pravda* 29 March 1985) and Ukrainian (*Pravda Ukrainy* 26 March 1985, FBIS Soviet Union 9 April 1985) parties. Also see the discussion in *Pravda* 18 April 1985.

47 'O sozyve ocherednogo . . . '.

48 'O sozyve ocherednogo . . . '.

49 For example, see *Pravda* 20 April 1985, 18 July 1985, 5 September 1985.

50 *Leningradskaia Pravda* 23 March 1986, FBIS Soviet Union 6 May 1986.

51 *Pravda* 18 July 1985. For a CC decision emphasising the need for increased personal responsibility, improved party performance in production matters and further improvement in the conditions of intra-party life, see the CC decision on the work of the party committee in the Ministry of the Machine Tool and Instrument Industry, *Pravda* 13 December 1985.

52 For example, 'Povyshat' trebovatel'nost'', *Pravda* 18 March 1985 and I. Shalimova, 'Attestatsiia – sredstvo povysheniia kompetentnosti kadrov', *Partiinaia zhizn'* 12, June 1985, pp. 32–5. Also the report of the Leningrad obkom plenum, *Pravda* 21 March 1985, and the Belgorod obkom plenum, *Pravda* 31 March 1985.

53 At the XXVII Congress a new set of regulations governing the Central Auditing Commission was introduced, but this concerned only financial matters and their correct disposition within the party. *KPSS v rezoliutsiiakh i resheniiakh s'ezdov, konferentsii i plenumov Ts.K. KPSS* (Moscow, 1989), XV, pp. 181–2.

54 For example, *Pravda* 27 March 1985.

55 Respectively *Pravda* 27 March 1985 and *Sovetskaia Rossiia* 19 April 1985, FBIS Soviet Union 25 April 1985.

56 Section 4(b) of the Rules. *Pravda* 7 March 1986. For a prefiguring of this, see Grishin's comments in *Moskovskaia Pravda* 19 March 1985, FBIS Soviet Union 2 April 1985.

57 'Iz besedy . . . '. Also 'Perestroika neotlozhna, ona kasaetsia vsekh i vo vsem', *Pravda* 2 August 1986.

58 'Politicheskii doklad . . . '. On failure to respond to criticism, see *Pravda* 1 November 1985.

59 *Sovetskaia Rossiia* 4 June 1985, FBIS Soviet Union 14 June 1985.

60 *Pravda* 23 March 1985 & 20 June 1985.

61 *Pravda* 27 July 1985 for the report of a conference in the CC. Also see the issue for 5 August 1985.

62 For example, *Pravda* 20 March 1985, 2 September 1985, 29 May 1986 & 29 December 1986.

63 For example, see Yel'tsin's letter in *Pravda* 23 May 1986. For the article which prompted this, see *Pravda* 13 May 1986.

64 *Pravda Ukrainy* 26 March 1985, FBIS Soviet Union 9 April 1985.

65 Section 28 of the Rules, *Pravda* 7 March 1986.

66 Section 19(e) of the Rules, *Pravda* 7 March 1986.

67 Quoting Leningrad leader Solov'ev, *Leningradskaia Pravda* 23 March 1986, FBIS Soviet Union 6 May 1986.

68 Section 27 of the Rules, *Pravda* 7 March 1986.

69 In his speech to the XXVII Congress, Gorbachev specifically contrasted collectivism with situations where the role of the plenum and the bureau were downgraded and instructions were issued by one individual. He cited the example of the CC of the Kirgiz Communist Party. 'Politicheskii doklad . . . '.

70 M. S. Gorbachev, 'Nastoichivo dvigat'sia vpered', *Izbrannye*, II, pp. 210–24, and 'Korennoi vopros ekonomicheskoi politiki partii', *Pravda* 12 June 1985, 'Iz besedy . . . '. The ideology too needed to be updated to take account of recent problems and developments. See the CC decision on the journal *Kommunist* and its tasks, which included further development of theory to make it applicable to contemporary problems. *Kommunist* 12, 1986, pp. 3–10. This article did, however, reaffirm the continuing role and importance of Marxism-Leninism.

71 *Pravda Ukrainy* 1 June 1985, FBIS Soviet Union 11 June 1985.

72 *Pravda* 6 April 1985.

73 For example, see the editorial in *Pravda* 12 May 1986. This also refers to the need for a change in the organisation, style and methods of work.

74 The new Rules made it incumbent upon those giving recommendations for party membership to assist candidates in 'their ideological-political growth'. Section 5 of the Rules, *Pravda* 7 March 1986.

75 'Politicheskii doklad . . . '.

76 This is also reflected in the way discussions of party responsibility for poor economic performance continued to be couched in the style of the Brezhnev period. For example, see *Pravda* 4 July 1986 (Nizhnevartovskii gorkom), 10 December 1986 (Perm obkom) and 18 January 1987 (Krasnoiarsk kraikom).

77 For example, see respectively the articles under the same name, 'Ob izmeneniiakh v Ustave KPSS', *Kommunist* 17, 1985, pp. 79–83 & 18, 1985, pp. 61–5.

78 'Iz besedy . . . '.

79 For example, *Pravda* 31 October 1986.
80 Respectively sections 24, 26 and 28.
81 For example, see 'O proektakh novoi redaktsii Programmy KPSS, izmenenii v Ustave KPSS, Osnovykh napravlenii ekonomicheskogo i sotsial'nogo razvitiia SSSR na 1986–1990 na period do 2000 goda', *Pravda* 16 October 1985; 'Politicheskii doklad . . . ' and 'O piatiletnem plane ekonomicheskogo i sotsial'nogo razvitiia SSSR na 1986–1990 gody i zadachakh partiinykh organizatsii po ego realizatsii', *Pravda* 17 June 1986. Also see the report of Volgograd obkom plenum, *Pravda* 25 March 1985.
82 'O sozyve . . . '.
83 'O sozyve . . . '.
84 In Krasnodar, *Pravda* 20 September 1986.
85 One indication of this was the accident at Chernobyl, which seems to have brought home to Gorbachev the way the communication and control problems of the Soviet structure had not been altered by the measures introduced hitherto.
86 For some discussion of this, see T. H. Rigby, 'Old style Congress – New style leadership?', Miller, Miller and Rigby, pp. 33–5.
87 This was much noted by Western observers. For example, see Gustafson and Mann, 'Gorbachev's first year'.

### 3 The move to institutional reform

1 See the interview with Krasnodar kraikom first secretary Ivan Polozkov in 'The Second Russian Revolution. III The Yel'tsin file', BBC Television, 1991. According to Polozkov, Gorbachev told him about his plans for multi-candidate elections in September 1986, but regional leaders did not receive the actual proposals until the night before the plenum opened.
2 See Gorbachev's speech to the trade unions in *Pravda* 26 February 1987.
3 Thane Gustafson and Dawn Mann, 'Gorbachev's next gamble', *Problems of Communism* 36, 4, July–August 1987, p. 13.
4 *Kazakhstanskaia Pravda* 26 December 1986, FBIS Soviet Union 8 January 1987.
5 *Kazakhstanskaia Pravda* 1 January 1987, FBIS Soviet Union 8 January 1987.
6 *Pravda* 7 January 1987. This followed up on an article entitled 'Old connections' dating from 11 October 1986. For Kolbin's acknowledgement that many of the criticisms made of the Kazakh situation were just, see *Pravda* 9 March 1987. For reports about the expulsion of some who were guilty of corrupt or illegal activity, see *Kazakhstanskaia Pravda* 12 & 13 February 1987, FBIS Soviet Union 12 March 1987.
7 *Kazakhstanskaia Pravda* 4 January 1987, FBIS Soviet Union 29 January 1987.
8 'O rabote Permskogo obkoma KPSS', 3 December 1986. *Pravda* 10 December 1986.
9 Domestic Service 20 January 1987. FBIS Soviet Union 22 January 1987. For details on the process of certification, which was to cover all senior officials

of the CC apparatus except CC secretaries and was to be conducted twice every five years, see *Kazakhstanskaia Pravda* 21 January 1987, FBIS Soviet Union 9 February 1987.

10 'O perestroike i kadrovoi politike partii', *Pravda* 28 January 1987.

11 'O perestroike i kadrovoi politike partii', *Pravda* 29 January 1987. Also the editorial in *Pravda* 31 January 1987.

12 *Pravda* 10 February 1987, *Sovetskaia Rossiia* 19 February 1987, FBIS Soviet Union 5 March 1987.

13 See *Sovetskaia Rossiia* 19 February 1987, FBIS Soviet Union 5 March 1987.

14 *Partiinaia zhizn'* 11, 1988, p. 15. For a discussion of one such election, see E. Nikitina, 'Plenum raikoma izbiraet pervogo sekretaria', *Partiinaia zhizn'* 5, 1987, pp. 32–5 Also see *Pravda* 28 March 1987.

15 Although as Nikitina notes, there was scope for lower-level nomination of candidates, at least in the instance she is discussing.

16 *Literaturnaia Gazeta* 25 February 1987, FBIS Soviet Union 25 March 1987.

17 For example, *Pravda Ukrainy* 3 March 1987, FBIS Soviet Union 13 March 1987.

18 For example, see the editorial in *Pravda* 7 March 1987.

19 *Kazakhstanskaia Pravda* 15 March 1987, FBIS Soviet Union 1 April 1987. He was addressing the plenum of the CC KCP.

20 For his assertion that former leaders of the KCP had pressured judicial organs to enable relatives who had committed criminal activity to avoid responsibility, see *Kazakhstanskaia Pravda* 24 March 1987, FBIS Soviet Union 9 April 1987.

21 *Pravda* 20 March 1987. For Ukrainian leader Shcherbitskii's comments, see *Pravda Ukrainy* 25 March 1987, FBIS Soviet Union 10 April 1987. For the removal of the first secretary, see *Pravda Ukrainy* 21 April 1987, FBIS Soviet Union 28 April 1987.

22 See the comments by Shcherbitskii at the plenum of the Ukrainian CC. *Pravda Ukrainy* 25 March 1987, FBIS Soviet Union 10 April 1987.

23 *Pravda* 2 April 1987. For criticism of the Uzbek bureau for leniency with corrupt officials, see *Pravda* 21 December 1987. For criticism of favouritism and protectionism under former Kirgiz leader Usubaliev, see *Pravda* 6 May 1987.

24 *Pravda* 26 April 1987.

25 *Pravda* 27 April 1987.

26 Shcherbitskii actually put his finger on one of the problems here when he said that some personal accountability reports 'lacked an analytical attitude . . . Omissions were frequently merely stated, but their causes were not revealed, and no proposals were made to eliminate them . . . [and they] referred to difficulties and immediate problems only in passing'. *Pravda Ukrainy* 28 April 1987, FBIS Soviet Union 12 May 1987.

27 As opposed to the general principles. All supported the principle of democratisation, whatever that meant. There was also some support for an influx of new forces into party bodies, although not all put the implications of this quite as starkly as the first secretary of Rakitianskii raikom: 'for

decades now we have zealously led people up the official ladder. The name of this phenomenon is the nomenklatura barrier. I am all for breaking out of this nomenklatura circle and giving scope to fresh forces.' *Pravda* 16 May 1987.

28 *Pravda* 31 May 1987.
29 *Pravda* 18 June 1987. The resolution was dated 8 June.
30 *Pravda* 16 July 1987.
31 'O zadachakh partii po korennoi perestroike upravleniia ekonomikoi', *Pravda* 26 June 1987.
32 'O sozyve XIX Vsesoiuznoi konferentsii KPSS', *Pravda* 27 June 1987. Gorbachev had mentioned such a conference in his address to the January plenum, but it had not been taken up at the time.
33 Formally the authority and responsibilities of the conference were uncertain, but Gorbachev hoped that it would be able to replace part of the CC, as similar gatherings had done in the past. By May 1988 among the 306 full members of the CC, more than 40 were 'dead souls', having left the posts that had at the time of the XXVII Congress entitled them to a seat. Michel Tatu, '19th Party Conference', *Problems of Communism* 3–4, May–August 1988, p. 6.
34 One possible reflection of the continuing strength of this opposition may be that during this period many of the criticisms of party organisations for not adequately assisting improved production performance repeated the model of such instructions from the Brezhnev period and failed to make any significant reference to democratisation or lower level obstruction. For example, see *Pravda* 21 April 1987 (Altai kraikom), 4 December 1987 (Cheliabinsk obkom), 25 February 1987 (Rostov oblast).
35 *Sovetskaia Rossiia* 9 July 1987, FBIS Soviet Union 13 July 1987.
36 *Pravda Ukrainy* 17 July 1987, FBIS Soviet Union 27 July 1987.
37 *Pravda* 29 July 1987.
38 *Pravda* 2 August 1987.
39 *Leningradskaia Pravda* 26 July 1987. FBIS Soviet Union 14 August 1987.
40 For one discussion, see Jeffrey Hahn, 'An experiment in competition: the 1987 elections to the local soviets', *Slavic Review* 47, 3, Fall 1988, pp. 434–47.
41 *Sovetskaia Rossiia* 9 August 1987, FBIS Soviet Union 20 August 1987.
42 *Pravda* 8 August 1987.
43 For example, see *Pravda* 8 August 1987 (Tajikistan), 16 August 1987 (Uzbekistan and Kirgizia).
44 *Pravda* 27 August 1987.
45 See the articles in *Pravda* 20 July 1987 & 17 September 1987.
46 See FBIS Soviet Union 28 September 1987.
47 *Pravda* 8 October 1987.
48 *Pravda* 31 October 1987.
49 *Izvestiia* 26 October 1987.
50 The image of a local party leadership cut off from what was happening around it was perfectly conjured up by Gorbachev in October 1987:

Enough of sitting inside offices, inside mansions built in decades past. These mansions, too, should be opened up so that party committees and district executive committees occupying them become full of life. The country is abuzz, it needs new ideas, action and discussion. And yet everything is calm inside offices with their parquet floors and carpeting and schedule of receiving hours. Can you imagine a revolution having been made in that way, according to a schedule? ('Partiia revolutsiia – partiia perestroika', *Pravda* 14 October 1987)

51 *Pravda* 1 November 1987.
52 *Pravda* 14 November 1987. On the need for glasnost and democratisation of party life, see the CC decision on the state of affairs in Vladimir, *Pravda* 11 November 1987.
53 *Sovetskaia Rossiia* 26 November 1987, FBIS Soviet Union 4 December 1987.
54 *Trud* 29 December 1987, FBIS Soviet Union 5 January 1988.
55 The report noted that members and candidates of the obkom bureau were criticised for 'their obsolete, imperious style of leadership. This was confirmed right here at the plenum. Obkom secretary S. Saydaliev tried to "put in their place those who had overstepped the mark" by shouting at them. That episode prompted the plenum participants to include in the resolution a point on the need for a party attitude toward criticism.'( ibid.) For the report of a meeting in Kiev oblast characterised by a purely formalist approach, see *Pravda* 10 December 1987. Interestingly, Gorbachev's own book, which was sent to the publishers in October 1987, offered no substantial discussion of the issue of party reform, although he did criticise the way slackness and corruption were hidden behind false reporting. M. S. Gorbachev, *Perestroika i novoe myshlenie dlia nashei strany i dlia vsego mira* (Moscow, 1987), pp. 16–18.
56 *Pravda* 27 December 1987.
57 *Pravda* 2 February 1988.
58 *Pravda* 27 January 1988.
59 *Sotsialisticheskaia Industriia* 22 December 1987, FBIS Soviet Union 5 January 1988.
60 *Selskaia zhizn'* 22 December 1987, FBIS Soviet Union 5 January 1988.
61 *Bakinskii Rabochii* 26 January 1988, FBIS Soviet Union 12 February 1988.
62 *Pravda* 27 January 1988.
63 *Sovetskaia Estoniia* 19 January 1988, FBIS Soviet Union 10 February 1988.
64 *Pravda Ukrainy* 27 December 1987, FBIS Soviet Union 11 January 1988.
65 *Pravda* 26 January 1988.
66 *Pravda* 20 December 1987.
67 *Leningradskaia Pravda* 20 December 1987, FBIS Soviet Union 26 January 1988.
68 *Pravda* 29 January 1988.
69 See the report of the plenum in *Izvestiia* 6 January 1988. For the plenum resolution, see *Kommunist* (Erevan) 30 December 1987, FBIS Soviet Union 14 January 1988.
70 *Pravda* 18 January 1988.

71 *Pravda* 21 January 1988.

72 For example, *Sotsialisticheskaia Industriia* 23 December 1987, FBIS Soviet Union 5 January 1988 (Komi oblast); *Leningradskaia Pravda* 20 December 1987, FBIS Soviet Union 26 January 1988 (Leningrad obkom); *Pravda Ukrainy* 23 January 1988 (Ukraine), FBIS Soviet Union 1 February 1988.

73 For example, the Tajik plenum was criticised for a half-hearted and purely formal self-criticism. *Pravda* 30 December 1987.

74 For example, *Leningradskaia Pravda* 20 December 1987, FBIS Soviet Union 26 January 1988 (Leningrad oblast); *Bakinskii Rabochii* 26 January 1988 (Azerbaijan), FBIS Soviet Union 12 February 1988.

75 *Pravda* 26 December 1987.

76 *Pravda* 20 December 1987.

77 *Pravda Ukrainy* 27 December 1987, FBIS Soviet Union 11 January 1988.

78 *Pravda Ukrainy* 24 January 1988, FBIS Soviet Union 1 February 1987.

79 Shcherbitskii's report to the plenum. *Pravda Ukrainy* 23 January 1988, FBIS Soviet Union 1 February 1988. He also reported that the CC nomenklatura had been cut by almost 33 per cent.

80 *Bakinskii Rabochii* 26 January 1988, FBIS Soviet Union 12 February 1988.

81 *Pravda* 16 February 1988.

82 For a more critical evaluation of meetings in Ukraine, see *Pravda Ukrainy* 16 February 1988. For central criticism of the Kiev party organisation for complacency, failure to give leadership to perestroika, and the refusal to restructure intra-party life, see *Pravda* 31 January 1988. For the report of a meeting called to discuss this criticism and a central interpretation of this meeting, see respectively *Pravda Ukrainy* 17 March 1988, FBIS Soviet Union 29 March 1988 and *Pravda* 19 March 1988.

83 Indeed, the problem of late payment of membership dues which was becoming apparent at this time (*Izvestiia Ts.K. KPSS* 4, 1989, p. 24) reflects a party with severe problems of morale let alone enthusiasm.

84 *Sovetskaia Rossiia* 7 February 1988, FBIS Soviet Union 16 February 1988. For example, it was reported that in Astrakhan oblast, five raikom first secretaries and one third of PPO secretaries were elected by secret ballot from among several candidates. *Pravda* 5 May 1988. This report details the, mainly unsatisfactory, reaction of Astrakhan obkom to an earlier CC CPSU resolution critical of its performance (entitled 'The lotus is withering').

85 *Partiinaia zhizn'* 22, 1988, p. 8.

86 For example, see N. Tiurin, 'Vremia konkretnykh del, vremia konkretnoi otvetsvennosti', *Kommunist* 18, 1987, pp. 43–4. Also see 'Demokratizatsiia partii – demokratizatsiia obshchestvo', *Kommunist* 2, 1988, pp. 26–30; 3, 1988, pp. 35–9; 4, 1988, pp. 85–9; 5, 1988, pp. 41–5. For one particularly outspoken comment, see V. Selivanov, 'O sile i avtoritete partii', *Pravda* 2 May 1988.

87 For example, *Kommunist* 3, 1988, p. 37; *Partiinaia zhizn'* 6, 1988, p. 26 & 10, 1988, p. 38; *Sovetskaia Kul'tura* 17 May 1988, FBIS Soviet Union 7 June 1988.

88 *Partiinaia zhizn'* 5, 1988, p. 41.

89 *Moscow News* 10 April 1988, p. 8.

90 *Kommunist* 9, 1988, p. 35.

91 *Moscow News* 20 March 1988, p. 8; 24 April 1988, p. 8; & 15 May 1988, p. 13.

92 *Sovetskaia Rossiia* 7 February 1988, FBIS Soviet Union 16 February 1988; *Sovetskaia Rossiia* 13 March 1988, FBIS Soviet Union 18 March 1988; *Izvestiia* 30 April 1988; *Sovetskaia Kul'tura* 28 April 1988, FBIS Soviet Union 4 May 1988.

93 *Moscow News* 12 June 1988, p. 8 and Radio Liberty Research Bulletin RL258/88, 17 June 1988, p. 8.

94 *Kommunist* 4, 1988, pp. 86–7; *Partiinaia zhizn'* 6, 1988, p. 29; 8, 1988, p. 49; 9, 1988, p. 48; 12, 1988, p. 32; *Pravda* 15 March 1988 & 17 March 1988; *Sovetskaia Kul'tura* 28 April 1988, FBIS Soviet Union 4 May 1988. Determination of the size of the apparatus by its own raikom rather than the CC was also advocated. *Partiinaia zhizn'* 3 February 1988.

95 *Kommunist* 5, 1988, pp. 42 & 43–5. The letter on p. 42 entitled 'The costs of the nomenklatura' criticised the privileges of this group and the way party organs defended 'obvious degenerates, swindlers, bribe-takers and thieves.'

96 *Pravda* 30 April 1988.

97 The charge that elected bodies were filled from above was a common one during this discussion. For example, see *Pravda* 9 March 1988; *Partiinaia zhizn'* 4, February 1988.

98 *Literaturnaia Gazeta* 4 May 1988, FBIS Soviet Union 5 May 1988. There was also a complaint that 'when it comes to the "top man" or other people in direct authority over us, any outburst of criticism still very often smacks of panegyrics.' *Pravda* 14 February 1988.

99 *Pravda* 28 May 1988.

100 For example, *Partiinaia zhizn'* 5 March 1988. For one call to give the party a clear 'constitutional status' in society, see *Pravda* 31 May 1988.

101 *Pravda* 16 May 1988. This letter came from a non-party member.

102 'Tezisy Tsentral'nogo Komiteta KPSS k XIX Vsesoiuznoi partiinoi konferentsii (Odobreny Plenumom Ts.K. KPSS 23 maia 1988 goda)', *Pravda* 27 May 1988.

103 See the interesting, positive, evaluation of the Theses in a discussion involving Rector of the Higher Party School V. Shostakovskii in *Sovetskaia Kul'tura* 23 June 1988, FBIS Soviet Union 14 July 1988. The discussants conclude that democratisation is essential to break the unaccountable power of the apparatus, but that democratisation can be carried out effectively within the bounds of the single party.

104 'O sozyve XIX vsesoiuznoi konferentsii KPSS', *Pravda* 27 June 1987. This was modified by a brief set of injunctions issued by Gorbachev in May 1988. For a discussion of the course of the elections, see Aryeh L. Unger, 'The Travails of Intra-Party Democracy in the Soviet Union: The Elections to the 19th Conference of the CPSU', *Soviet Studies* 43, 2, 1991, pp. 329–54.

105 See the reports in *Pravda* 4 June 1988; *Komsomolskaia Pravda* 22 May 1988, FBIS Soviet Union 25 May 1988 (for the situation at MGU); and *L'Unita* 5 June 1988, FBIS Soviet Union 16 June 1988. Not all gained election in

Moscow; some were elected from other areas e.g. Boris Yel'tsin from Karelia.

106 For reports, see *Sovetskaia Rossiia* 1 June 1988, FBIS Soviet Union 7 June 1988 and *Argumenty i fakty* 23, 4–10 June 1988, FBIS Soviet Union 7 June 1988.

107 *Pravda* 6 June 1988.

108 *L'Unita* 12 June 1988, FBIS Soviet Union 17 June 1988 and *Izvestiia* 18 June 1988.

109 For example, for discussions of one instance of this, in Cheliabinsk, see *Pravda* 21 May 1988 and *Sotsialisticheskaia Industriia* 1 June 1988, FBIS Soviet Union 10 June 1988. For other examples of disputes over nominations, see Unger, 'Travails', pp. 333–4 & 339–43.

110 *Sovetskaia Kul'tura* 2 June 1988, FBIS Soviet Union 6 June 1988.

111 *Komsomolskaia Pravda* 15 May 1988, FBIS Soviet Union 17 May 1988.

112 *Pravda* 1 June 1988 and *Literaturnaia Gazeta* 25 May 1988, FBIS Soviet Union 2 June 1988. Also *Sovetskaia Kul'tura* 26 May 1988, FBIS Soviet Union 9 June 1988.

113 *Pravda* 13 June 1988.

114 *Sovetskaia Kul'tura* 21 April 1988 and *Sotsialisticheskaia Industriia* 12 April 1988, both in FBIS Soviet Union 26 April 1988.

115 This may be reflected in the admission that Politburo sessions tended to last the whole day and often into the night, with discussion ranging over a wide array of issues. *Izvestiia Ts.K. KPSS* 2, pp. 246 & 256.

116 For an argument that Ligachev was not a conservative but part of the consensus with Gorbachev, see Jeffrey Surovell, 'Ligachev and Soviet Politics', *Soviet Studies* 43, 2, 1991, pp. 355–74. While Ligachev was part of the consensus and was willing to move with it, he was at the more cautious end of that consensus.

117 This process of a radicalising agenda producing more reservations among leaders explains why it was so difficult for Gorbachev to stack the leading organs with unambiguous supporters of his programme; those who supported the programme at one point were likely to have serious reservations about it once it had moved on in a more radical direction.

118 In this regard see the moderate evaluation of Stalin given by Gorbachev in his address for the seventieth anniversary of the revolution. 'Oktiabr' i perestroika: revoliutsiia prodolzhaetsia', *Pravda* 3 November 1987.

119 For the letter, entitled 'Ne mogu postupat'sia printsipami', *Sovetskaia Rossiia* 13 March 1988. For the official response, reputedly written by Yakovlev, 'Printsipy perestroiki: revoliutsionnost' myshlenniia i deistvii', *Pravda* 5 April 1988.

120 On this see Angus Roxburgh, *The second Russian revolution* (London, BBC Books, 1991), p. 112.

121 Including laws on cooperatives, enterprise autonomy, and privately based consumer and service operations.

122 Important here were the public demonstrations in August 1987 in the Baltic capitals over the 1939 Nazi–Soviet treaty and the beginnings of trouble over Nagorno-Karabakh in February 1988.

123 'The second Russian revolution. III. The Yel'tsin File'. It is not clear what effect these had. It seems to have had little effect on the performance of PPOs. The first round of personnel changes brought in other members of the former Grishin machine to replace those removed, but the second round involved bringing people from the enterprises. Personal communication, Moscow November 1991.

124 A stenographic report of the plenum has been published in *Izvestiia Ts.K. KPSS* 2, 1989, pp. 209–87. Yel'tsin's speech is on pp. 239–41.

125 For Yel'tsin's discussion of the plenum and subsequent events, see Boris Yel'tsin, *Ispoved' na zadannuiu temu* (Moscow, 1990), pp. 79–90. For one discussion of the Yel'tsin affair, see Seweryn Bialer, 'The Yeltsin affair: the dilemma of the left in Gorbachev's revolution', Seweryn Bialer (ed), *Inside Gorbachev's Russia. Politics, Society and Nationality* (Boulder, CO, Westview Press, 1989), pp. 91–119.

## 4 The programme for change

1 M. S. Gorbachev, 'O khode realizatsii reshenii XXVII s'ezda KPSS i zadachakh po uglubleniiu perestroiki', *Pravda* 29 June 1988.

2 Once again this involved a direct clash between Yel'tsin and Ligachev, principally over Yel'tsin's request for political rehabilitation. The speeches were published in *Pravda* 29 June–2 July 1988. Also see *XIX vsesoiuznaia konferentsiia kommunisticheskoi partii sovetskogo soiuza, 28 iunia–1 iulia 1988 goda. Stenograficheskii otchet* (Moscow, 1988) 2 vols. On the Conference, see Stephen White, 'Gorbachev, Gorbachevism and the party conference', *The Journal of Communist Studies* 4, 4, December 1988, pp. 127–60; Michel Tatu, '19th CPSU conference', *Problems of Communism* 37, 3–4, May–August 1988, pp. 1–15.

3 'O demokratizatsii sovetskogo obshchestva i reforme politicheskoi sistemy', *Pravda* 5 July 1988. Formally the resolutions were adopted on 1 July but were not released until 5 July, presumably so they could be reviewed by the Politburo on 4 July.

4 This was to involve the elimination of the Committee of Party Control and the Central Auditing Commission, and the creation of a single Central Control and Auditing Commission.

5 'O bor'be s biurokratizmom', *Pravda* 5 July 1988.

6 'O glasnosti', *Pravda* 5 July 1988.

7 'O pravovoi reforme', *Pravda* 5 July 1988.

8 M. S. Gorbachev, 'O prakticheskoi rabote po realizatsii reshenii XIX vsesoiuznoi partiinoi konferentsii', *Pravda* 30 July 1988.

9 'O prakticheskoi rabote po realizatsii reshenii XIX vsesoiuznoi konferentsii KPSS', 'Ob otchetakh i vyborakh v partiinykh organizatsiiakh', and 'Ob osnovnykh napravleniiakh perestroiki partiinogo apparata', *Pravda* 31 July 1988.

10 See the resolution 'Ob otchetakh i vyborakh v partiinykh organizatsiiakh', *Pravda* 31 July 1988. For an editorial which linked the campaign with democratisation, see *Pravda* 3 August 1988.

11 *Pravda* 18 August 1988.
12 'Instruktsiia o provedenii vyborov rukovodiashchikh partiinykh organov', *Partiinaia zhizn'* 16 August 1988, pp. 30–35. This Instruction was adopted on 12 August. It replaced the instruction of the same name adopted on 29 March 1962 and amended on 2 July 1966 and 7 August 1973. For one discussion, see John Lowenhardt, 'Democratization of party elections in the Soviet Union. Central Committee CPSU Instructions on elections, 1937–1988', *Acta Politica* 1, January 1989.
13 For criticisms, see for example *Moscow News* 37, 11 September 1988.
14 *Pravda* 31 August 1988.
15 *Pravda Ukrainy* 11 October 1988, FBIS Soviet Union 25 October 1988. He also reported that more than 25 per cent of organisers, 33 per cent of shop organisation secretaries and 30 per cent of PPO secretaries were replaced.
16 *Pravda* 5 December 1988. According to a report at the gorkom plenum, more than a third of party leaders were elected on a competitive basis. *Moskovskaia Pravda* 6 January 1989, FBIS Soviet Union 18 January 1989.
17 *Pravda* 12 December 1988.
18 M. S. Gorbachev, 'Narashchivat' intellektual'nyi potentsial perestroiki', *Pravda* 8 January 1989.
19 *Pravda* 21 January 1989. Interestingly, Leningrad oblast first secretary Solov'ev used similar language: 'A number of collectives have nominated noncontroversial and 'convenient' people rather than those who are businesslike and enterprising.' *Pravda* 26 December 1988.
20 *Pravda* 13 February 1989.
21 For example, *Sotsialisticheskaia Industriia* 1 February 1989, FBIS Soviet Union 9 February 1989.
22 *Pravda* 21 January 1989. Also see his earlier comments, *Pravda* 12 December 1988.
23 *Pravda* 23 August 1988.
24 *Pravda* 13 February 1989.
25 *Pravda* 23 December 1988.
26 For example, *Pravda* 16 August 1988, 18 October 1988 and *Pravda Ukrainy* 11 October 1988, FBIS Soviet Union 25 October 1988.
27 *Pravda Ukrainy* 22 January 1989, FBIS Soviet Union 2 February 1989.
28 For example, see the reports in *Pravda* 15 December 1988 (Bukhara oblast conference proceeded in the old superficial and uncritical fashion) and 28 January 1989 (corruption in Azerbaijan – citing earlier articles about a particular secretary's 'patrimony').
29 *Pravda* 13 December 1988. Also see the preceding issue.
30 *Moscow News* 1, 1 January 1989. The six were Grigorii Baklanov, Alexander Gelman, Daniil Granin, Elem Klimov, Roald Sagdeev and Mikhail Ul'ianov. Also see Dawn Mann, 'Results of the 1988 CPSU Report-and-Election Campaign', RL February 24, 1989, pp. 4–7.
31 *Izvestiia Ts.K. KPSS* 1, 1989, pp. 81–6.
32 'Ob obrazovanii komissii Ts.K. KPSS i reorganizatsii apparata Ts.K. KPSS

v svete reshenii XIX vsesoiuznoi partiinoi konferentsii', *Pravda* 1 October 1988.

33 'O komissiiakh tsentral'nogo komiteta KPSS', *Pravda* 29 November 1988.

34 'O komissiiakh . . . '.

35 See *Izvestiia Ts.K. KPSS* 1, 1989, p. 86. The twenty departments prior to the reorganisation are listed here.

36 M. S. Gorbachev, 'Narashchavit' intellektual'nyi potentsial perestroiki', *Pravda* 8 January 1989. This involved a reduction of 536 responsible and 143 technical workers. *Izvestiia Ts.K. KPSS* 6, 1989, p. 116.

37 'O reorganizatsii apparata mestnykh partiinykh organov', *Spravochnik partiinogo rabotnika* 29, 1989 (Moscow, 1989), pp. 307–9. This was a decision of the Politburo dated 10 September. For central adoption of local recommendations regarding structure, see 'O predlozheniiakh ts.k. kompartii soiuznikh respublik, kraikomov, obkomov partii po strukture i shtatam apparata mestnykh partiinykh organov', (Politburo decision 31 October), *Spravochnik* . . . , pp. 309–12. For the adoption of proposals by a series of local party organisations for the establishment of control-auditing commissions, see 'Ob obrazovanii kontrol'no-revizionnykh komissii v riade partiinykh organizatsii' (Politburo decision 12 November), *Spravochnik* . . . , pp. 313–16. Also see the report in *Moskovskaia Pravda* 12 February 1989, FBIS Soviet Union 22 February 1989.

38 For example, see *Pravda Ukrainy* 11 October 1988, FBIS Soviet Union 25 October 1988 (Ukraine); TASS 25 October 1988, FBIS Soviet Union 26 October 1988 (Latvia); *Zaria Vostoka* 23 November 1988, FBIS Soviet Union 9 December 1988 (Georgia); TASS 7 December 1988, FBIS Soviet Union 8 December 1988 (Uzbekistan); *Pravda* 12 December 1988 (Moscow oblast), *Moskovskaia Pravda* 6 January 1988 (Moscow), FBIS Soviet Union 18 January 1989. According to a report in early 1989, during the second half of 1988 local party organs lost 7000 posts in the reorganisation compared with the 700 from the CC apparatus. *Izvestiia Ts.K. KPSS* 4, 1989, p. 24.

39 *Pravda* 5 December 1988. Interview with V.K. Mesiats from Moscow obkom.

40 Respectively, *Pravda* 28 January, 11 & 28 February, 14, 15 & 19 March 1989. For an argument that, at least until April 1989, only the Commission on Legal Policy was fulfilling any substantive function, see Alexander Rahr, 'Who is in Charge of the Party Apparatus?', Radio Liberty, *Report on the USSR* 1, 15, 14 April 1989, pp. 21–22. According to Volgograd first secretary Kalashnikov, the commissions 'have not done much so far' *Pravda* 27 April 1989. For a report that commissions in Ukraine had begun work, see Shcherbitskii's comments in *Pravda Ukrainy* 22 January 1989, FBIS Soviet Union 2 February 1989.

41 'O merakh po osushchestvleniiu politicheskoi reformy v oblasti gosudarstvennogo stroitel'stva', *Pravda* 29 November 1988.

42 'Ob izmeneniiakh i dopolneniiakh Konstitutsii (Osnovnogo Zakona) SSSR', *Pravda* 3 December 1988.

43 'O vyborakh narodnykh deputatov SSSR', *Pravda* 4 December 1988.
44 *Pravda Ukrainy* 25 December 1988, FBIS Soviet Union 6 January 1989.
45 *Pravda Ukrainy* 22 January 1989, FBIS Soviet Union 2 February 1989.
46 For example, see the discussion with L. A. Onikov in *Pravda* 2 January 1989.
47 For example, at the end of November Gorbachev told the Supreme Soviet that the party was the only force that 'can unify and integrate the diverse and at times contradictory social interests into a single party'. *Pravda* 30 November 1988. Also his speech to the January 1989 plenum. *Pravda* 11 January 1989.
48 *Pravda* 2 March 1989.
49 *Pravda* 5 October 1988.
50 See *Sovetskaia Kul'tura* 6 October 1988, FBIS Soviet Union 14 October 1988. Also see the comments by Onikov in *Pravda* 2 January 1989.
51 Onikov, *Pravda* 2 January 1989.
52 For example, see the admission about passivity and stage managing in South Sakhalin in *Pravda* 31 August 1988. For the summary report, see *Izvestiia TS.K. KPSS* 3, 1989, pp. 14–24. This reflected considerable ambivalence about the new procedures.
53 'O khode raionnykh i gorodskikh partiinykh konferentsii', *Izvestiia Ts.K. KPSS* 1, 1989, pp. 94–8.
54 According to the summary report, the following results were achieved (with 1985 figures in brackets where available):

| | |
|---|---|
| PPOs where the work of the committee, bureau or secretary was deemed unsatisfactory | 0.8% (0.1%) |
| PPO secretaries elected from two or more candidates | 48.1% |
| Change of PPO secretaries | 37.0% (25.4%) |
| Shop organisations in which secretary elected from two or more candidates | 50.2% |

In Moscow, the figure for competitive election of secretaries was 33%. *Izvestiia Ts.K. KPSS* 3, 1989, pp. 18–27.
55 *Izvestiia Ts.K. KPSS* 4, 1989, p. 38.
56 For references on this relating to Moscow oblast and Kiev, see respectively *Pravda* 12 December 1988 and *Pravda Ukrainy* 25 December 1988. In the first nine months of 1988 the number of members and candidates leaving the party increased 36.5 per cent compared with the same period in 1987. *Izvestiia Ts.K. KPSS* 1, 1989, p. 134.
57 *Pravda* 1 July 1988.

## 5 Reform out of control

1 Run off elections were held on 9 April in those 149 districts where two or more candidates split the vote and none received the necessary 50 per cent. In the 199 districts where one or two candidates were nominated but none received 50 per cent, new nominations as well as new elections had to be held. First round elections were held on 14 May and the second round on

21 May. For a discussion of and statistics from the election, see Jeffrey W. Hahn, 'The Soviet state system', in Stephen White, Alex Pravda and Zvi Gitelman (eds.), *Developments in Soviet politics* (London, Macmillan, 1990), pp. 92–7. Also Max E. Mote, 'Electing the USSR Congress of People's Deputies', *Problems of Communism* 38, 6, November–December 1989, pp. 51–6; and Peter Lentini, 'Reforming the electoral system: The 1989 elections to the USSR Congress of People's Deputies', *The Journal of Communist Studies* 7, 1, March 1991, pp. 69–94.

2  Of the 2,250 seats in the Congress of People's Deputies, 1,500 were to be filled by direct popular election. The remaining 750 seats were allocated to public organisations, with specific numbers of seats being set aside for specific organisations. The CPSU was allocated 100 seats, although of course party members also stood in the popular constituencies and in the constituencies of other organisations.

3  This list was selected from a larger list of 312 potential candidates. Of the 100, 52 were elected unanimously; among Politburo members, there were 10 votes against Ryzhkov, 12 against Gorbachev and 78 against Ligachev. Lentini, 'Reforming the Electoral System', p. 87.

4  The extent of the rejection of the party in Moscow is reflected in the following table which shows candidates' and winners' prior membership of party committees:

|  | Candidates | Winners |
|---|---|---|
| CC | 1 | 0 |
| Moscow gorkom | 10 | 3 |
| Raikoms | 27 | 1 |

Brendan Kiernan and Joseph Aistrup, 'The 1989 Elections to the Congress of People's Deputies in Moscow', *Soviet Studies* 43, 6, 1991, p. 1,055.

5  *Pravda* 13 April 1989.

6  For example, see *Izvestiia* 16 April 1989 (Georgia), *Pravda* 20 April 1989 and *Leningradskaia Pravda* 7 April 1989 (Leningrad), FBIS Soviet Union 21 April 1989.

7  *Pravda* 8 April 1989.

8  See John P. Willerton Jr, 'The political leadership', in White, Pravda and Gitelman (eds.), *Developments* p. 62. For full figures, see Elizabeth Teague, 'Fall of representation of party apparatus in CPSU Central Committee', Radio Liberty, *Report on the USSR* 1, 19, May 12 1989, p. 4.

9  *Pravda* 27 April 1989.

10  *Pravda* 27 April 1989.

11  *Pravda* 27 April 1989.

12  *Pravda* 27 April 1989.

13  *Pravda* 27 April 1989. For some other comments on the informals, see the speeches by Miasnikov and Mesiats.

14  For example, see the speeches of Bobovikov, Miasnikov, and Kolbin.

15  The plenum speakers did provide some evaluations of the progress thus

far achieved in some of the reforms initiated at the XIX Conference. The different views on the effect of the reorganisation in the apparatus have been noted. In a press conference at the end of the plenum, Medvedev noted that before the restructuring of the CC apparatus there had been 20 departments but that this had been reduced to eight (*sic*), while the apparatus had been cut by 40 per cent. FBIS Soviet Union 26 April 1989. According to Kalashnikov in the plenum, the differentiation between party and state remained only on paper. Party bodies were clearly finding it difficult to withdraw from economic affairs. See the report of the Committee for Party Control from April 1989, *Izvestiia Ts.K. KPSS* 5, 1988, pp. 61–2. However one report said that in the first quarter of 1989, the CC received half the number of communications on economic questions as in the same time the previous year, a figure suggesting some progress in withdrawing from economic affairs. *Izvestiia Ts.K. KPSS* 5, 1989, p. 6. The decline in apparatus functions is suggested by the following figures for the number of questions discussed by CC departments:

| | 1986 | 1987 | 1988 | 1989 | 1/1–20/6/1990 | Total |
|---|---|---|---|---|---|---|
| Party construction & cadre work | 24 | 56 | 10 | 12 | 12 | 114 |
| Ideology | 20 | 73 | 17 | 9 | 7 | 126 |
| Social-economic | 26 | 60 | 12 | 10 | 2 | 110 |
| Agrarian | 18 | 23 | 5 | 1 | — | 47 |
| International | 3 | 36 | 4 | 4 | 4 | 51 |
| State-law | 7 | 18 | 5 | 13 | 5 | 48 |
| Defence | 2 | 4 | 2 | 1 | 1 | 10 |
| National relations | — | — | — | — | 2 | 2 |
| General | 6 | 1 | 3 | 2 | 2 | 14 |
| Chancellery | 2 | 3 | — | 2 | 1 | 8 |
| Total | 108 | 274 | 58 | 54 | 36 | 530 |

*Izvestiia Ts.K. KPSS* 9, 1990, p. 23.

16 Interestingly, in the open letter to Gorbachev by six supporters of reform in January 1989, reference was made to 'the dictatorship of mediocrities' in the party centre and the sabotage of reform by party officials. *Moscow News* 1, 1 January 1989.

17 For example, see *Pravda* 29 April 1989.

18 'Programma deistvii po itogam aprel'skogo (1989g) Plenuma Ts.K. KPSS', *Izvestiia Ts.K. KPSS* 7, 1989, pp. 7–13. However, this was a bland, opaque document that was clearly inadequate to meet the looming challenges.

19 For some comments on this, see Anatoly Sobchak, *For a new Russia* (New York, The Free Press, 1992).

20 On these early parties, see Vera Tolz, *The USSR's emerging multiparty system* (New York, Praeger, 1990); Vladimir Brovkin, 'Revolution from below: informal political associations in Russia 1988–1989', *Soviet Studies* 42, 2, April 1990, pp. 233–57; Michael E. Urban, 'The Soviet multi-party system. A Moscow roundtable', *Russia and the World* 18, 1990.

21 *Pravda* 23 December 1989.

22 For a discussion of the miners' strike activity, see Theodore Friedgut and Lewis Siegelbaum, 'Perestroika from below: the Soviet miners' strike and its aftermath', *New Left Review* 181, 1990, pp. 5–32 and Peter Rutland, 'Labor unrest and movements in 1989 and 1990', *Soviet Economy* 6, 4, 1990, pp. 345–84.

23 M. S. Gorbachev, 'Perestroika raboty partii – vazneishaia kliuchevaia zadacha dnia', *Pravda* 19 July 1989. For a review of some of the complaints and fears of party secretaries both at this meeting and more generally, see Vladimir Brovkin, 'First party secretaries: an endangered Soviet species?', *Problems of Communism* 39, 1, January–February 1990, pp. 15–27.

24 'Po-novomu osmyslit' funktsii i rol' partii v obshchestve' and 'Zakliuchitel'noe slovo M.S. Gorbacheva na soveshchanii v Ts.K. KPSS', *Pravda* 21 July 1989. Little practical seems to have come from the meeting. The Politburo decision on the meeting was bland. 'O realizatsii polozhenii doklada t. Gorbacheva M.S., predlozhenii i zamechanii vyskazannykh na soveshchanii pervykh sekretarii ts.k. kompartii soiuznykh respublik, kraikomov i obkomov partii', *Izvestiia Ts.K. KPSS* 9, 1989, pp. 9–11.

25 Although this was ambiguous because Bobykin was referring to discussions about the role of the party in contemporary life.

26 According to the deputy chief of the Organizational Party Work Department of the CC, about 10,000 low-level party leaders had been replaced in elections with multiple candidacies and secret ballots. Radio Liberty Research Bulletin RL422/88, September 23, 1988, p. 8.

27 According to the then second secretary of Moscow gorkom, Yuri Prokof'ev, 'We have reduced the apparat of the Moscow City Party Committee by one-third and abolished all the sectoral departments. But nothing has changed: the Party's functions in society remain the same. And the reduced apparat – today these are really competent, qualified people – operates in the old way.' 'Reforming the Party', *Moscow News* 36, 3 September 1989, p. 5.

28 In this connection, he said that what was needed was a second secretary of the CC, even if officially the office was not called this.

29 For other comments on the performance of the CC, see the comments by Kemerovo first secretary Mel'nikov and Volgograd first secretary Kalashnikov. *Pravda* 27 April 1989.

30 See above, chapter 4. The commissions met on an irregular basis. For the dates of their meetings, see *Izvestiia Ts.K. KPSS* 9, 1990, pp. 25–9. Also see below.

31 Radio Liberty, *Report on the USSR* 1, 5, 3 February 1989, p. 3.

32 The commissions were to be recast at the March 1990 plenum.

33 For example, *Leningradskaia Pravda* 29 November 1989, FBIS Soviet Union 21 December 1989.

34 For example, for criticism of the failures of the Moldavian CC Bureau to give leadership, see *Pravda* 12 May 1989 & 4 October 1989.

35 The reference was to a 'majority of raikoms' in Moscow. *Moskovskaia Pravda*

22 June 1989, FBIS Soviet Union 1 August 1989. In the same speech, by Moscow first secretary Zaikov, the gorkom is also accused of failing to give adequate leadership.

36 It is unclear whether the irregularity of reports about Politburo deliberations reflects a lower level of activity or a changed policy on reporting. For one discussion, see Dawn Mann, 'The Challenges Facing Gorbachev', Radio Liberty, *Report on the USSR* 1, 35, 1 September 1989, p. 15. There were thirty-four meetings of the Politburo and Secretariat in 1989. *Izvestiia Ts.K. KPSS* 1, 1990, p. 3. Reports of Politburo sessions in late 1989 show no reduction in the range of issues discussed in this body, further reflecting the difficulty in separating the party from the state.

37 TASS 3 August 1989, FBIS Soviet Union 7 August 1989.

38 Between January 1989 and June 1990, the CC commissions met on the following number of occasions: Party Construction and Cadre Policy 4; Ideology 5; Socio-economic 5; Agrarian 6; International 4; Legal 4. *Izvestiia Ts.K. KPSS* 9, 1990, p. 24. A list of the topics discussed at these sessions will be found on pp. 25–9. For reports on the work of the commissions in Latvia see *Sovetskaia Latviia* 29 April 1989, FBIS Soviet Union 12 May 1989 and in Estonia *Sovetskaia Estoniia* 5 May 1989, FBIS Soviet Union 17 May 1989. For a report of the work of the Commission on Party Building and Cadre Policy, see *Pravda* 4 June 1989.

39 *Izvestiia Ts.K. KPSS* 12, 1989, p. 6. At the September 1989 plenum four new CC secretaries were appointed, suggesting an enhanced role for this body.

40 Of the others, that of April 1989 brought about major personnel changes in the CC, September 1989 dealt with nationality issues and the XXVIII Congress, 25–6 December 1989 discussed events in Lithuania, and the February 1990 plenum dealt with the draft party platform.

41 One qualification is necessary here. Baltic representatives refused to participate in measures critical of Lithuania, and Boris Yel'tsin voted against the Draft Platform of the CC at the February plenum.

42 This was at the joint plenum of the Leningrad obkom and gorkom in November 1989. *Leningradskaia Pravda* 29 November 1989, FBIS Soviet Union 21 December 1989.

43 The author was M. V. Maliutin. *Sovetskaia Kul'tura* 4 July 1989, FBIS Soviet Union 1 August 1989.

44 *Pravda* 24 October 1989.

45 *Sotsialisticheskaia Industriia* 22 August 1989, FBIS Soviet Union 23 August 1989.

46 *Pravda* 19 June 1989.

47 *Sovetskaia Rossiia* 2 March 1990.

48 *Sotsialisticheskaia Industriia* 5 August 1989, FBIS Soviet Union 7 August 1989.

49 *Sovetskaia Rossiia* 9 July 1989, FBIS Soviet Union 3 August 1989. For the argument that what was needed was to replace the economic emphasis in cadres' qualifications and work with political-organisational work, see

*Pravda* 2–3 May 1989. According to the Chancellery of the CC, responsible workers in the obkoms, kraikoms and republican CCs had been reduced by 27.7%. *Izvestiia Ts.K. KPSS* 6, 1989, p. 116.

50 Interview with Prokof'ev. *Pravda* 27 November 1989.

51 *Pravda* 2 January 1990.

52 *Sovetskaia Latviia* 20 June 1989, FBIS Soviet Union 21 June 1989. In December Vagris argued that the CPL would not sever its relations with the CPSU but would use its independence to transform those relations. *TASS* 5 December 1989, FBIS Soviet Union 6 December 1989.

53 *Sovetskaia Estoniia* 10 September 1989, FBIS Soviet Union 2 October 1989. Also see the comments by first secretary Vialias in *New Times* 16–22 January 1990. The Democratic Platform also supported federalisation. See the comments of one of its founders Vladimir Lysenko in *Pravda* 4 February 1990.

54 *Sovetskaia Litva* 26 February 1989, FBIS Soviet Union 21 March 1989. For the discussion of the move to an independent party, see Alfred Erich Senn, 'Toward Lithuanian independence: Algirdas Brazauskas and the CPL', *Problems of Communism* 39, 2, March–April 1990, pp. 21–8.

55 *Sovetskaia Litva* 28 June 1989, FBIS Soviet Union 26 July 1989.

56 See the speeches of Artrauskas and Brazauskas, *Sovetskaia Litva* 17 & 18 October 1989, FBIS Soviet Union 7 November 1989.

57 For example, on 16 November the entire Lithuanian party Politburo attended a full meeting of the CPSU Politburo in Moscow, while Gorbachev explicitly warned against moves to establish a separate party. Respectively, *Sovetskaia Litva* 18 November 1989, FBIS Soviet Union 27 December 1989, and *Pravda* 3 December 1989. Medvedev had visited Vilnius personally to deliver Gorbachev's message. *Pravda* 2 December 1989. For Lithuanian party leader Brazauskas' response, see *Sovetskaia Litva* 2 December 1989, FBIS Soviet Union 4 January 1990.

58 *Sovetskaia Rossiia* 21 December 1989, FBIS Soviet Union 21 December 1989. For Brazauskas' speech, see *Sovetskaia Litva* 20 December 1989, FBIS Soviet Union 19 January 1989.

59 CC plenum, 30 September 1989. FBIS Soviet Union 7 November 1989.

60 *Pravda Ukrainy* 20 October 1989, FBIS Soviet Union 8 December 1989. The Leningrad party organisation declared 'we reject the idea of the conversion of the CPSU into a confederation of parties of the union republics. The CPSU should remain a single international party with a single programme and statutes.' *Leningradskaia Pravda* 29 November 1989, FBIS Soviet Union 21 December 1989. A similar position was adopted by the Belorussian party (*Sovetskaia Belorussiia* 19 October 1989, FBIS Soviet Union 8 December 1989). By the end of the year its position mirrored that of the centre around Gorbachev: a 'new status of the union republican communist party within a renewed CPSU, the strengthening of its independence and the right to decide organisational-structural, cadre, financial and other questions within the limits of the CPSU Programme and Rules'. *Sovetskaia Belorussiia* 31 December 1989, FBIS Soviet Union 1 February 1990. For an argument in

favour of proportional representation by republics in the formation of
leading organs, see Vagris' address to the plenum of the Latvian CC on 23
January, FBIS Soviet Union 7 February 1990.

61 For example, see the report of Gorbachev's meeting with the first
secretaries from the Baltic republics (*Pravda* 16 September 1989), the
nationality policy adopted at the September plenum (*Pravda* 24 September
1989) and the discussion of changes in the party Rules in *Pravda*
12 November 1989. Also the comments by Medvedev at a press conference
following the December plenum. TASS 9 December 1989, FBIS Soviet
Union 11 December 1989 and the CC's appeal 'K sovetskomu narodu'.
*Pravda* 12 December 1989.

62 *Izvestiia Ts.K. KPSS* 11, 1989, p. 4. For some of these, see *Izvestiia Ts.K. KPSS*
1, 1990, pp. 75–87 & 2, 1990, pp. 68–72.

63 For the argument in favour of this by first secretary Brazauskas, see his
comments to the CPLith CC plenum on 1 December 1989, *Sovetskaia Litva*
2 December 1989, FBIS Soviet Union 4 January 1990. He specifically
criticised the view, promoted by the centre, that Lenin was opposed to a
federal party. For Gorbachev's response, see his speech to the CC 'V edinstve
partii – sud'ba perestroiki', *Pravda* 26 December 1989 and the leading
article 'Internatsional'noe edinstvo KPSS', *Pravda* 28 December 1989.

64 At a session of the Latvian Supreme Soviet in mid-January, the Latvian
Communist party was declared to be the lineal descendant of the LCP that
had operated in underground conditions in the 1920s and 1930s and
that its incorporation into the AUCP(b) had been non-voluntary and
coercive. *Krasnaia zvezda* 18 January 1990, FBIS Soviet Union 23 January
1990. The same session of the Supreme Soviet removed the communist
party's monopoly position from the republic's constitution.

65 The Lithuanian party had declared its independence at the XX Congress on
20 December. On 21 December 160 delegates held a party conference and
declared their continued adherence to the CPSU.

66 This even while becoming more accepting of the drive for secession on
the part of the Lithuanians. The change from opposing such a move to
understanding that it was probably inevitable seems to have been brought
about by his visit to Vilnius in early January 1990.

67 Specifically, they were to have the right independently to handle organisational, cadre and financial questions and to engage in publishing activity.
The presence of the republican party leaders in the proposed new
Presidium was meant to entrench a role for these parties in the discussion
of national issues, while the CCs of the republican parties were to be able
to demand discussion of a question at a CC plenum if they disagreed with
a decision of the party's central leadership organs. 'K gumannomu
demokraticheskomu sotsializmu', *Pravda* 13 February 1990.

68 This plenum was specifically devoted to the party's national policy. For
Gorbachev's speech, see *Pravda* 20 September 1989. It had been mooted in
the draft platform on national policy published prior to the plenum.
'Natsional'naia politika partii v sovremennykh usloviiakh (platforma

KPSS)', *Pravda* 17 August 1989. For a letter urging the establishment of a Russian party and basing this on the party's nationality policy, while questioning the adequacy of a Russian Bureau, see *Pravda* 4 September 1989. A joint meeting of the Leningrad gorkom and obkom in November supported this. *Izvestiia Ts.K. KPSS* 12, 1989, pp. 46–50.

69 'Ob obrazovanii rossiiskogo biuro tsk kpss', *Pravda* 10 December 1989.

70 *Pravda* 10 December 1989.

71 'K gumannomu . . .' *Pravda* 13 February 1990. Also see Gorbachev's speech to the March plenum, *Pravda* 12 March 1990.

72 For one, unconvincing, attempt to distinguish between these two cases, see the interview with CC Secretary Manaenkov in *Pravda* 9 November 1989.

73 For example, see the programme of the newly united Leningrad obkom and gorkom, *Pravda* 11 March 1990. An initiative committee to establish such a party was established in Leningrad in February 1990. TASS 9 February 1990, FBIS Soviet Union 15 February 1990. Headed by Boris Gidaspov, the unified Leningrad organisation was a major conservative bastion in Russia.

74 *Le Monde* 25 May 1989, FBIS Soviet Union 2 June 1989.

75 *Pravda* 14 June 1989. This was in the context of disagreement over the status of Marxism-Leninism, especially compared with international human values. Compare *Leningradskaia Pravda* 29 November 1989, FBIS Soviet Union 21 December 1989 with Prokof'ev in *Moscow News* 7, 18 February 1990.

76 For example, *Moskovskaia Pravda* 22 June 1989, FBIS Soviet Union 1 August 1989 (Zaikov) and *Sovetskaia Rossiia* 9 July 1989, FBIS Soviet Union 3 August 1989.

77 For example, Salutskii in *Pravda* 4 February 1990.

78 For example, see the Draft Programme of the Estonian party in *Sovetskaia Estoniia* 10 September 1989, FBIS Soviet Union 2 October 1989; *Pravda* 11 October 1989 and *Moscow News* 7, 18 February 1990.

79 *Sovetskaia Kul'tura* 4 July 1989, FBIS Soviet Union 1 August 1989.

80 *Sotsialisticheskaia Industriia* 22 August 1989, FBIS Soviet Union 23 August 1989. Also Razumov in *Pravda* 12 November 1989, and the platform of the Leningrad party organisation in *Leningradskaia Pravda* 29 November 1989, FBIS Soviet Union 21 December 1989. In the Programme of the Belorussian party, rather than endorsing this principle it called for unity of action following adoption of a decision, no persecution of those who express a different constructive opinion, and consideration and defence of the viewpoint of the minority if it is not at variance with the requirements of the CPSU Programme and Rules. *Sovetskaia Belorussiia* 31 December 1989, FBIS Soviet Union 1 February 1990.

81 For example, see *Sovetskaia Kul'tura* 13 November 1989, FBIS Soviet Union 14 December 1989 (Riga gorkom secretary Klausten); *Leningradskaia Pravda* 23 November 1989, FBIS Soviet Union 2 January 1990 (discussion at joint plenum of Leningrad obkom and gorkom); *Sovetskaia Kul'tura* 7 December

1989, FBIS Soviet Union 13 December 1989 (Shostakovskii); *Komsomolskaia Pravda* 27 January 1990, FBIS Soviet Union 30 January 1990 (Shostakovskii).

82 The Democratic Platform is discussed in greater detail in the following chapter.

83 For example, see the interview with V. Shostakovskii, Rector of Moscow Higher Party School in *Sovetskaia Kul'tura* 6 October 1988, FBIS, Soviet Union Daily Report 14 October 1988. The Platform adopted by the CC of the Estonian Communist Party prior to the September 1989 CC plenum called for a review of the 1921 ban on fractions and for the toleration of the formation of platforms inside the party. Elizabeth Teague, 'Estonian Party Publishes Draft Program', Radio Liberty, *Report on the USSR* 1, 38, 22 September 1989, p. 20.

84 *Pravda* 6 February 1990.

85 'K gumannomu . . . '.

86 *Pravda* 3 March 1990.

87 See the comments in the July meeting by Zaikov and Masaliev. Also see Zaikov's comments to the Moscow gorkom plenum, *Moskovskaia Pravda* 22 June 1989, FBIS Soviet Union 1 August 1989. For the abolition by Tiumen obkom of 2000 nomenklatura positions, which would leave only about 100, see *Izvestiia* 21 February 1990. For criticism of a continuing nomenklatura approach in Uzbekistan, see *Pravda Vostoka* 29 April 1989, FBIS Soviet Union 11 May 1989.

88 *Izvestiia Ts.K. KPSS* 2, 1989, p. 7.

89 For example, FBIS Soviet Union 11 September 1989 (Kaliningrad obkom), *Pravda* 25 October 1989 (Sakhalin obkom), *Pravda* 1 December 1989 (Karelian obkom), *Sovetskaia Belorussiia* 23 November 1989, FBIS Soviet Union 5 January 1990 (Gomel' obkom), and *Pravda* 28 February 1990 (Kaluga obkom).

90 *Pravda* 10 July 1989. In September a report in *Pravda* noted that in the last report and election campaign (1988) only half the PPO secretaries were elected on a multi-candidates basis, with even fewer at higher levels. *Pravda* 12 September 1989.

91 *Pravda* 1 December 1989.

92 *Izvestiia* 3 February 1990.

93 *Pravda* 4 February 1990. For local party leaders having difficulty in acting in the new style and under new conditions, see *Pravda* 9 October 1989. For the call for leaders with new qualities, with speaking ability, analytical capacity and lively individuality, see *Pravda* 16 October 1989.

94 For example, see the editorial in *Pravda* 12 September 1989. Also see Polozkov's comments in *Sovetskaia Rossiia* 9 July 1989, FBIS Soviet Union 3 August 1989. In October 1989 the Commission on Party Construction and Cadre Policy reviewed the further democratisation of cadre policy, discussed practical measures for dismantling the formal-nomenklatura mechanism of cadre policy and recommended the abolition of the records and monitoring nomenklatura located in the apparatus of party committees. See the reports in *Pravda* 15 October 1989 and *Izvestiia Ts.K. KPSS*

11, 1989, p. 4. The Commission decided the CC would pass responsibility for vetting 800 posts to lower level committes, which would in turn give up the right to vet 12,000 lesser posts. Following the April 1989 plenum, appointments of secretaries in the regions of Russia followed a different pattern to the earlier period: no longer were people who had spent some time in Moscow as CC Inspectors sent to the regions. In a move that may reflect sensitivity to pressures for multi-candidate secret ballot elections, people from within the region (and who were therefore known by the electorate) were usually promoted. Elizabeth Teague and Dawn Mann, 'Gorbachev's dual role', *Problems of Communism* 39, 1 January–February 1990, p. 12.

95 For explicit recognition of this see *Pravda* 24 October 1989. For a call for a thorough assessment of personnel policy, see *Pravda* 16 October 1989.

96 According to Onikov in July 1989, while every stratum of society had been embraced by rapid democratisation, internal party democracy had 'become frozen at the pre-perestroika level'. *Pravda* 10 July 1989. In January he had claimed that democratic procedures in the party were even more restricted than under Stalin. *Pravda* 2 January 1989. Also *Leningradskaia Pravda* 29 November 1989, FBIS Soviet Union 21 December 1989.

97 *Pravda* 3 September 1989. This is also reflected in the figures for the election of responsible officials from two or more candidates cf 1988:

|  | 1988 | 1989 |
| --- | --- | --- |
| PPO secretaries | 48.1% | 42.9% |
| Shop organisation secretaries | 50.2% | 43% |
| Party group organisers |  | 35.5% |

*Izvestiia Ts.K. KPSS* 3, 1989, p. 18 & 2, 1990, p. 67. Elections with multiple candidacies were reported to be 50 per cent greater in 1989 than 1987. *Izvestiia Ts.K. KPSS* 2, 1990, p. 66.

98 For example, *Sovetskaia Kul'tura* 7 December 1989 FBIS Soviet Union 13 December 1989, *Pravda* 6 December 1989, *Komsomolskaia Pravda* 27 January 1990, FBIS Soviet Union 30 January 1990 and *Pravda* 4 February 1990. This was not included in the draft regulations governing this matter published in late February 1990. These regulations also did not make competition mandatory. *Pravda* 27 February 1990.

99 For example, *Sovetskaia Kul'tura* 7 December 1989, FBIS Soviet Union 13 December 1989.

100 *Moskovskaia Pravda* 22 June 1989, FBIS Soviet Union 1 August 1989.

101 *Moscow News* 1, 7 January 1990. The decision of January 1989 to publish proceedings had not been fully implemented.

102 *Pravda* 10 February 1990.

103 *Izvestiia* 19 January 1990.

104 *Pravda* 15 February 1990.

105 *Pravda* 26 February 1990.

106 *Pravda* 1 March 1990.

107 *Trud* 6 February 1990 FBIS Soviet Union 15 February 1990, *Pravda* 13 February 1990.

108 *Izvestiia* 8 February 1990 and *Sovetskaia Rossiia* 14 February 1990, FBIS Soviet Union 15 February 1990.

109 *Izvestiia* 3 February 1990.

110 *Izvestiia* 4 February 1990.

111 *Pravda* 28 January 1990.

112 *Sovetskaia Rossiia* 2 March 1990, FBIS Soviet Union 8 March 1990.

113 For example, Gorbachev adviser Georgii Shakhnazarev, reported in Radio Liberty, *Report on the USSR* 468/89, 22 September 1989. For a call for the removal of this article, see *Sovetskaia Estoniia* 18 November 1989, FBIS Soviet Union 14 December 1989 (Estonian Supreme Soviet). For calls for dialogue with informals, see *Pravda* 8 August 1989 & 10 October 1989. For the report of a discussion in the Academy of the Social Sciences entitled 'O probleme odnopartiinosti i mnogopartiinosti', *Izvestiia Ts.K. KPSS* 1, 1990, pp. 69–74.

114 For example, Mikhail Gorbachev, 'Na perelomnom etape perestroiki', *Pravda* 31 March 1989 and 'Sotsialisticheskaia ideia i revoliutsionnaia perestroika', *Pravda* 29 November 1989. In the latter he argued in favour of the continuation of single party rule because the party was the guarantor of socialism, the only effective integrating force in the country, had launched perestroika and was leading it forward, and could become an effective democratic force by democratising itself. Of these, only the first was a traditional formal justification for party rule. The others were all related to the party's current performance and could be evaluated by observers in a more immediate sense than could talk of the move towards socialism. In this sense Gorbachev was reasserting the position he had espoused since becoming General Secretary: the party had to earn its position of leadership.

115 *Sovetskaia Litva* 8 December 1989, FBIS Soviet Union 18 January 1990. Latvia did the same on 11 January 1990. *Izvestiia* 13 January 1990.

116 'Ob avangardnoi roli KPSS', *Pravda* 8 December 1989.

117 'Vystuplenie M.S. Gorbacheva na Plenume TsK KPSS po voprosam II S'ezda narodnykh deputatov SSSR', *Pravda* 10 December 1989.

118 For example,*Sovetskaia Estoniia* 8 December 1989, FBIS Soviet Union 11 January 1990 (Vialias from Estonia), *Pravda* 2 January 1990 (Sokolov from Belorussia), Salutskii in a roundtable discussion in *Pravda* 4 February 1990. Also see the article by S. Afanas'ev in *Pravda* 21 February 1990. Here Afanas'ev argued for a new law to govern the activities of 'the party and other socio-political movements'. The comments of Yakovlev are also interesting. Aleksandr Yakovlev, *Muki prochiteniia bytiia. Perestroika: nadezhdy i real'nosti* (Moscow, 1991), pp. 87–129. Also the election platform adopted by Leningrad communists, *Leningradskaia Pravda* 29 November 1989, FBIS Soviet Union 21 December 1989.

119 'K sovetskomu narodu', *Pravda* 12 December 1989.

120 *Pravda* 6 February 1990.
121 The new Article 6 read:

> The CPSU, other political parties, trade unions, youth, social organisations and mass movements participate in shaping the policies of the Soviet state and in running state and social affairs through their representatives elected to the Congress of People's Deputies as well as in other ways.

122 For an early example of this, see the comments of Politburo member Vadim Medvedev in an interview with a French newspaper:

> There is no conflict between a multi-party system and socialist society, as experience proves. The existence of one or several parties in a socialist society is a matter of historical practice, specific conditions, and tradition. In our country after the revolution there were for some time representatives of other parties in the soviets and even in the government . . . As for the single party system, there is no conflict between it and democracy. It does not exclude democracy as long as the party acts democratically, within the framework of a socialist rule-of-law state, and is under the people's constant supervision. Just as a single-party system is not synonymous with anti-democracy, neither is a multi-party system any kind of guarantee against undemocratic government methods. The important thing is a society's opportunity to represent the interests of individuals and social groups, to compare them and to give them consideration.
> *Le Monde* 25 May 1989, FBIS Soviet Union 2 June 1989.

The degree to which these comments reflect Medvedev's real position is unclear. See his comments one month later at footnote 123. For other comments, see *Leningradskaia Pravda* 29 November 1989, FBIS Soviet Union 21 December 1989; *Sovetskaia Kul'tura* 30 November 1989 (Latvia), FBIS Soviet Union 14 December 1989; *Komsomolskaia Pravda* 27 January 1990 (Shostakovskii of the Democratic Platform), FBIS Soviet Union 30 January 1990; *Pravda* 21 February 1990; *Izvestiia* 10 March 1990.

123 FBIS Soviet Union 10 May 1989. Vialias was addressing the Estonian CC plenum. For a similar view from Latvian first secretary Vagris, see *Sovetskaia Latviia* 20 June 1989, FBIS Soviet Union 21 July 1989. For attacks on informals, see *Moskovskaia Pravda* 22 June 1989, FBIS Soviet Union 1 August 1989 and *Leningradskaia Pravda* 29 November 1989, FBIS Soviet Union 21 December 1989.
124 *Moskovskaia Pravda* 23 June 1989, FBIS Soviet Union 14 July 1989.
125 *Pravda* 2 January 1990.
126 *Pravda* 21 February 1990. A similar argument will be found in *Sovetskaia Belorussiia* 28 December 1989, FBIS Soviet Union 2 February 1990. For an argument that a multi-party system is a breeding ground for the owners of capital, see *Pravda* 7 March 1990.
127 *Sovetskaia Rossiia* 9 July 1989, FBIS Soviet Union 3 August 1989.
128 *Sovetskaia Rossiia* 26 August 1989, FBIS Soviet Union 8 September 1989.

129 *Izvestiia Ts.K. KPSS* 3, 1990, p. 124. Entry figures were as follows:

|      | To full | To candidate |
|------|---------|--------------|
| 1985 | 609,927 | 654,233 |
| 1986 | 640,719 (+5.0%) | 663,070 (+1.4%) |
| 1987 | 607,201 (−5.2%) | 585,294 (−11.7%) |
| 1988 | 522,884 (−13.9%) | 438,886 (−25.0%) |

*Izvestiia Ts.K. KPSS* 2, 1989, p. 138.

The marked decrease in entry to candidate membership reflects the drop in the party's popular authority. During 1989, the total number of full members fell by 119,612. *Izvestiia Ts.K. KPSS* 2, 1989, p. 138 & 4, 1990, p. 113.

130 *Sovetskaia Latviia* 29 April 1989, FBIS Soviet Union 12 May 1989.

131 *Moskovskaia Pravda* 22 June 1989, FBIS Soviet Union 1 August 1989.

132 *Pravda* 4 February 1990.

133 *Pravda* 10 October 1989. The figure of 18,000 in 1988 compared with 4,000 in 1986. *Izvestiia Ts.K. KPSS* 11, 1989, pp. 36–40.

134 *Pravda* 12 November 1989.

135 *Izvestiia Ts.K. KPSS* 8, 1989, p. 11.

136 *Leningradskaia Pravda* 31 January 1990, FBIS Soviet Union 22 February 1990.

137 *Pravda* 31 January 1990.

138 See the report of a questionnaire conducted in Moscow in mid-1989. *Izvestiia Ts.K. KPSS* 11, 1989, p. 71. In January 1990, for the lead-up to the XXVIII Congress, the Politburo decided to strengthen the enquiry-reception centre of the CC to handle citizens' enquiries. This was presumably designed in part to project the party as more concerned for and less isolated from the people and their concerns. For the decision and a list of the CC members and candidates who would be available in the period leading up to the congress, see *Izvestiia Ts.K. KPSS* 7, 1990, pp. 7–16. Subsequent issues of the journal contain reports of the operation of the centre. For one argument about the lack of rank-and-file control and the party being in a 'state of siege', see the comments by T. Samolis in *Pravda* 18 September 1989.

139 *Sovetskaia Estoniia* 12 May 1989, FBIS Soviet Union 2 June 1989. For the same claim regarding Lithuania, see the comments of the Committee for Party Control dated 9 October 1989. *Izvestiia Ts.K. KPSS* 11, 1989, pp. 36–40.

140 *Sovetskaia Moldaviia* 12 May 1989, FBIS Soviet Union 6 June 1989.

141 *Pravda* 19 June 1989.

142 *Pravda* 12 November 1989.

143 *Sovetskaia Rossiia* 9 July 1989, FBIS Soviet Union 3 August 1989.

144 *Sotsialisticheskaia Industriia* 5 August 1989, FBIS Soviet Union 7 August 1989.

145 *Izvestiia Ts.K. KPSS* 11, 1989, p. 28.

146 Of 86 party organisations, 35 were unable to fund their own activities and

had to rely upon central subsidies, while 33 per cent of PPOs were refusing to forward the dues that had been paid by members. *Izvestiia Ts.K. KPSS* 6, 1989, pp. 117–19.
147 *Pravda* 2 January 1990.
148 *Moskovskaia Pravda* 22 June 1989, FBIS Soviet Union 1 August 1989.
149 *Sotsialisticheskaia Industriia* 5 August 1989, FBIS Soviet Union 7 August 1989.
150 *Sotsialisticheskaia Industriia* 22 August 1989, FBIS Soviet Union 23 August 1989. A public opinion poll conducted in June showed that more than 50 per cent of respondents believed the authority of party members with whom they worked was low. *Pravda* 16 October 1989.
151 *Sovetskaia Rossiia* 25 October 1989, FBIS Soviet Union 31 October 1989.
152 For example, see the roundtable in *Pravda* 4 February 1990.
153 *Sovetskaia Rossiia* 21 January 1990, FBIS Soviet Union 2 February 1990.
154 *Komsomolskaia Pravda* 16 January 1990, FBIS Soviet Union 26 January 1990.
155 *Izvestiia Ts.K. KPSS* 7, 1989, p. 98.
156 For example, *Moskovskaia Pravda* 22 June 1989, FBIS Soviet Union 1 August 1989 and *Sovetskaia Rossiia* 9 July 1989, FBIS Soviet Union 3 August 1989.
157 *Pravda* 25 June 1989.
158 *Leningradskaia Pravda* 29 November 1989, FBIS Soviet Union 21 December 1989.
159 *Pravda* 14 March 1990.
160 For example, *La Repubblica* 8 February 1990 FBIS Soviet Union 14 February 1990 (Yuri Afanas'ev); *Pravda* 21 February 1990 (Prokof'ev speaking about the forthcoming congress).
161 *Pravda* 4 February 1990 (V. Lysenko of the Democratic Platform).
162 *Izvestiia* 4 February 1990. For details on the party budget, see *Pravda* 12 March 1990.
163 For example, see the Politburo decision 'O rabote partiinykh organizatsii po ukrepleniiu svoikh riadov i obnovleniiu sostava KPSS v usloviiakh uglubleniia perestroiki i politicheskoi reformy' of 21 July 1989. *Izvestiia Ts.K. KPSS* 8, 1989, pp. 7–9.
164 For one linking of the party regaining authority in society with renewal through the forthcoming report and election campaign, see the Politburo decision of 2 August 1989 'O provedenii otchetov i vyborov v partiinykh organizatsiiakh v 1989 godu'. *Izvestiia Ts.K. KPSS* 9, 1989, pp. 7–9.
165 Although it was at this time that such innovations as the abolition of candidate status were mooted.
166 Agence France Presse, 4 February 1990, FBIS Soviet Union 5 February 1990.
167 *Pravda* 5 February 1990.
168 *Pravda* 6 February 1990.
169 'K gumannomu, demokraticheskomu sotsializmu', *Pravda* 13 February 1990.
170 His name was Shaliev. *Pravda* 9 February 1990. The speeches were

published in *Pravda* 6–9 February 1990. Also see the positive comments by Yakovlev at this time. Yakovlev, 'Muki . . .'.

171 *Pravda* 12 March 1990.

172 The speeches from the plenum will be found in *Pravda* 12, 17, 18, 19 & 20 March 1990.

173 *Pravda* 19 March 1990.

174 Although a set of broad principles was enunciated by the centre. *Pravda* 17 March 1990.

175 Indeed, the establishment of an executive presidential structure was seen as a way of ensuring decisions were implemented in the face of the withdrawal of the party from a direct role in the economy.

176 *Pravda* 16 March 1990.

177 At the 9 December 1989 plenum, Ivashko was elected a full member of the Politburo and Frolov became a CC secretary. For one discussion of the balance of forces within the Politburo at this time, see Richard Sakwa, *Gorbachev and his reforms 1985–1990* (New York, Philip Allan, 1990), pp. 18–19.

## 6 The lead-up to the Congress

1 The party did well in rural areas, where there may have been a greater tendency to rely on those with 'experience'; in most rural oblasts and krais communists supported by the local apparatus usually won office. Gregory G. Embree, 'RSFSR election results and roll call votes', *Soviet Studies* 43, 6, 1991, p. 1,066. For a discussion of the situation at provincial levels, see Joel C. Moses, 'Soviet provincial politics in an era of transition and revolution, 1989–91', *Soviet Studies* 44, 3, 1992, pp. 479–509. Also see the discussions of Yaroslavl, and Leningrad, Perm' and Arkhangel'sk in respectively Jeffrey W. Hahn, 'Local Politics and Political Power in Russia: The Case of Yaroslavl'', *Soviet Economy* 7, 4, 1991, pp. 322–41 and Mary McAuley, 'Politics, Economics, and Elite Realignment in Russia: A Regional Perspective', *Soviet Economy* 8, 1, 1992, pp. 46–88.

2 See the discussion in Timothy J. Colton, 'The Moscow Election of 1990', *Soviet Economy* 6, 4, 1990, pp. 285–344.

3 For the statement by Moscow gorkom first secretary Prokof'ev that the party organisation accepted the desire by the soviet to have its own newspaper and that they were currently working out concrete measures for dividing paper, printing facilities etc., see his address to the XXVIII Conference of the Moscow city party organisation, *Moskovskaia Pravda* 15 June 1990.

4 On Leningrad party first secretary Gidaspov, see Andrei Chernov, ' The Last First Secretary, or three myths about Boris Gidaspov', *Moscow News* 25, 1–8 July 1990.

5 *Moscow News* 26, 8–15 July 1990. For another example, see the report in the same issue about Ivan Polozkov's 'opposition to the new legislative power'.

6 *Izvestiia Ts.K. KPSS* 8, 1990, p. 145. For one party discussion of other forces on the political stage, see *Izvestiia Ts.K. KPSS* 4, 1990, pp. 150–6.

7 Gorbachev at the XXVIII Congress, *Pravda* 3 July 1990. The concern about its ability to get by in this new situation is also reflected in the attempt to turn *Pravda* into a more effective instrument of propaganda and communication with society as a whole. See the CC resolution in *Pravda* 7 April 1990.

8 Preamble to the 1986 Rules. Graeme Gill, *The rules of the Communist Party of the Soviet Union* (London, Macmillan, 1988), p. 228.

9 For example, see the 'Pozitsiia Moskovskoi gorodskoi partiinoi organizatsii k XXVIII s'ezdu KPSS', *Moskovskaia Pravda* 17 June 1990 and *Pravda* 6 June 1990.

10 *Sovetskaia Rossiia* 21 June 1990.

11 For example, *Moskovskaia Pravda* 17 June 1990.

12 For example, see *Sovetskaia Rossiia* 20 June 1990 and 21 June 1990 (especially the speech by Kemerovo obkom first secretary Mel'nikov).

13 *Moskovskaia Pravda* 16 June 1990.

14 *Sovetskaia Rossiia* 21 June 1990.

15 Respectively *Pravda* 23 May 1990 and 19 May 1990.

16 *Pravda* 20 June 1990. The letter claimed that in the current CC workers constituted 11 per cent of the membership compared with 29.1 per cent in the party as a whole. Only 5 per cent of the delegates to the XIX Conference of the party were workers.

17 *Moskovskaia Pravda* 15 June 1990.

18 *Pravda* 28 June 1990.

19 *Argumenty i fakty* 24, 16–22 June 1990.

20 *Sovetskaia Rossiia* 20 June 1990. The speaker was V. A. Tiul'kin, who was delivering a co-report from the initiative congress of communists of Russia.

21 *Sovetskaia Rossiia* 21 June 1990.

22 For example, see the open letter to Gorbachev in *Pravda* 16 May 1990. For an assertion of faith in socialist ideals, see *Pravda* 28 May 1990. Also see the discussions in *Pravda* 11 June 1990 and 18 June 1990.

23 *Moskovskaia Pravda* 17 June 1990.

24 *Moskovskaia Pravda* 15 June 1990. This position was repeated in the resolution of the conference. 'Positsiia Moskovskoi gorodskoi partiinoi organizatsii k XXVIII s'ezdu KPSS', *Moskovskaia Pravda* 17 June 1990.

25 *Sovetskaia Rossiia* 20 June 1990. The speaker was V. N. Lysenko, giving the co-report of the Democratic Platform to the Russian conference.

26 *Pravda* 28 June 1990.

27 *Pravda* 20 June 1990. The venue was the conference of Russian party organisations.

28 *Pravda* 16 May 1990.

29 For one example of this, see the article entitled 'V chem prichiny neudach?' in *Pravda* 14 May 1990. This declared that the party had to consist of like-minded people and could not include people with different ideas about the

aims of the movement and the methods of achieving them. It called for monolithic organisation and getting rid of those who differed.

30 *Pravda* 12 May 1990.

31 For example, *Pravda* 23 May 1990 and 6 June 1990.

32 Both Politburo report and CC letter are in *Pravda* 11 April 1990.

33 It was entitled 'For consolidation on the basis of the principles of perestroika', *Pravda* 16 April 1990.

34 *Pravda* 2 June 1990. Also see the Platform of the Democratic Platform, *Pravda* 3 March 1990.

35 For example, see the argument that fractions reflecting different views and interests could exist in the party, but these had to be in the open. *Pravda* 28 May 1990. For the view that by the end of 1989 there were already eight distinct tendencies in the party, see Vyacheslav Shostakovskii, 'Obnovliaia kontseptsii partii', *Politicheskoe obrazovanie* 12, 1989, pp. 5–12, cited in Ronald J. Hill, 'The CPSU: From monolith to pluralist?', *Soviet Studies* 43, 2, 1991, p. 224.

36 For example, see 'Chto partiia poteriala?', *Pravda* 6 June 1990.

37 'K gumannomu, demokraticheskomu sotsializmu', *Pravda* 13 February 1990.

38 For example, the view that minority views should always find representation in the protocols of party meetings and representatives of those views should gain membership in party bodies.

39 The speaker was Moscow gorkom first secretary Prokof'ev, *Moskovskaia Pravda* 15 June 1990.

40 For a discussion of the origins and development of the Democratic Platform, see Igor Chubais, 'The democratic opposition: an insider's view', Radio Liberty, *Report on the USSR* 3, 18, 3 May 1991, pp. 4–15. Also Michael McFaul & Sergei Markov, *The Troubled Birth of Russian Democracy. Parties, Personalities and Programs* (Stanford, Hoover Institution Press, 1993), pp. 94–95.

41 The composition of delegates was said to be as follows: 40 per cent from educational institutions and research institutes, 20 per cent from industrial enterprises, 5 per cent workers and 20 per cent full-time party function-aries. Some 60 per cent were party members of more than ten years party standing. *Moscow News* 15, 15–22 April 1990. For Shostakovskii's view of the conference, see *Komsomolskaia Pravda* 27 January 1990.

42 *Moscow News* 15, 15–22 April 1990.

43 For example, the Moscow oblast conference was held in Moscow on 26–7 May. The conference adopted a 'Programmatic Declaration' and the three positions regarding the future of the association evident at the national conference emerged. See the reports in *Komsomolskaia Pravda* 29 May 1990 and *Moscow News* 22, 10–17 June 1990. The documents from the conference are in *Izvestiia Ts.K. KPSS* 8, 1990, pp. 129–32. Differences with the CC platform are drawn out explicitly here.

44 *Glasnost'* 2, 21 June 1990. This seems to represent a strengthening of the view that the party could not reform itself. An earlier survey reported

corresponding figures of 34 per cent, 47 per cent and 3 per cent. *Argumenty i fakty* 21, 26 May–1 June 1990. The figures are provided by a Democratic Platform spokesman Lisitsyn, but the population of the survey is wider than that of delegates to the conference. For another report of the national conference, see *Moskovskaia Pravda* 19 June 1990.

45 For some, perhaps including the leadership of the Platform, this course may have been adopted less because of a belief that the party could be transformed from within than because of a desire both to weaken the party as much as possible and, by withdrawing as a group after the congress, gaining a share of the party's assets. Some may also have been concerned to hold onto their jobs as long as possible.

46 For example, *Pravda* 21 February and 3 March 1990, *Sovetskaia Rossiia* 20 June 1990, and *Moskovskaia Pravda* 17 June 1990. For interviews with leading figures, see *Pravda* 4 February 1990.

47 'Ne soglasen', *Pravda* 21 May 1990.

48 For example, for the view that the theses of the Democratic Platform were closer to reality than the Platform of the CC, see 'V neskol'ko strok', *Pravda* 28 May 1990.

49 For example, 'Za kem idti?', *Pravda* 16 May 1990. Also see the comments by Vadim Medvedev, 'S chem idem k s'ezdu', *Pravda* 19 May 1990.

50 For example, see *Pravda* 11 March, 17 March, 23 May and 30 May 1990.

51 For example, one writer argued that all too often those who simply favoured greater democratisation in the party were labelled supporters of the Platform. In fact, he declared, the radicals had little support in the PPOs. 'Ne delat' pugal', *Pravda* 23 May 1990. A survey of party members taken in April asked about the respondent's attitude to the Democratic Platform. It elicited the following responses: do not know it 12 per cent; know it but undecided 36 per cent; actively support it and willing to join it if a new party is formed 15 per cent; do not agree with it 17 per cent; no answer 19 per cent. *Argumenty i fakty* 25, 23–9 June 1990. On the question of what the most important course of action for the party was in current circumstances, the same survey elicited the following responses: organisational split and the formation of two separate parties 19 per cent; cleansing of the party from conservatives 51 per cent; cleansing of the party from those who deviate from socialist ideals 35 per cent.

52 *Pravda* 11 April 1990.

53 For example, see 'Status dlia partkluba', *Pravda* 14 May 1990, and the speeches by Krasil'nikov at the Moscow city conference and Lysenko at the Russian conference in, respectively, *Moskovskaia Pravda* 17 June 1990 and *Sovetskaia Rossiia* 20 June 1990.

54 *Moscow News* 19, 15 April 1990.

55 *Pravda* 8 May 1990.

56 *Glasnost'* 2, 21 June 1990.

57 Among delegates to the founding congress of the Russian Communist Party, a poll gained the following answers to the question of which platform they supported:

|              | Full support | Partial support | No support |
|--------------|--------------|-----------------|------------|
| CC           | 45           | 44              | 2          |
| Demo. platform | 5          | 48              | 12         |
| Marx. platform | 3          | 44              | 12         |

*Izvestiia Ts.K. KPSS* 7, 1990, p. 37.

Corresponding figures for delegates to the XXVIII Congress were:

|              |    |    |    |
|--------------|----|----|----|
| CC           | 49 | 38 | 2  |
| Demo. platform | 5 | 41 | 12 |
| Marx. platform | 3 | 37 | 11 |

*Izvestiia Ts.K. KPSS* 8, 1980, p. 135.

The figures are less than 100 per cent because some delegates did not answer the question. After hearing the reports of the different platforms at the XXVIII Congress, 30 per cent and 23 per cent of delegates respectively said that their confidence in the Democratic Platform and Marxist Platform had declined. *Izvestiia Ts.K. KPSS* 8, 1980, p. 135.

58 'K voprosu ob antagonizme', pp. 1–2. This is a study compiled by three members of the Club of Electors , L. Efimova, A. Sobianin and D. Iur'ev.

59 *Glasnost'* 2, 21 June 1990. According to another report, there were representatives from six union republics. *Pravda* 19 June 1990. The II Conference was also reported in *Moskovskaia Pravda* 19 June 1990.

60 *Glasnost'* 2, 21 June 1990.

61 *Pravda* 14 April 1990.

62 In particular see 'Konsolidatsiia eshche vozmozhna?', *Pravda* 13 June 1990. Also *Argumenty in fakty* 14, 7–13 April 1990.

63 See the speeches by Buzgalin at the Moscow city conference and Kolganov at the Russian conference in, respectively, *Moskovskaia Pravda* 17 June 1990 and *Sovetskaia Rossiia* 20 June 1990.

64 *Glasnost'* 2, 21 June 1990.

65 For example, see the report on the Kazakh party congress, *Pravda* 29 May 1990.

66 Throughout this period all speakers were insistent that a new communist party for the Russian Republic had to be within the CPSU and not contribute to the breakup of that organisation.

67 For example, see articles in *Pravda* 6 June 1990, 7 June 1990, 12 June 1990 and 18 June 1990.

68 *Argumenty i fakty* 21, 26 May–1 June 1990.

69 For a discussion of this, see Robert W. Orttung, 'The Russian Right and the dilemmas of party organisation', *Soviet Studies* 44, 3, 1992, pp. 445–78.

70 This was opposed by the Leningrad 'Initiative Committee for the Preparation of the Founding Congress of the Russian Communist Party on Leninist Principles' which wanted delegates directly elected by the PPOs so that the gathering would have the right to found the RCP. Orttung, 'Russian Right', pp. 459–60.

71 See the interview with some members of the organising committee in *Sovetskaia Rossiia* 1 June 1990.

72 This was certainly the charge made by spokesmen for the organising committee and the initiative congress (see below), I. P. Osadchin and V. A. Tiul'kin, *Sovetskaia Rossiia* 20 June 1990. For the admission that the Bureau had worked weakly, with the hint that this may have been due to its small staff (30 people) and lack of a means of mass information, see the interview with CC Secretary Manaenkov, *Pravda* 5 May 1990. It met only three times to ratify decisions taken elsewhere. *Izvestiia Ts.K. KPSS* 9, 1990, p. 24.

73 For example, see the comments by Osadchin and Tiul'kin, *Sovetskaia Rossiia* 20 June 1990. Manaenkov admitted earlier opposition to the formation of an independent party in the interview in *Pravda* 5 May 1990, while Gorbachev's position at the earlier plena has already been noted. The Bureau was a compromise between those who wanted a Russian party and those in the leadership who feared that this would provide an institutional base that would weaken national party organs. Orttung, 'Russian Right', p. 459.

74 The first initiative committee was established in Leningrad in February 1990. Orttung, 'Russian Right', p. 457.

75 Gorbachev opposed this, declaring that the conference should only discuss the establishment of the party. He criticised the way in which decisions at this congress ignored the views of the central leadership and of the rank-and-file. *Pravda* 28 April 1990. He was opposed in part because he feared that the RCP, with almost 60 per cent of all CPSU members and with a conservative leadership, would dominate the national party. For his proposal that once the party was established, decisions in CPSU leadership bodies might require a majority of communist parties as well as delegates, see *Izvestiia* 13 May 1990.

76 This chronology has been reconstructed from *Pravda* 5 May 1990, 10 June 1990 and 11 June 1990 and *Sovetskaia Rossiia* 20 June 1990.

77 The conservative credentials of the initiative movement, which opposed both the shift of power to the soviets and the establishment of a market economy, was clear to all. *Pravda* 20 June 1990.

78 *Pravda* 12 May 1990.

79 A stenographic record was published in *Sovetskaia Rossiia* 20–6 June 1990. For a survey of delegates' views, see *Izvestiia Ts.K. KPSS* 7, 1990.

80 *Pravda* 21 June 1990.

81 Some 48 per cent of delegates saw the absence of a clear theoretical orientation as a cause of the crisis in society. This was the largest number of respondents for any cause, including economic difficulties. The equivalent figure at the XXVIII Congress was 44 per cent. Respectively *Izvestiia Ts.K. KPSS* 7, 1990, pp. 36–8 and 8, 1990, p. 133.

82 On Polozkov, see the unflattering portrait drawn in *Moscow News* 26, 8–15 June 1990.

83 Many opposed this move. As a form of protest, instead of passing on

membership dues, some PPOs retained them within the organisation. This occurred, for example, in the party organisation in the Institute for International Economy and Foreign Relations. Personal communication, Moscow November 1991.

84 Among these were the party organisations of *Kommunist, Literaturnaia Gazeta,* Radio Moscow, Novosti, IMEMO, the Institute of Oriental Studies and the Institute of the Economy of World Socialist Systems. For one reference, see *Moscow News* 26, 8–15 June 1990.

85 For example, see *Pravda* 5 May 1990.

86 *Argumenty i fakty* 23, 9–15 June 1990, *Pravda* 16 May 1990.

87 *Pravda* 4 June 1990, *Moskovskaia Pravda* 16 June 1990 and 17 June 1990, *Sovetskaia Rossiia* 21 June 1990.

88 *Moskovskaia Pravda* 17 June 1990.

89 *Sovetskaia Rossiia* 20 June 1990. The speaker was Osadchin giving the co-report from the Organising Committee.

90 For one complaint about the way this had been operating see the speech by Yakutsk obkom first secretary Prokop'ev at the Russian conference. *Sovetskaia Rossiia* 21 June 1990.

91 *Sovetskaia Rossiia* 22 June 1990. Also *Pravda* 21 June 1990.

92 This point was also made by Moscow first secretary Prokof'ev in an interview in *Moscow News* 26, 9–16 July 1990. Mel'nikov's comments are in *Sovetskaia Rossiia* 21 June 1990.

93 For example, see *Pravda* 16 May 1990, *Moskovskaia Pravda* 15 June 1990 (Prokof'ev) and *Sovetskaia Rossiia* 21 June 1990 (Mel'nikov).

94 Although there were also complaints about an excess of 'spontaneous meeting democracy' and the instability this brought to leading organs. For example, see 'Kto vyderzhivaet shtorm', *Pravda* 23 May 1990 and *Sovetskaia Rossiia* 21 June 1990 (Okhokhonin).

95 Also often present here was the view that conference/congress delegates should retain the authority mandated to them until the following conference/congress to enable them to play a continuing authoritative role in party affairs. One effect of this could have been for them to exercise significant influence on elected bodies. *Moskovskaia Pravda* 16 June 1990.

96 *Moskovskaia Pravda* 17 June 1990. For calls for individual reports, see *Moskovskaia Pravda* 17 June 1990, *Sovetskaia Rossiia* 21 June 1990 and 22 June 1990.

97 Prior to the congress, the following members and candidates were interviewed: Kriuchkov and Usmanov (21/6), Vorotnikov and Pugo (22/6), Yakovlev and Girenko (23/6), Zaikov and Luk'ianov (24/6), Sliun'kov (25/6), Shevardnadze and Razumovskii (26/6), Yazov and Stroev (27/6), Biriukova (28/6), Medvedev and Baklanov (29/6), Ligachev and Masliukov (30/6) and Frolov (1/7). Politburo members who did not appear at this time were Gorbachev and Ryzhkov.

98 *Moskovskaia Pravda* 15 June 1990.

99 *Pravda* 14 May 1990 and 30 May 1990.

100 For example, see *Pravda* 28 May 1990 and *Sovetskaia Rossiia* 21 June 1990 (Prokop'ev).
101 *Pravda* 21 May 1990. For criticism of the view that the apparatus was the source of all that was bad, see *Pravda* 6 April 1990.
102 *Pravda* 6 June 1990.
103 The writer also suggested a series of measures for improvement, one effect of which would have been to reduce the apparat by 35%–40%. *Pravda* 4 June 1990. Consistent with this was the charge that the CC apparatus had become divided into isolated otdels and therefore lacked an overall perspective. *Sovetskaia Rossiia* 22 June 1990 (Chaptynov).
104 The correspondent asserted that of forty-four gorkoms and raikoms in Volgograd oblast, only fourteen could financially support themselves. *Pravda* 6 June 1990.
105 He also disputed the charges of excessive secrecy in the work of the apparatus. *Pravda* 30 May 1990.
106 For some comments, see *Moskovskaia Pravda* 16 June 1990 (Tikhomirov) and *Sovetskaia Rossiia* 21 June 1990 (Prokop'ev). Both were critical.
107 For example, *Moskovskaia Pravda* 17 June 1990. For calls for the strengthening of the PPOs, see *Pravda* 23 May 1990 and 13 June 1990.
108 This was the view of the Moscow city party committee draft position for the XXVIII Congress. *Pravda* 11 June 1990.
109 For example, see the report in *Rabochaia Tribuna* 8 May 1990.
110 For charges of passivity, see *Pravda* 2 June 1990 and 6 June 1990. For the call to establish a culture of democracy and participation in the party to enable members to espouse and defend their ideals, see *Pravda* 9 June 1990.
111 *Moskovskaia Pravda* 15 June 1990.
112 For this charge, see *Moskovskaia Pravda* 15 June 1990 (Prokof'ev). More generally, see *Pravda* 14 June 1990.
113 For example, the Democratic Platform. See *Moskovskaia Pravda* 17 June 1990 (Stupnikov).
114 For example, see *Sovetskaia Rossiia* 21 June 1990 (Makashov) and 22 June 1990 (Boiko).
115 *Moskovskaia Pravda* 17 June 1990 (Mileiko).
116 One development which gave force to this conviction was the ANT scandal. For the official party reaction, see *Izvestiia Ts.K. KPSS* 6, 1990, pp. 18–24.
117 For explicit linkages drawn between party membership developments and disillusionment, see *Rabochaia Tribuna* 8 May 1990, *Moskovskaia Pravda* 15 June 1990 (Prokof'ev) and *Sovetskaia Rossiia* 21 June 1990 (Mel'nikov).
118 *Moskovskaia Pravda* 16 June 1990 (Prokof'ev) and 17 June 1990 ('Pozitsiia Moskovskoi gorodskoi partiinoi organizatsii k XXVIII s'ezdu KPSS'). On disillusionment in one factory, see *Pravda* 13 June 1990.
119 *Moskovskaia Pravda* 17 June 1990 (V.S. Afanas'ev).
120 *Pravda* 21 May 1990.

121  Actual figures were:

|                        | Nov. 1989 | June 1990 |
|------------------------|-----------|-----------|
| CC                     | 24%       | 27%       |
| Enterprise comm/bureau | 6%        | 19%       |
| Raikom/gorkom          | 4%        | 14%       |
| Obkom/kraikom          | 4%        | 11%       |

The partial results of this survey were reported in a number of places. These are from *Glasnost'* 3, 28 June 1990. A survey conducted in mid-April asked party members what aspects of the party's activity most needed renewal. The following responses were elicited: theoretical bases of the party 40 per cent; ideological activities 36 per cent; organisational relations between different levels of the party 50 per cent; structure of the apparat 35 per cent; long term policy 23 per cent; short term policy 27 per cent; methods of party work 36 per cent. *Argumenty i fakty* 25, 23–9 June 1990.

122  *Pravda* 25 June 1990. Only 18 per cent were firmly convinced that the party was the leading political force while another 14 per cent were reported to be of this opinion but less firmly so.

123  *Moscow News* 25, 1–8 July 1990.

124  'O srokakh sozyva XXVIII s'ezda KPSS, provedeniia otchetno-vybornoi kampanii b partii, norme predstavitel'stva i poriadke izbraniia delegatov s'ezda', *Materialy plenuma tsentral'nogo komiteta KPSS 11, 14, 16 Marta 1990g* (Moscow, 1990), pp. 180–88. Local party organisations were given the power to choose how delegates were selected. Some 26 per cent of delegates were selected in the traditional way, indirectly by conferences at lower levels. The remainder were elected in single or multi-member constituencies. See the report of the Mandates Commission head Manaenkov in *Pravda* 5 July 1990.

125  *Moscow News* 23, 17–24 June 1990. For the view that this level of apparat representation would ensure that the Congress had a conservative disposition, see *Pravda* 14 June 1990.

126  *Pravda* 2 June 1990. According to Gorbachev aide Shakhnazarov, local bosses fixed the election of congress delegates. 'The second Russian revolution. VI. End of the beginning', BBC Television 1991.

127  Respectively *Pravda* 19 May 1990, 9 June 1990 and 2 June 1990.

128  *Glasnost'* 2, 21 June 1990.

129  *Argumenty i fakty* 21, 26 May–1 June 1990. For the report of his success in Belgorod and the argument that he had been incorrectly and without his knowledge included in the electoral list in the election at which he failed, see *Argumenty i fakty* 22, 2–8 June 1990. According to one report, in a field of 15, Yel'tsin received 86 per cent of the vote. *Moscow News* 23, 17–24 June 1990.

130  *Pravda* 3 July 1990. For discussions of the Congress, see Giuletto Chiesa, 'The 28th Congress of the CPSU', *Problems of Communism* 39, 4, July–August 1990, pp. 24–38; John Gooding, 'The XXVIII Congress of the

CPSU in perspective', *Soviet Studies* 43, 2, 1991, pp. 237–54; and Ronald J. Hill, 'The Twenty-eighth CPSU Congress', *The Journal of Communist Studies* 7, 1, March 1991, pp. 95–105; and Stephen White, 'The Politics of the XXVIII Congress', E.A. Rees (ed), *The Soviet Communist Party in Disarray. The XXVIII Congress of the Communist Party of the Soviet Union* (London, Macmillan, 1992), pp. 29–60.

131 For example, according to Azeri chief Mutalibov, a 'gap has developed between the helmsman of perestroika and all the rest of the party masses'. *Pravda* 4 July 1990. Also see the speeches of people like Gurenko, Nazarbaev and Golazov in *Pravda* 6 July 1990 and Luchinskii and Masaliev in *Pravda* 8 July 1990.

132 An attempt had been made to discredit Yakovlev at the opening of the Congress by the anonymous circulation of a false document purporting to be a verbatim transcript of an address Yakovlev had given. See Alexander Yakovlev, *Muki prochiteniia bytiia. Perestroika: nadezhdy i real'nosti* (Moscow, 1991), pp. 206–10.

133 See the analysis in Chiesa, 'The 28th Congress', pp. 32–3.

134 *Pravda* 11 July 1990.

135 At a closed meeting with regional party leaders, Gorbachev was vigorously criticised for the failures of perestroika and the consequences of this for the country. Gorbachev responded by threatening to resign, an act which moderated the stance of the regional leaders. 'The second Russian revolution. VI. End of the Beginning', BBC Television, 1991.

136 Although congress delegates did change the name of the proposed commission on economic reform to remove the word 'market' from it.

137 Of the 4,538 ballots cast, 3,411 were for and 1,116 against Gorbachev, while his rival, a party functionary from Kiselevsk, Teimuraz Avaliani received 501 votes for and 4,026 against. Eleven ballots were invalid.

138 Throughout the months preceding the Congress, there was some discussion of these proposals. A useful selection will be found in the issues of *Izvestiia Ts.K. KPSS* 4, 1990, pp. 16–20; 5, 1990, pp. 24–7; 6, 1990, pp. 32–6; and 7, 1990, pp. 9–31. The new party Rules were published in *Pravda* 18 July 1990.

139 This meant that only Gorbachev and Ivashko were re-elected from the pre-Congress Politburo. Its membership was Gorbachev, Ivashko, Burakevicius (Lithuanian CP), Dzasokhov (CC Secretary), Frolov (Pravda editor), Gumbaridze (Georgian CP), Gurenko (Ukrainian CP), Karimov (Uzbek CP), Luchinskii (Moldavian CP), Makhkamov (Tajik CP), Masaliev (Kirgiz CP), Movsisian (Armenian CP), Mutalibov (Azeri CP), Nazarbaev (Kazakh CP), Niiazov (Turkmen CP), Polozkov (Russian CP), Prokof'ev (Moscow gorkom), Rubiks (Latvian CP), Semenova (CC Secretary), Shenin (CC Secretary), Sillari (Estonian CP), Sokolov (Belorussian CP), Stroev (CC Secretary), and Yanaev (CC Secretary). Candidate membership was abolished.

140 This does not mean that there was a dramatic shift in the identity of the people exercising power. Of the former Politburo members, Kriuchkov,

Medvedev, Primakov, Ryzhkov, Shevardnadze, Yakovlev and Yazov all became members of the Presidential Council.

141 The secretaries and their responsibilities were Ivashko (leadership and socio-economic policy), Dzasokhov (ideology), Shenin and Manaenkov (party construction and cadre policy), Semenova (women's movement), Stroev (agricultural policy), Yanaev and Falin (international links), Girenko (international relations), Kuptsov (links with socio-political organisations and movements), and Baklanov (party organisation in the defence complex). The five rank-and-file members were Aninskii, Gaivoronskii, Mel'nikov, Teplenichev and Turgunova.

142 In the April–July period, only the Ideology, Agrarian and International commissions met, each on one occasion. *Izvestiia Ts.K. KPSS* 9, 1990, pp. 25–9.

143 Russia 124, Ukraine 40, Kazakhstan 22, Uzbekistan 18, Belorussia 12, Georgia 11, Azerbaijan 10, Tajikistan 10, Turkmenistan 9, Kirgiziia 8, Latvia 7, Moldavia 7, Armenia 7, Estonia 6, Lithuania 6, organisation in military 11, in KGB 1, in MVD 1.

144 These were negotiated with the Council of Representatives of Delegations at the Congress. A full list of the bodies represented will be found in *Izvestiia Ts.K. KPSS* 8, 1990, pp. 3–4.

145 Evan Mawdsley, 'The 1990 Central Committee of the CPSU in Perspective', *Soviet Studies* 43, 5, 1991, p. 900. There was also a significant reduction in Great Russian representation, from 71.1 per cent to 51.9 per cent.

146 Mawdsley, 'The 1990 Central Committee', p. 907. Also on mass representatives, see William A. Clark, 'Token Representation in the CPSU Central Committee', *Soviet Studies* 43, 5, 1991, pp. 913–29.

147 Mawdsley, 'The 1990 Central Committee', p. 907.

148 This was to replace the central auditing and control organs and had been foreshadowed at the XIX Conference. It had been introduced on a trial basis in a number of party organisations in early 1989. *Izvestiia Ts.K. KPSS* 3, 1989, pp. 5 & 31–2.

149 A survey indicated that only 19 per cent of delegates thought the CPSU should become a parliamentary party. *Pravda* 13 July 1990.

150 The draft presented to the plenum had been passed to a commission headed by Medvedev for revision. For a discussion of some proposals, see *Izvestiia Ts.K. KPSS* 5, 1990, pp. 20–3; 6, 1990, pp. 25–31; 7, 1990, pp. 9–31. For the congress resolution on the platform, entitled 'K gumannomu, demokraticheskomu sotsializmu', see *Pravda* 13 July 1990.

151 See the interview with Vladimir Lysenko in McFaul & Markov, pp. 100–13, esp. p. 103.

152 The Congress report of the Central Auditing Commission on party finances was enlightening here. *Pravda* 4 July 1990. According to this report, 58 per cent of party funds came from membership dues, 41.6 per cent from the profits of publishing houses and other enterprises, and 0.4 per cent other income. Declining membership levels and publications subscriptions threatened this basis. Not all party organisations were able to

finance their operations from their own resources and therefore required central subsidies. In 1989, fifty of eighty-six republican, krai and oblast organisations received subsidies; between 40 per cent and 75 per cent of the expenditure of the Kirgiz, Tajik and Turkmen parties came from this source. These demands would be even greater for 1990. The late payment of membership dues was increasing; in the fourth quarter of 1989 279,000 members were late in making their payments, by 1 April 1990 this had risen to 670,000. There had also been an increase in the under-payment of dues and some organisations had refused to transfer dues to other committees.

## 7 The party imploding

1 A survey of party members at the end of October–early November 1990 showed that only 18 per cent believed the congress had positively influenced the state of affairs in the party, and only 3 per cent believed the authority of the pary in society was rising (cf. 67 per cent who believed it was falling). *Izvestiia Ts.K. KPSS* 1, 1991, p. 59. Even congress delegates as a body were ambivalent about the results of the congress, an attitude which mirrored that of the population as a whole. *Izvestiia Ts.K. KPSS* 10, 1990, pp. 70–72.

2 *Krasnaia zvezda* 16 March 1991, FBIS Soviet Union 27 March 1991. For one discussion of the range of tendencies in the party at the end of 1990, see Alexander Yakovlev, *Predislovie, Obval, Posleslovie* (Moscow, 1992), 'Obval', esp. pp. 161–8.

3 *Pravda* 21 July 1990. For an attack on the Democratic Platform and the Marxist Platform, the former for seeking to break up the party, the latter to erode its ideological-theoretical positions, see the statement of the Bureau of the CC of the Belorussian Communist Party, *Sovetskaia Belorussia* 20 June 1990, FBIS Soviet Union 1 August 1990.

4 See the joint statement with the Coordinating Council of the Marxist Platform in the CPSU, *Pravda* 1 August 1990. It was earlier published in *Moskovskaia Pravda* 27 July 1990. For an interview with a leader of the Working Group of Communist Reformers of the Democratic Platform in the CPSU, Georgii Gusev, see *Rabochaia Tribuna* 27 July 1990, FBIS Soviet Union 9 August 1990. For one discussion of the fate of the Democratic Platform and the establishment of the Republican Party of Russia, see Igor Chubais, 'The Democratic Opposition: An Insider's View', Radio Liberty, *Report on the USSR* 3, 18, 3 May, 1991, pp. 12–15.

5 In the words of spokesman Vladimir Bezuglov, *Komsomolskaia Pravda* 12 September 1990, FBIS Soviet Union 19 September 1990. Also see the interview with A. Dimitriev and V. Lipitskii, both Democratic Platform members of the CC of the Communist Party of the RSFSR, *Rabochaia Tribuna* 29 September 1990, FBIS Soviet Union 12 October 1990.

6 See the interview with Shostakovskii in *New Times* 31, 31 July–6 August 1991, pp. 8–9. He also discusses the circumstances of his sacking as

Rector of the Higher Party School on 13 July. Also his 'Oshibki ili zakonomernost'?', *Perspektivy* 3, 1991, pp. 38–47 where responsibility for the party's inability to democratise is attributed to the tradition created by Lenin.

7 On its attempts to gather support, see the report in *Sovetskaia Rossiia* 4 August 1990, FBIS Soviet Union 13 August 1990.

8 For one report from Belorussia, see *Sovetskaia Molodezh* 17 July 1990, FBIS Soviet Union 21 August 1990. It also led to splits from republican communist parties. For the case of Moldavia, see TASS 12 March 1991, FBIS Soviet Union 12 March 1991.

9 This charge was voiced at the CC plenum in October by S. A. Kalinin. *Pravda* 10 October 1990.

10 See the reports in *Izvestiia* 14 November 1990 and TASS 17 November 1990, FBIS Soviet Union 19 November 1990. The conference was attended by 230 delegates from 50 republics, territories and regions of Russia.

11 *Krasnaia zvezda* 13 December 1990, FBIS Soviet Union 11 January 1991.

12 Along with Rutskoi, Silaev, Popov, Sobchak, Shatalin, Petrakov and Vol'skii, Shevardnadze and Yakovlev formed the Movement for Democratic Reform in July 1991. This organisation came to nothing.

13 *Pravda* 31 October 1990, TASS 17 & 18 November 1990, FBIS Soviet Union 19 November 1990, and *Glasnost'* 21, 1 November 1990.

14 *Pravda* 15 July 1991. The platform was very critical of the party leadership and the way it ignored the party masses, and accused it of centrism and of committing serious errors.

15 See the report of the congress in *Sovetskaia Rossiia* 3 July 1991, FBIS Soviet Union 12 July 1991. Also see *Rossiiskaia Gazeta* 27 July 1991. Initially this was the initiative Congress of the Communists of Russia and was instrumental in the creation of the RCP. Its initial congress was held in three stages, April, June and October 1990. *Izvestiia Ts.K. KPSS* 4, 1991, pp. 51–6. This article also discusses other groups in the party in Leningrad, including the Left Centre (members of the former Democratic Platform who remained in the CPSU) and Edinstvo. Headed by Nina Andreeva, Edinstvo had been established in May 1989; further conferences were held in April and October 1990. Also see the discussion in Robert W. Orttung, 'The Russian Right and Dilemmas of Party Organisation', *Soviet Studies* 44, 3, 1992, pp. 470–1.

16 According to member of the coordinating council of the Marxist Platform Alexander Buzgalin, this was designed to consolidate the efforts of communist-democrats and communist Marxists to achieve radical transformation within the communist party. TASS 18 November 1990,FBIS Soviet Union 19 November 1990.

17 Moscow Radio Rossii, 21 January 1991, FBIS Soviet Union 25 January 1991.

18 *Pravda* 8 January 1991, *Krasnaia zvezda* 29 May 1991, FBIS Soviet Union 5 June 1991, and Moscow Radio Rossii, 10 August 1991, FBIS Soviet Union 12 August 1991. The May meeting was for the Platform in Ukraine.

19 For the decisions of the joint CC-CCC plenum of 25 April 1991 on the work

of communists in the soviets, see *Izvestiia Ts.K. KPSS* 6, 1991, pp. 17–24. This recognised the danger of anti-communist forces using the soviets and emphasised the need for both party organisation and activity in this realm. The essentials of this position were confirmed by a Politburo decision of 3 June 1991. *Izvestiia Ts.K. KPSS* 8, 1991, pp. 15–17.

20 *Pravda* 11 February 1991.

21 For a report (denied) that at the Third Congress of People's Deputies they wanted to remove Yel'tsin, see *Sovetskaia Rossiia* 30 March 1991, FBIS Soviet Union 8 April 1991.

22 TASS 2 April 1991, FBIS Soviet Union 3 April 1991. According to another report, only 7 per cent of the Communists of Russia group had agreed to join the new organisation. TASS 12 April 1991, FBIS Soviet Union 15 April 1991, citing Ivashko.

23 See the comments by Grigorii Vodolazov in Moscow Russian Television Network, 17 June 1991, FBIS Soviet Union 20 June 1991.

24 A similarly named body was also established in Belorussia. Vilnius Radio, 16 June 1991, FBIS Soviet Union 20 June 1991. According to Rutskoi in late June, the number of members of this new body was already somewhere between 3.5 to 3.8 million communists. Moscow Russian Television 27 June 1991, FBIS Soviet Union 28 June 1991.

25 For an interesting appeal for the establishment of such groups at all levels, see *Izvestiia* 11 April 1991. Among the authors were Latsis, Lipitskii (Member of CC RCP) and Vodolazov.

26 For example, Rutskoi was condemned by the Kursk obkom plenum for his perceived attempts to split the party. He had been elected as a deputy from Kursk oblast. *Izvestiia* 16 April 1991.

27 For one criticism of the leadership of the Russian party by Rutskoi, see the interview with him in *Argumenty i fakty* 17, April 1991 and his speech to a plenum of the CC RCP in May in *Sovetskaia Rossiia* 15 May 1991, FBIS Soviet Union 16 May 1991. In the latter he said he intended to remain a member of the CPSU and justified Communists of Russia under Article 16 of the Rules of the CPSU which provided for socio-political movements. The newspaper quoted the text of Section IV Article 6 providing for party groups/factions in the soviets.

28 Moscow Radio Rossii 11 July 1991, FBIS Soviet Union 12 July 1991. For the CPSU's official reaction, including a defence of the RCP, see *Pravda* 27 July 1991. For the initial programmatic statement of the new party, see *Rossiiskaia Gazeta* 18 July 1991.

29 Rutskoi in *Rossiiskaia Gazeta* 3 August 1991. For the resolution of its constituent conference, see *Rossiiskaia Gazeta* 7 August 1991. It was declared that the 'Democratic Party of Communists of Russia be created within the CPSU as a voluntary socio-political association operating within the framework of the laws of the USSR and the RSFSR by parliamentary methods'. The party also supported Yel'tsin, including his decree eliminating political party organisation in state organs (see below), a position hotly opposed by the Russian party leadership.

30 Interfax 7 August 1991, FBIS Soviet Union 8 August 1991. For an attack upon the new party, see *Sovetskaia Rossiia* 10 August 1991, FBIS Soviet Union 14 August 1991. For a formal protest from the council of the Democratic Party of Communists of Russia about the declaration by the CC CPSU Secretariat that the decisions of the DPCR conference were *ultra vires* and invalid and also the expulsion of Rutskoi and Lipitskii, see *Rossiiskaia Gazeta* 10 August 1991.

31 *Izvestiia* 9 August 1991.

32 For a report about the Uzbek party becoming autonomous within the CPSU, see *Izvestiia* 7 November 1990. In Armenia a push to make the party independent was defeated by a move to assert its autonomy. *Pravda* 29 November 1990. In December the Georgian party declared itself independent of the CPSU. TASS 8 December 1990, FBIS Soviet Union 10 December 1990. In February 1991 a survey of party members found that 40% supported a federal party and 39% opposed it. *Pravda* 26 February 1991.

33 *Argumenty i fakty* 26, 30 June–6 July 1990.

34 For example, see *Komsomolskaia Pravda* 12 September 1990, FBIS Soviet Union 19 September 1990. Also see chapter 6, n. 84.

35 *Moskovskaia Pravda* 24 July 1990, FBIS Soviet Union 15 August 1990.

36 *Sovetskaia Rossiia* 19 August 1990. An alarming aspect of this was that 90,000 of the departures were workers. Also see *Pravda* 5 September 1990.

37 For a report see *Sovetskaia Rossiia* 22 July 1990.

38 See the interview with Polozkov in *Pravda* 6 August 1990. For a commentary on this interview, which characterises Polozkov's views as 'very conservative, even reactionary', see *Moscow News* 32, 10–26 August 1990. Also *Moscow News* 34, 2–9 September 1990.

39 *Sovetskaia Rossiia* 21 August 1990. The draft criticised many of the practical steps of perestroika as having been 'inconsistent and have left in the background the socialist essence and focus of perestroika' and committed the RCP to 'the socialist orientation of the transition to a regulated market economy'. It also rejected depoliticisation of the military and security apparatus. For comment upon the draft, see *Pravda* 17 August 1990.

40 For a report on this which also reflects disagreement over how best to proceed with the creation of the party, see *Sovetskaia Rossiia* 19 August 1990. Also the pre-congress interview with Polozkov in *Krasnaia zvezda* 4 September 1990, FBIS Soviet Union 5 September 1990. The draft was designed by a group including representatives of the Marxist Platform, Initiative Congress of Communists of Russia, the Reformer Communists Section of the Democratic Platform in the CPSU and the Preparatory Committee for the RSFSR Communist Party Constituent Congress.

41 For a report on a news conference with Polozkov on 29 August, see *Izvestiia* 30 August 1990. For a call for the postponement of the congress because 'in its present composition [the congress] does not reflect the interests and positions of Russia's communists' and most Russian communists would not accept 'such a declarative [meaning lacking in specific proposals for

action] and, to a considerable degree, conservative programme', see the appeal from Ufa communists reported in *Izvestiia* 2 September 1990.

42 *Pravda* 5 September 1990.

43 *Izvestiia* 6 September 1990.

44 Criticism of the draft along some of these lines even came from within the conservative Leningrad party apparatus. *Leningradskaia Pravda* 31 August 1990, FBIS Soviet Union 27 September 1990.

45 Although the CC Secretariat only began to function with a full complement toward the beginning of October. *Pravda* 15 November 1990.

46 Report of comments by Polozkov, Moscow Television Service, 6 September 1990, FBIS Soviet Union 7 September 1990.

47 *Izvestiia* 7 September 1990.

48 *Rabochaia Tribuna* 29 September 1990, FBIS Soviet Union 12 October 1990. The speakers were Dimitriev and Lipitskii of the Democratic Platform within the CPSU.

49 *Moskovskaia Pravda* 6 October 1990, FBIS Soviet Union 23 October 1990.

50 *Sovetskaia Rossiia* 19 October 1990, FBIS Soviet Union 22 October 1990.

51 *Sovetskaia Rossiia* 19 October 1990, FBIS Soviet Union 22 October 1990.

52 *Sovetskaia Rossiia* 24 October 1990, FBIS Soviet Union 26 October 1990. The two statements were separated by a congress of Democratic Russia from which a hard anti-communist line emanated, but this was not a change in position for many of those elements of which Democratic Russia consisted. This episode reflects, at best, a profound misjudgement on the part of the RCP leadership about the nature of the views of those who made up Democratic Russia.

53 *Pravda* 21 November 1990. The commissions (and their chairmen) were problems of party building (A. N. Il'in), humanitarian and ideological problems (G. A. Ziuganov), socio-economic policy and links with workers' movement (A. G. Mel'nikov), agrarian policy and links with peasants' movement (V. I. Kashin), work with public associations and ethnic and youth policy (I. I. Antonovich), problems of the women's movement (N. P. Silkova), and ties with soviets of people's deputies (A. S. Sokolov).

54 *Sovetskaia Rossiia* 16 November 1990, FBIS Soviet Union 14 December 1990.

55 *Pravda* 15 November 1990.

56 *Pravda* 15 December 1990. Also see the report of the meeting of the RCP CC Politburo in *Sovetskaia Rossiia* 16 February 1991, FBIS Soviet Union 28 February 1991.

57 *Sovetskaia Rossiia* 28 February 1991, FBIS Soviet Union 7 March 1991.

58 For a sustained defence of the conservative position, including an expression of support for the so-called 'black colonels', see Polozkov's address to the March 1991 CC RCP plenum. Also the speeches of Stoliarov and Antonovich. *Sovetskaia Rossiia* 7 & 9 March 1991, FBIS Soviet Union 15 March 1991. The whole plenum was a vigorous assertion of conservative views, with significant attacks upon Gorbachev. For one discussion of this, see *Moscow News* 11, 17–24 March 1991.

59 TASS 12 May 1991, FBIS Soviet Union 14 May 1991.

60  See the discussion of readers' letters by T. Samolis in *Pravda* 1 July 1991.
61  Rumours of Polozkov's removal had preceded the second stage of the foundation congress of the RCP in September 1990. Such rumblings increased during 1991.
62  See the statement by the RCP CC Politburo and CCC Presidium which, while acknowledging the right of democratisation within the party, confirms the opposition to fractions and tries to justify the existence of the RCP. *Pravda* 27 July 1991.
63  For Polozkov's speech, TASS 6 August 1991, FBIS Soviet Union 7 August 1991. For the CC CPSU Draft Programme entitled 'Socialism, Democracy, Progress', see *Pravda* 8 August 1991.
64  The resolutions are in *Sovetskaia Rossiia* 8 August 1991, FBIS Soviet Union 9 August 1991. One of these vigorously rejects Yel'tsin's departisation decree.
65  TASS 2 August 1990, FBIS Soviet Union 3 August 1990. A further 120,000 died while only 125,000 joined during the same period. Of those expelled, 160,000 were workers and peasants.
66  *Pravda* 14 August 1990.
67  *Pravda* 9 October 1990. The reporter was Ivashko.
68  *Moskovskaia Pravda* 6 October 1990, FBIS Soviet Union 23 October 1990.
69  *Sovetskaia Moldova* 2 September 1990, FBIS Soviet Union 27 September 1990. The final group, those who pursued speculative aims, were accused of joining the party out of career and selfish aims and their loss was considered positive. By mid-October it was reported that in 1990 in Moldova 7,000 had handed in their membership cards and a further 4,000 had been expelled, with only 1,400 new members joining. TASS 16 October 1990, FBIS Soviet Union 17 October 1990.
70  *Pravda* 10 October 1990.
71  For example, see the reported comments of Boris Gidaspov in *Gudok*, 2 December 1990, FBIS Soviet Union 13 December 1990.
72  *Pravda* 18 October 1990.
73  For one appeal by party veterans for the youth to remain in the party, see *Pravda* 8 January 1991.
74  *Pravda* 12 January 1991.
75  *Pravda* 4 January 1991. The party's membership was eroding more in Russia and the Baltic republics than elsewhere in the Soviet Union. Harasymiw, 'Changes in Party's Composition', pp. 144–152. Membership did not fall in the military; it grew by 3.7% in 1990. Radio Liberty, *Report on the USSR*, 3, 8, 22 February 1991.
76  *Moskovskaia Pravda* 10 February 1991, FBIS Soviet Union 15 March 1991. For one attempt to explain membership loss by Shenin, see *Rabochaia Tribuna* 14 March 1991, FBIS Soviet Union 20 March 1991. For criticism of the party's hypocrisy in criticising those who left the party, see *Rossiiskaia Gazeta* 19 June 1991. For an overview of the disillusionment among party members, see Stephen White, 'The CPSU and its Members in Late Communist Russia', Unpublished. I am grateful to Stephen White for allowing me to see this paper prior to publication.

77 It was reported that as of 1 February, at least half the members of the Georgian Communist Party were not paying membership dues and that more than 27 per cent of members had left the party. *Izvestiia* 8 February 1991.

78 *Pravda* 2 March 1991.

79 This is reflected in the lower entry and higher departure rates in the third quarter of that year: of all of those entering and leaving the party during the first nine months of 1990, respectively 25 per cent and 64 per cent occurred in the third quarter, immediately following the congress. *Izvestiia Ts.K. KPSS* 12, 1990, p. 81.

80 *Sovetskaia Rossiia* 7 March 1991, FBIS Soviet Union 15 March 1991. The speaker was Polozkov. The dimensions of the problem are reflected at the local level in the experience of Cheliabinsk oblast party organisation. Entry figures were as follows: 1986 6,000; 1989 750; 1990 81; first quarter of 1991 4. Departures: 1986 53; 1989 2,000; 1990 almost 22,000; first quarter of 1991 3,500. *Izvestiia Ts.K. KPSS* 6, 1991, pp. 55 & 57.

81 *Pravda* 6 May 1991. The number of entrants to the party was also reported to have risen, from 108,000 in 1990 to 46,000 in the first quarter of 1991. This takes no account of those who remained in the party but took no part in its affairs. Towards the end of 1990, this was said to be 30 per cent of the membership. *Izvestiia Ts.K. KPSS* 1, 1991, p. 60.

82 *Pravda* 26 July 1991.

83 For example, see the programme suggested by CC Secretary Manaenkov in *Pravda* 6 August 1991.

84 Harasymiw, 'Changes in Party's Composition', pp. 142–143.

85 *Pravda Ukrainy* 26 June 1990, FBIS Soviet Union 1 August 1990. He also reported that in 1988 the Ukrainian party transferred R48 million and in 1989 R51 million to the CC CPSU.

86 *Izvestiia Ts.K. KPSS* 8, 1990, pp. 91–8. Membership dues amounted to slightly more than R1.6 billion and income from publishing activity to R1 billion. Of expenditure, R1.913 billion was reported to be for the upkeep of local party authorities and development of their physical plant and just over R51 million on central party establishments and the CC apparatus (the latter R22.305 million). Wages of senior officials of party committees constituted R460.95 million and of full-time party organisation officials R282.5 million. *Uchitelskaia Gazeta* 28, July 1990, FBIS Soviet Union 14 August 1990.

87 The projection for the entire year 1990 was a deficit for local party organs of R104,600,000, which had to be made up by the centre. *Izvestiia Ts.K. KPSS* 8, 1990, p. 91. For Gidaspov's explanation of the financial problems of Leningrad obkom and possible solutions: structural reorganisation or entry into commercial entrepreneurial activity, see *Leningradskaia Pravda* 31 August 1990, FBIS Soviet Union 27 September 1990.

88 Although virtually all publications suffered a drop in subscriptions, this seems to have been greater for the party's political journals and newspapers. See figures in *Izvestiia Ts.K. KPSS* 2, 1991, p. 58.

89 *Pravda* 14 September 1990. For an argument by CCC Chairman Pugo that the budgetary problems meant that action needed to be taken on non-payment of dues, see *Pravda* 12 October 1990.
90 TASS 17 October 1990, FBIS Soviet Union 18 October 1990. Also see *Izvestiia Ts.K. KPSS* 5, 1991, p. 71.
91 *Izvestiia Ts.K. KPSS* 10, 1990, p. 100. As well as reducing expenditure, party organs were called upon to become involved in commercial enterprises. After the coup, there were reports that the party leadership had sought to send significant amounts of funds abroad or to transform them into real estate. For example, *Time* 9 September 1991, p. 42.
92 *Pravda* 3 November 1990. For new rules on handling the party's financial arrangements, see 'Mechanism for forming, executing and monitoring CPSU budget', *Pravda* 17 December 1990. These provided, *inter alia*, for the independence of the union republican parties in 'the formation and execution of their budgets'. A revised version of these rules was published in *Pravda* 28 June 1991 and *Izvestiia Ts.K. KPSS* 7, 1991, pp. 17–21. It was estimated that as at 1 January 1991, 1.3 million communists did not pay their party dues, amounting to over R5.5 million. *Rabochaia Tribuna* 2 March 1991, FBIS Soviet Union 7 March 1991.
93 *Nezavisimaia Gazeta* 8 August 1991, FBIS Soviet Union 15 & 16 August 1991.
94 Moscow Television Service, 5 November 1990, FBIS Soviet Union 6 November 1990, p. 39. The speaker was Ivashko. He also acknowledged that the party had a foreign currency account, but argued that this was a new development; formerly foreign funds, which he claimed only came from subscriptions from communists working abroad, were placed in a single pool with government funds. He claimed that at present the party's foreign currency account contained a mere R2 million, an amount that was not even sufficient to cover the foreign inks required to meet the party's publishing commitments. In December he said the party's foreign currency roubles amounted to just over R6 million. *Pravda* 13 December 1990. That Ivashko's comments were disingenuous to say the least, see the reports in *Nezavisimaia Gazeta* 8 August 1991, FBIS Soviet Union 15 & 16 August 1991.
95 *Pravda* 6 February 1991. For the speech by CC Administrator of Affairs N. E. Kruchina on which this decision was based, see *Pravda* 5 February 1991. During his speech, Kruchina revealed that as of 1 October 1990, one in five communists was in arrears in Vologda, Kirov and Moscow oblast organisations and one in six in Moscow city, Novgorod, Novosibirsk, Sverdlovsk and Cheliabinsk party organisations.
96 *Rabochaia Tribuna* 2 March 1991, FBIS Soviet Union 7 March 1991.
97 For example, see the comments by the chairman of the Central Auditing Commission's new commission 'On monitoring the implementation of the CPSU budget and auditing financial and economic activity', G. G. Veselkov, *Pravda* 8 January 1991. He was commenting on the draft of the 'Instruction on the registration of party membership dues and the financial and economic activity of the CPSU organisations' published in *Pravda* 30 October 1990 and adopted at the joint CC–CCC plenum in January 1991.

*Izvestiia Ts.K. KPSS* 3, 1991, pp. 46–55. This was part of a series of normative-methodological documents adopted at this plenum in an endeavour to bring to reality the changes in the party Rules adopted at the XXVIII Congress. They are to be found in *Izvestiia Ts.K. KPSS* 3, 1991, pp. 18–64.

98 Both are exposed in *Nezavisimaia Gazeta* 8 August 1991, FBIS Soviet Union 15 & 16 August 1991. In this issue was published details of the implementation of the 1990 budget and figures for the 1991 budget. In 1989 the party appears to have begun to establish cooperatives and banks as commercial enterprises to bolster party resources. For one report, see Radio Liberty, *Report on the USSR* 2, 42, 19 October 1990, p. 48.

99 *Pravda* 29 July 1991.

100 This position was supported by the Democratic Platform. *Argumenty i fakty* 4–10 August 1990.

101 *Uchitelskaia Gazeta* 28, July 1990, FBIS Soviet Union 14 August 1990 and *Nezavisimaia Gazeta* 8 August 1991, FBIS Soviet Union 15 & 16 August 1991.

102 For example, see the comments by Gidaspov in *Leningradskaia Pravda* 31 August 1990, FBIS Soviet Union 27 September 1990 and Pugo, *Pravda* 12 October 1990.

103 *Pravda* 13 October 1990.

104 For example, see the discussion in *Sovetskaia Rossiia* 18 September 1990, FBIS Soviet Union 28 September 1990.

105 TASS 8 October 1990, FBIS Soviet Union 11 October 1990.

106 *Pravda* 7 February 1991.

107 *Pravda* 31 October 1990, *Rabochaia Tribuna* 2 November 1990 & 1 December 1990, FBIS Soviet Union 16 November 1990 & 18 December 1990.

108 *Pravda* 29 April 1991.

109 See the report in *Vecherniaia Moskva* 19 November 1990, FBIS Soviet Union 25 January 1990. Some buildings were passed into party hands as late as 21 February 1990, just prior to the local elections in which the party clearly believed it would not do well.

110 *Argumenty i fakty* 20, May 1991. A poll in early 1991 showed a majority in favour of the nationalisation of party property. *Moscow News* 13, 31 March–7 April 1991.

111 For the seizure of Kemerovo oblast party printing works, see *Izvestiia* 8 June 1991.

112 *Pravda* 15 September 1990. A total of 603 people were to be cut, leaving 890 with jobs. Moscow Television 12 October 1990, FBIS Soviet Union 16 October 1990. This was on top of a reduction of 536 ranking CC officials in 1989. TASS 9 October 1990, FBIS Soviet Union 10 October 1990.

113 *Moskovskaia Pravda* 26 July 1990, FBIS Soviet Union 14 August 1990.

114 *Izvestiia* 15 September 1990.

115 TASS 16 October 1990, FBIS Soviet Union 17 October 1990.

116 *Izvestiia Ts.K. KPSS* 10, 1990, p. 6. Those remaining within the competence of the CC would be party functionaries, party press organ leaders and heads of scientific and educational institutions subordinate to the CC.

117 For example, Maykom gorkom. *Izvestiia* 5 September 1990.
118 *Sovetskaia Belorussia* 16 September 1990, FBIS Soviet Union 12 October 1990.
119 For example Moscow Domestic Service 6 August 1990, FBIS Soviet Union 6 August 1990, (Kaliningrad), *Izvestiia* 16 September 1990 (Belorussia). For criticism of the abolition of raikoms in Nagorno-Karabakh, see the comments by Iu.I. Mkrtumian to the October CC plenum, *Pravda* 11 October 1990.
120 For example, Moscow Domestic Service 19 September 1990, FBIS Soviet Union 20 September 1990, (Archangelsk), *Izvestiia* 18 September 1990 (Kharkov).
121 *Pravda* 10 September 1990.
122 *Komsomolskaia Pravda* 25 September 1990, FBIS Soviet Union 27 September 1990.
123 *Pravda* 17 September 1990.
124 For example, Shenin in *Sovetskaia Kul'tura* 22 December 1990, FBIS Soviet Union 3 January 1991. Also *Sovetskaia Moldova* 4 December 1990, FBIS Soviet Union 28 January 1991.
125 See the comments by Gidaspov, *Leningradskaia Pravda* 31 August 1990, FBIS Soviet Union 27 September 1990.
126 *Pravda* 12 October 1990. The speaker was A.A. Pomorov from Tomsk. For one discussion of the parlous state of many of the PPOs, see *Rabochaia Tribuna* 3 November 1990, FBIS Soviet Union 13 November 1990. Although in the report and election campaign of 1990, only 1.2 per cent of committees, bureaux and secretaries were declared to have worked unsatisfactorily compared to 0.9 per cent in 1988. *Izvestiia Ts.K. KPSS* 5, 1991, p. 70.
127 *Pravda* 2 February 1991. Shenin also acknowledged that there had been an improvement in the working of some PPOs. For an editorial endorsing Shenin's views, see *Pravda* 6 February 1991. Also see the comments of E. N. Makhov, first deputy chairman of the CCC CPSU, *Pravda* 4 February 1991 and Shenin again in *Pravda* 2 March 1991. The number of PPO secretaries elected from two or more candidates in the report and election meetings of 1990 was 44 per cent, a drop of 4.5 per cent compared with 1988. *Izvestiia Ts.K. KPSS* 5, 1991, p. 70.
128 *Rabochaia Tribuna* 5 February 1991, FBIS Soviet Union 12 February 1991. The report also noted that the disintegration of the party in Moldova was occurring on the right bank of the Dnestr, but on the left bank and in the south (the homes of the ethnically Russian and Gagauz population in Moldova) the party remained healthy and was in the process of splitting from its republican centre.
129 *Pravda* 2 March 1991. The number of PPOs had dropped from 441,949 on 1 January 1989 to 385,726 on 1 January 1991, or 12.7 per cent. Compare the figures in *Izvestiia Ts.K. KPSS* 2, 1989 p. 142 & 6, 1991, p. 46.
130 For example, see Prokof'ev's comments about Moscow gorkom, *Sovetskaia Rossiia* 30 November 1990, FBIS Soviet Union 14 December 1990.
131 For example, *Pravda* 24 December 1990 (on Irkutsk obkom).

132  *Pravda* 2 July 1991, referring to the situation in Belorussia.
133  *Pravda* 3 March 1991.
134  *Pravda* 2 February 1991.
135  *Pravda* 11 October 1990.
136  *Pravda* 6 March 1991.
137  *Rabochaia Tribuna* 14 March 1991, FBIS Soviet Union 20 March 1991. On the need for improved information links within the party, see *Pravda* 6 June 1991.
138  *Pravda* 28 March 1991. For a call for the PPOs to reactivate themselves as independent actors, see *Pravda* 1 May 1991. On the need to improve their performance, *Pravda* 1 June 1991 & 7 June 1991.
139  The Council of PPO Secretaries attached to the CC and subordinate to the Secretariat was established on 12–13 May 1991 in accord with the party Rules and a decision of the Secretariat of 22 January 1991. The Council was seen as a forum for the concerns of the PPOs, an arena within which their problems could be discussed, and a channel for them into leading party ranks. For its establishment, composition and statute, see *Izvestiia Ts.K. KPSS* 8, 1991, pp. 67–70. Councils were also established at other levels in different parts of the country. See pp. 50–1 for examples.
140  Such conferences were held in various parts of the country in the late winter and spring of 1991; more than 50 per cent of all PPO secretaries participated. The main report of these conferences suggests that many PPOs were having great difficulty in adjusting to changing circumstances. See the report in *Izvestiia Ts.K. KPSS* 8, 1991, pp. 44–52.
141  For a call for the PPOs to reassert their role, see *Pravda* 24 June 1991.
142  *Sovetskaia Rossiia* 18 September 1990, FBIS Soviet Union 28 September 1990.
143  *Golos Armenii*, 3 October 1990, FBIS Soviet Union 31 October 1990. However, according to a poll published in *Pravda* 26 February 1991, 63 per cent of communists was convinced that the party could lead the country out of the crisis, although only 38 per cent adhered to this opinion without reservation.
144  The speaker was Tajik first secretary K. M. Makhkamov, *Pravda* 23 July 1990. The charge was ironic in light of the fact that new electoral regulations for the party introduced in October 1990 did not make competition mandatory. *Pravda* 30 October 1990.
145  For the report of one meeting to discuss the need for the formation of such fractions, see *Sovetskaia Rossiia* 20 September 1990, FBIS Soviet Union 24 September 1990.
146  *Sovetskaia Rossiia* 3 July 1991, FBIS Soviet Union 12 July 1991.
147  See the comments which hint at this in *Sovetskaia Rossiia* 18 September 1990, FBIS Soviet Union 28 September 1990.
148  For a discussion of this, and the way that many in the apparatus felt threatened by it, see the comments by CC Secretary Shenin in *Sovetskaia Kul'tura* 22 December 1990, FBIS Soviet Union 3 January 1991.
149  For example, see the comments by Ivashko at the October CC plenum, *Pravda* 9 October 1990, comments by Shenin in *Pravda* 2 March 1991, and

the resolution of the joint CC–CCC RCP plenum of 6 March 1991, *Sovetskaia Rossiia* 15 March 1991, FBIS Soviet Union 21 March 1991. On the need to improve work in the soviets, see the resolution of the joint CC–CCC plenum of April 1991 based on a CC commission report on this question, *Pravda* 30 April 1991 and the follow-up decision of the Politburo. *Pravda* 5 June 1991.

150 For a report of the abolition of a party committee in one of the Donetsk coal mines, see TASS 9 July 1990, FBIS Soviet Union 10 July 1990. For a discussion, and criticism, of this, see *Rabochaia Tribuna* 25 July 1990, FBIS Soviet Union 7 August 1990. On the proposal in the Uralmash plant to remove party committees, see *Izvestiia* 10 April 1991. Also see the report in *Moscow News* 34, 2–9 September 1990.

151 For example, in the English Language Faculty at Moscow Linguistic University. *Izvestiia Ts.K. KPSS* 12, 1990, p. 13.

152 See the comments from the CC Secretariat meeting. *Pravda* 6 May 1991. On education, see the Secretariat decisions of 2 October and 5 November 1990. *Izvestiia Ts.K. KPSS* 11, 1990, pp. 12–14 & 12, 1990, p. 12; on legal organs the Secretariat decision of 16 October 1990, *Izvestiia Ts.K. KPSS* 11, 1990, p. 20. For a defence of the continued presence of party organs in legal bodies based in part upon appeals to international treaties protecting human rights, see *Izvestiia Ts.K. KPSS* 11, 1990, pp. 21–3.

153 On Moldova, see Moscow Domestic Service, 4 August 1990, FBIS Soviet Union 6 August 1990.

154 For some details, see the report of the CC Secretariat session in TASS 17 October 1990, FBIS Soviet Union 18 October 1990. For the depoliticisation of the Armenian KGB in accord with the republic's independence declaration of 23 August 1990, see Armenpres 25 September 1990, FBIS Soviet Union 27 September 1990. For a protest by the RCP against the decision by the Russian Supreme Soviet to prohibit activity by PPOs in internal affairs organs subordinate to the Ministery of Internal Affairs, see *Sovetskaia Rossiia* 12 May 1991, FBIS Soviet Union 15 May 1991. For party members in the Russian Supreme Court suspending their party membership, see *Izvestiia* 7 August 1991, and for those in the Kirgiz Ministry of Justice, *Izvestiia* 26 July 1991. On 26 September 1990 the Lithuanian parliament approved a bill banning 'political parties of other states, their sections or organisations', from being established or functioning in Lithuania. TASS 26 September 1990, FBIS Soviet Union 27 September 1990.

155 *Vedomosti S'ezda narodnykh deputatov SSSR i Verkhovnogo Soveta SSSR* 37, 12 September 1990, p. 908. The practical effect of this decree was minimal.

156 *Izvestiia* 22 July 1991.

157 For example, the Bureau of the All-Army Committee of the CPSU, TASS 23 July 1991, FBIS Soviet Union 24 July 1991; CC–CCC RCP, *Sovetskaia Rossiia* 24 July 1991, FBIS Soviet Union 26 July 1991; CC CPSU in a resolution at the end of the 25–26 July plenum, *Pravda* 27 July 1991; also see *Pravda* 24 July 1991. For one discussion offering different views, see *Izvestiia* 25 July 1991.

158 This call, of course, raised the whole question of the relationship between republican and all-union authority, a point which enabled the decree's supporters to dismiss the relevance of such an appeal.

159 For example, Boris Gidaspov, *Pravda* 10 August 1991.

160 *Pravda* 1 August 1991, citing and criticising a report from *Izvestiia* 27 July 1991 to this effect.

161 For example, see the report in *Komsomolskaia Pravda* 6 August 1991, FBIS Soviet Union 9 August 1991. This report also cited cases where party organisations did not act in accord with the decree's provisions. For one report, see *Moscow News* 33, 18–25 August 1991.

162 *Sovetskaia Rossiia* 8 August 1991, FBIS Soviet Union 9 August 1991.

163 *Rossiiskaia Gazeta* 10 August 1991.

164 For some of these arguments see *Leningradskaia Pravda* 31 August 1990, FBIS Soviet Union 27 September 1990. (Gidaspov); *Pravda* 9 October 1990 (Ivashko); TASS 17 October 1990, FBIS Soviet Union 18 October 1990 (CC Secretariat); *Rabochaia Gazeta* 24 November 1990, FBIS Soviet Union 17 December 1990 (member of Ukrainian Politburo V. E. Ostrozhinskii). For criticism of the calls for the depoliticisation of law enforcement organs, see *Pravda* 28 July 1990.

165 On the expulsion from the party of an official who sought to implement a state decision to ban party organisation in educational establishments in Russia, see *Komsomolskaia Pravda* 23 March 1991, FBIS Soviet Union 27 March 1991.

166 TASS 27 July 1990, FBIS Soviet Union 27 July 1990. In August 1990 only 18.8 per cent of respondents said they would vote for the party in a multi-party election, and 80.7 per cent believed the party's prestige had declined in the last two–three years. *Vestnik* August 1990, p. 27.

167 *Moscow News* 30, 5–12 August 1990.

168 *Izvestiia* 30 November 1990. The corresponding 'against' figures were 24 per cent, 36 per cent and 38 per cent.

169 Greater trust was put in Democratic Russia by 49 per cent; the corresponding figures in November had been 14 per cent for the CPSU and 42 per cent for Democratic Russia. *Vecherniaia Moskva* 6 March 1991, FBIS Soviet Union 11 April 1991.

170 *Novoe Vremia* 12, March 1991, FBIS Soviet Union 12 April 1991.

171 For example, see the reports in *Pravda* 28 July 1990. On May Day 1990, the Soviet leadership left the mausoleum in the face of anti-communist chanting and slogans carried by demonstrators following the official May Day march.

172 *Vecherniaia Moskva* 19 July 1990, FBIS Soviet Union 16 August 1990.

173 See the comments on this by Zaramenskii, deputy head of the CC Department for Work with Public and Political Organisations. *Sovetskaia Rossiia* 18 September 1990, FBIS Soviet Union 28 September 1990. On the party's failure to rebut charges against it in the press, see the comments by S.A. Kalinin at the October 1990 plenum. *Pravda* 10 October 1990. See Manaenkov's complaint about these criticisms, *Pravda* 16 October 1990. On

Democratic Russia, see the comments by Prokof'ev at the January 1991 plenum, *Pravda* 4 February 1991. Also see Prokof'ev's comments about organised opposition at the Moscow gorkom plenum. *Moskovskaia Pravda* 24 April 1991, FBIS Soviet Union 6 May 1991.

174 TASS 9 October 1990, FBIS Soviet Union 10 October 1990.

175 *Krasnaia Zvezda* 9 January 1991, FBIS Soviet Union 10 January 1991.

176 *Pravda* 12 October 1990; *Izvestiia* 12 November 1990; *Rabochaia Gazeta* 24 November 1990, FBIS Soviet Union 17 December 1990; *Pravda* 21 January 1991. For the situation in West Ukraine, where the term 'moral terror' was used, see *Izvestiia Ts.K. KPSS* 12, 1990, pp. 15–19.

177 See the report of the first session of the CC Commission for Socio-political Matters, *Sel'skaia zhizn'* 27 October 1990, FBIS Soviet Union 6 November 1990.

178 *Moscow News* 45, 18–25 November 1990. Another attempt to convene such a trial occurred in February 1991. *Pravda* 19 February 1991.

179 For example, see reports of meetings in *Sovetskaia Rossiia* 1 December 1990, FBIS Soviet Union 5 December 1990, and *Pravda* 19 December 1990. See some of the speeches at the January CC plenum in *Pravda* 5 February 1991 (particularly the speech by Malofeev). There was also a sense of bitterness about those who had left the party and now attacked it. For example, see the comments of CPU CC first secretary S. Gurenko, *Pravda* 11 July 1991.

180 For example, see the attempt to rally Lithuanian communists in *Pravda* 9 December 1990. For comments on the persecution of communists in Lithuania, see *Krasnaia Zvezda* 27 February 1991, FBIS Soviet Union 7 March 1991.

181 Yel'tsin was elected president of the RSFSR while Popov and Sobchak were elected mayors of Moscow and Leningrad respectively. Prokof'ev at least acknowledged that the party 'lost unconditionally' in these elections. TASS 20 June 1991, FBIS Soviet Union 20 June 1991. Also see the commentary in *Izvestiia* 20 June 1991.

182 For a discussion of registration by CC Secretary O. S. Shenin, see his comments to the January 1991 CC plenum, *Pravda* 2 February 1991. For the decision to register the party's statutes in accord with the law, which also involved inclusion in those statutes of a mechanism for ending party activity, see *Pravda* 6 February 1991. For reports of the registration, see *Pravda* 12 April 1991 and *Izvestiia Ts.K. KPSS* 6, 1991, pp. 43–8. Some republican parties also sought, and gained, registration at the republican level. For example in Tajikistan (TASS 7 May 1991, FBIS Soviet Union 9 May 1991), Belorussia (Minsk Radio 8 July 1991, FBIS Soviet Union 11 July 1991), Ukraine (TASS 22 July 1991, FBIS Soviet Union 23 July 1991) and Armenia (Interfax 13 August 1991, FBIS Soviet Union 14 August 1991).

183 See the comments by CC Secretary Yuri Manaenkov, *Glasnost'* 10 January 1991.

184 This may be hinted at in the judgement that the combination of the positions of party first secretary and chairman of the soviet 'has failed

the test of time'. *Sovetskaia Rossiia* 16 October 1990, FBIS Soviet Union 26 October 1990.

185 For example, Prokof'ev of Moscow, *Pravda* 14 August 1991 and Gidaspov of Leningrad, *Leningradskaia Pravda* 31 August 1991, FBIS Soviet Union 27 September 1990.

186 *Pravda* 10 September 1990.

187 For example, see the comments by Shenin, *Pravda* 2 March 1991 and the report of a Politburo discussion, *Pravda* 5 June 1991. One comment soon after the XXVIII Congress was interesting in this regard. Uzbek leader Karimov declared that it was more effective to exercise power through the party than it was through the presidential structure. *Pravda* 21 July 1990.

188 For the charge that the party apparatus still controlled local affairs, see *Moscow News* 46, 26 November–2 December 1990. This may also be reflected in the fact that a considerable proportion of regional party first secretaries continued to combine this position with that of soviet chairman. In December 1990, 41.8 per cent combined both positions, although in a further 29.4 per cent of positions the identity of the incumbent was unknown, so the proportion of combined incumbencies may have been over 50 per cent. Dawn Mann, 'Leadership of regional Communist Party committees and soviets', Radio Liberty, *Report on the USSR* 2, 51, 21 December 1990, pp. 15–25. On some resigning from the party to take up leading posts in the soviet following a June 1990 decision of the Russian Congress of People's Deputies forbidding chairmen of soviets simultaneously acting as first secretary of the party committee at that level, see Darrell Slider, 'The CIS: Republican Leaders Confront Local Opposition', RFE/RL Research Report 1, 10, 6 March 1992, p. 8.

189 *Pravda Ukrainy* 19 December 1990, FBIS Soviet Union 9 January 1991. On conflict in Lvov, see *Rabochaia Tribuna* 29 January 1991, FBIS Soviet Union 5 February 1991.

190 For example, on Kazakhstan see *Izvestiia* 2 February 1991, on Tajikistan *Pravda* 8 January 1991.

191 For a discussion of this, see *Izvestiia* 20 June 1991.

192 *Izvestiia* 16 October 1990.

193 A CC Department for Work with Socio-Political Organisations was created in early August, a CC Secretary was made responsible for this, and a standing CC Commission was created in early September.

194 See the comments by CC Secretary Kuptsov who had responsibility in this area. *Rabochaia Tribuna* 4 August 1990. For a Politburo decision of 24 January 1991 which was more ambiguous regarding the need for choice of the socialist path as an essential pre-requisite to relations, see *Izvestiia Ts.K. KPSS* 2, 1991, pp. 25–6. Also the discussion by Kuptsov, *Izvestiia Ts.K. KPSS* 5, 1991, pp. 4–9.

195 On the need for regular consultation with 'all political parties and movements', see the comments of Prokof'ev in *Pravda* 22 November 1990.

196 On the difficulties the party was experiencing in adjusting to the need to

cooperate with other forces, see the report of the meeting of the Social-Economic Commission, *Pravda* 13 November 1990.

197 *Pravda* 21 July 1990.

198 *Komsomolskaia Pravda* 27 July 1990, FBIS Soviet Union 1 August 1990. For a more positive view of the Congress, see *Rabochaia Tribuna* 15 July 1990 FBIS Soviet Union 25 July 1990 and *Sovetskaia Estoniia* 18 July 1990, FBIS Soviet Union 1 August 1990. For a call for the CC and the Soviet President to implement the decisions of the XXVIII Congress, see the joint CC–CCC RCP resolution of 15 November 1990, *Sovetskaia Rossiia* 16 November 1990, FBIS Soviet Union 14 December 1990.

199 *Pravda* 26 July 1990. Also 26 February and 6 March 1991. For the view that old principles still dominated and rank-and-file views were ignored in the election of party leaders, see the letter from A. Kozlov in *Pravda* 3 September 1990.

200 *Sovetskaia Belorussiia* 20 June 1990, FBIS Soviet Union 1 August 1990. For similar complaints about lack of leadership in the Belorussian party, see *Pravda* 5 December 1990.

201 See the report of the Leningrad obkom plenum, *Pravda* 31 August 1990. Also see the criticisms coming from Kiev obkom, *Pravda* 10 December 1990.

202 *Pravda* 26 February 1991. For the comments of local party leaders from the Cheliabinsk oblast party organisation about the problems they faced, which in part involved the absence of a clear sense of direction, see *Izvestiia Ts.K. KPSS* 6, 1991, pp. 54–7.

203 *Pravda* 12 October 1990. Also see the CCC resolution on discipline in the party for a similar evaluation:

> The CPSU Central Control Commission plenum considers that the state of affairs which has taken shape in the party and the poor level of intra-party discipline are in many respects attributable to inadequate theoretical, ideological, political and organisational work on the part of the CPSU Central Committee, its Politburo, and party committees and to systematic laggardness in political assessments and the formulation of proper measures and preventive actions to eliminate negative phenomena in the life of the party and society.' (*Pravda* 6 March 1991)

204 *Pravda* 10 October 1990. Also see other speeches from the October plenum in Pravda 11 & 12 October 1990 (speeches by Mktrumian and Pomorov). For Polozkov's view that many decisions were out of step with reality and 'much was said, but little got done', see *Pravda* 5 September 1990.

205 *Pravda* 11 October 1990 (Kadochnikov, Buzgalin and Potapov). For the charge that party leading organs were being confronted with another *fait accompli* by the Supreme Soviet, see Prokof'ev in *Moskovskaia Pravda* 27 April 1991, FBIS Soviet Union 3 May 1991. He was referring to Gorbachev's anti-crisis programme. Also see the article by Ukrainian first secretary Gurenko in which he complained that leading party organs had not discussed important questions like privatisation. *Pravda* 11 July 1991. Also see *Pravda* 18 October 1990.

206 *Pravda* 18 October 1990.

207 Kalinin at the October 1990 plenum. *Pravda* 10 October 1990.

208 Shenin in *Golos Armenii* 3 October 1990, FBIS Soviet Union 31 October 1990.

209 *New Times* 49, 4–10 December 1990, pp. 7–11.

210 For example, *Leningradskaia Pravda* 21 November 1990, FBIS Soviet Union 5 December 1990; *Rabochaia Tribuna* 5 December 1990, FBIS Soviet Union 6 December 1990; *Pravda* 13 December 1990. For one affirmation by Gorbachev that he would continue to combine both posts, see *Pravda* 26 December 1990.

211 For one discussion of the course of this question at the plenum, see Prokof'ev's speech at the plenum in *Moskovskaia Pravda* 27 April 1991, FBIS Soviet Union 3 May 1991. For the *Pravda* editorial on the plenum, see *Pravda* 7 May 1991. The plenum of Leningrad obkom prior to the CC plenum brought up the question of the 'question of the party's political confidence' in Gorbachev. *Sovetskaia Rossiia* 16 April 1991, FBIS Soviet Union 17 April 1991. For the view that a move to unseat Gorbachev at the July 1991 plenum was blunted by Yel'tsin's decree banning party organisation in institutions in Russia, see *Rossiiskaia Gazeta* 31 July 1991. For the argument that this was not a conservative plot but simply reflected the anxiety in the party, see the comments of Ukrainian first secretary Gurenko, *Pravda* 11 July 1991.

212 Communists in the Solikamsk Magnesium Plant, *Rossiiskaia Gazeta* 12 July 1991.

213 *Pravda* 4 January 1991.

214 For one complaint about the way in which the Uzbek party criticised the centre but refused to turn a critical eye on its own performance, see *Pravda* 18 December 1990. For an attempt by Shenin to defend the centre against such attacks, see his interview in *Krasnaia zvezda* 16 March 1991, FBIS Soviet Union 27 March 1991. In November 1990 the Secretariat had adopted a decision designed to increase the flow of information about developments in the Politburo and Secretariat. *Izvestiia Ts.K. KPSS* 12, 1990, p. 4. For a later decision by the Secretariat about improving information links in the party, see *Izvestiia Ts.K. KPSS* 8, 1991, pp. 56–7.

215 *Moskovskaia Pravda* 24 April 1991, FBIS Soviet Union 6 May 1991.

216 *Pravda* 13 December 1990. For the draft of the union treaty, see *Pravda* 24 November 1990. The plenum also discussed privileges in the party.

217 TASS 3 February 1991, FBIS Soviet Union 4 February 1991. *Pravda* 4 February 1991. This, which was a joint plenum with the CCC, also discussed a series of party housekeeping matters.

218 For the plenum resolution, which supports the programme while offering a series of concrete suggestions for its improvement, see *Pravda* 30 April 1991. For a discussion of the plenum, see *Pravda* 7 May 1991.

219 The resolutions on the draft programme and Yel'tsin's decree are in *Pravda* 27 July 1991. The draft programme was adopted as an acceptable basis for further discussion, while the Yel'tsin decree was protested and an appeal made to the Committee for Constitutional Oversight and the Soviet

President and the Supreme Court to investigate the legality of the decree.

220 *Sovetskaia Estoniia* 18 July 1990, FBIS Soviet Union 1 August 1990.

221 See the report of its meeting in *Pravda* 15 September 1990. According to the monthly chronologies published in *Izvestiia Ts.K. KPSS*, the Politburo met on the following occasions: 16 November 1990, 16 January 1991, 30 January, 25 March, 24–25 April and 3 June 1991. According to one report, the Politburo met on 38 occasions in 1985, and only 9 in 1990. *Moscow News* 10, 10–17 March 1991.

222 *Golos Armenii* 3 October 1990, FBIS Soviet Union 31 October 1990.

223 *Golos Armenii* 3 October 1990, FBIS Soviet Union 31 October 1990.

224 Speech by Dzasokhov to October plenum. TASS 9 October 1990, FBIS Soviet Union 10 October 1990. According to the monthly chronologies in *Izvestiia Ts.K. KPSS*, the Secretariat met on the following occasions: 1990: October 2, 16, 23, November 5, 13, 27, December 5, January 8, 15, 22, February 7, 12, 22, 26, March 26, April 10, 13, 29, May 8, 14, 22, 28, and June 4, 11, 18, 25.

225 Moscow Domestic Service, 28 July 1990, FBIS Soviet Union 30 July 1990. Perhaps in response to this, *Pravda* carried frequent reports of Secretariat meetings.

226 The speaker was Dzasokhov. TASS 9 October 1990, FBIS Soviet Union 10 October 1990.

227 *Pravda* 13 September 1990. At the December 1990 plenum a commission on questions of the party's financial and economic activity was established.

228 TASS 9 October 1990, FBIS Soviet Union 10 October 1990.

229 See Shenin's discussion of these at the October plenum. *Pravda* 10 October 1990.

230 The capacity of these organs to play a dynamic role in policy formation was not aided by the cuts made to the CC apparatus, which was reduced by 40 per cent following the congress. *Pravda* 15 September 1990. For some details of the reorganisation of the apparatus, see Shenin's comments in *Pravda* 10 October 1990. Reports of the commissions' proceedings were published in *Izvestiia Ts.K. KPSS*

231 For example, see Gorbachev's speech to the October 1990 plenum, *Pravda* 9 October 1990, the article by L. Onikov in *Pravda* 4 December 1990, the CC statement of February 1991 entitled 'On the Current Situation and the Tasks of the Party', *Pravda* 4 February 1991, and A. Mel'nikov's article critical of the leadership in *Pravda* 14 May 1991.

232 For the judgement that the Congress had been a rebuff to conservative forces who nevertheless had shown their true colours by demanding a trial of Politburo members, see *Izvestiia* 27 July 1990. For the argument that the Congress was not a 'congress of apparatchiks', see Shenin's comments in *Golos Armenii* 3 October 1990, FBIS Soviet Union 31 October 1990.

233 See the interesting comment by Belorussian first secretary Sokolov, not a renowned reformer, 'I think all of us, particularly the professional party

workers, have not fully grasped that perestroika is the main ideology'. *Pravda* 31 July 1990.
234 *Nezavisimaia Gazeta* 3 August 1991. This article, by V. Lipitskii, argues that Gorbachev and his supporters produced the draft in this way because they knew that it would be unacceptable to the conservative elements in the party and that only by presenting them with a *fait accompli* at the plenum could they bring about a split in the party. Gorbachev's initial unwillingness to quit the party after the coup does not sit easily with the claim that he wished to split it in July. For the deliberations of the official commission established to draft the Programme, see *Izvestiia Ts.K. KPSS* 2, 1991, pp. 16–24 & 4, 1991, pp. 13–16.
235 *Pravda* 8 August 1991.
236 For the debates, see *Pravda* 26–29 July 1991. Gorbachev's speech is in the issue of 26 July.
237 For a discussion of this, see *Pravda* 20 July 1991. For the decision of the CC plenum to convene such a congress, see *Pravda* 27 July 1991.
238 For an argument that there were three trends in the party, bureaucratic-administrative socialism, orthodox traditional Marxism-Leninism, and social democracy, see *Izvestiia* 4 July 1991.

## 8 The end

1 For example, see Prokhanov's 'A Word to the People', *Sovetskaia Rossiia* 23 July 1991 and the call by the Initiative Group in *Sovetskaia Rossiia* 16 August 1991.
2 Reported in *Izvestiia* 21 August 1991. According to Valentin Falin, the Secretariat did not know about the plans for the coup and only one member, Shenin, was involved in any of the measures. Moscow Central Television 29 August 1991, FBIS Soviet Union 30 August 1991.
3 TASS 21 August 1991, FBIS Soviet Union 21 August 1991. For a stronger, anti-coup stance by the Secretariat, see *Pravda* 22 August 1991. This was, of course, when the the failure of the coup was manifest to all. Although see the report of a secret directive sent from the CC recommending that communists support the State Comittee for the State of Emergency. Moscow Central Television 23 August 1991, FBIS Soviet Union 28 August 1991, *Rossiiskaia Gazeta* 12 September 1991 and *Pravda* 23 October 1991.
4 See the report in *Pravda* 23 August 1991. According to one poll, responsibility for the actions of the Emergency Committee for the State of Emergency belonged to:

| party as a whole | 19% |
| party apparat | 32% |
| only higher party leadership | 32% |
| party not responsible at all | 8% |
| hard to say | 8% |

*Moscow News* 34–5, 1–8 September 1991.

5 For example, see the pieces in *Pravda* 21 (reporting the Omsk oblispolkom) and 23 August 1991. The newspaper's attempt to distance itself from the party in an attempt to survive should not be under-estimated here.

6 *Izvestiia* 26 August 1991.

7 *Rossiiskaia Gazeta* 27 August 1991.

8 *Izvestiia* 27 August 1991.

9 *Izvestiia* 30 August 1991.

10 *Rossiiskaia Gazeta* 27 August 1991.

11 *Rossiiskaia Gazeta* 30 August 1991. He had reaffirmed the elimination of party organisations from the armed forces and security organs by decree on 22 August. On party property, see *Izvestiia* 28 August 1991.

12 The suspension was lifted on 12 September, by which time the newspapers had registered themselves as independent, non-party publications.

13 *Rossiiskaia Gazeta* 9 November 1991.

14 According to the 1990 Law on Public Associations, a party could be banned only by the courts, not by presidential decree, except when a state of emergency had been declared. No state of emergency had been declared by the legitimate authorities at the time of Yel'tsin's decree. According to Yel'tsin's legal adviser, Sergei Shakhrai, this legislation did not apply to the CPSU because after October 1917 that organisation was not a party but 'some kind of state-political formation of a criminal nature'. *Moscow News* 21, 24 May 1992 and *Izvestiia* 25 May 1992. On this, also see *Izvestiia* 4 May 1992.

15 However some, including Popov, did argue that it was undemocratic to act in this way and that the party should be permitted to exist.

16 For example, see the comments on Azerbaijan in *Moscow News* 37, 15–22 September 1991. Also see the discussion in Darrell Slider, 'The CIS: republican leaders confront local opposition', RFE/RL Research Report, 1, 10, 6 March 1992, pp. 7–11. Also see the discussions in *Rossiiskaia Gazeta* 4 March 1992 and *Nezavisimaia Gazeta* 22 February 1992, and the important article by Gavriil Popov in *Izvestiia* 21, 24, 25 & 26 August 1992 in which he argues that, following the coup, power was held not by the democratic movement, but by reformist apparatchiks.

17 There was also considerable concern about the way in which former party officials were able to use their formal positions to gain wealth and set themselves up in the new emerging market. For example, *Rossiiskaia Gazeta* 2 & 11 March 1992, *Moscow News* 47, 24 November–1 December 1991 & 48, 1–8 December 1991.

18 For example, *Izvestiia* 22 & 28 October 1991, 10 February 1992 *Nezavisimaia Gazeta* 6 March 1992, *Izvestiia* 7 & 9 March 1992, and *Moscow News* 49, 8–15 December 1991. For a defence of the party's budget and the claim that it did not have major hard currency holdings, see *Glasnost'* 28, 30 July–5 August 1992.

19 For example, see the reports in *Pravda* 20 September 1991, *Nezavisimaia Gazeta* 18 & 25 February 1992. Among these groups were those with names

like the Socialist Workers' Party, Socialist Labour Party, and the All-Union Communist Party of Bolsheviks.

20 *Rossiiskaia Gazeta* 22 February 1992.

21 *Glasnost'* 22, 18–24 June 1992. For some organisational details about the proposed conference, see *Glasnost'* 28, 30 July–5 August 1992.

22 For details, see *Glasnost'* 34, 15–21 October 1992 & 35, 22–28 October 1992.

23 For some reports, see *Izvestiia* 18 March 1992, *Nezavisimaia Gazeta* 25 February 1992.

24 *Izvestiia* 14 March 1992.

25 In the elections to the Lithuanian legislature on 25 October and 15 November, the successor to the Lithuanian Communist Party, the Lithuanian Democratic Labour Party, achieved a majority of the seats.

26 Vera Tolz, Wendy Slater & Alexander Rahr, 'Profiles of the Main Political Blocs', RFE/RL Research Report 2, 20, 14 May 1993, p. 20.

27 *Nezavisimaia Gazeta* 7 October 1993.

28 For example, see the reports on privileges in *Pravda* 16 December 1990 and *Sovetskaia Rossiia* 13 July 1991.

29 For example, *Pravda* 28 December 1990.

# Bibliography

*Argumenty i fakty* 1985–92
*Glasnost'* 1990–2
*Izvestiia* 1985–92
*Izvestiia Ts.K. KPSS* 1989–91
*Kommunist* 1985–91
*Komsomolskaia Pravda* 1990
*Moscow News* 1985–92
*Moskovskaia Pravda* 1990
*New Times* 1985–91
*Nezavisimaia Gazeta* 1991–2
*Partiinaia zhizn'* 1985–91
*Pravda* 1985–91
*Rabochaia Tribuna* 1990
*Rossiiskaia Gazeta* 1991–2
*Sovetskaia Rossiia* 1990
*Spravochnik partiinogo rabotnika* (Moscow, 1985–91)
*Vedomosti S'ezda narodnykh deputatov SSSR i Verkhovnogo Soveta SSSR* 1990–1
*Vestnik* 1990

*Foreign Broadcasting Information Service Soviet Union* 1985–91
*KPSS v rezoliutsiiakh i resheniiakh s'ezdov, konferentsii i plenumov Ts.K. KPSS* (Moscow, 1989)
*Materialy plenuma tsentral'nogo komiteta KPSS 11, 14, 16 Marta 1990g* (Moscow, 1990)
*XIX vsesoiuznaia konferentsiia kommunisticheskoi partii sovetskogo soiuza, 28 iunia–1 iulia 1988 goda. Stenograficheskii otchet* (Moscow, 1988)
*XXVII s'ezd kommunisticheskoi partii sovetskogo soiuza 25 fevralia–6 marta 1986 goda. Stenograficheskii otchet* (Moscow, 1986)

Bialer, Seweryn, 'The Yeltsin Affair: The Dilemma of the Left in Gorbachev's Revolution', Seweryn Bialer (ed.), *Inside Gorbachev's Russia. Politics, Society and Nationality* (Boulder, Westview Press, 1989)
Brovkin, Vladimir, 'First Party Secretaries: An Endangered Soviet Species?', *Problems of Communism* 39, 1, January–February 1990

246

Brovkin, Vladimir, 'Revolution from Below: Informal Political Associations in Russia 1988–1989', *Soviet Studies* 42, 2, April 1990

Brown, Archie, 'The Power of the General Secretary of the CPSU', in T. H. Rigby, Archie Brown & Peter Reddaway (eds.), *Authority, Power and Policy in the USSR. Essays dedicated to Leonard Schapiro* (London, Macmillan, 1980)

Chiesa, Giuletto, 'The 28th Congress of the CPSU', *Problems of Communism* 39, 4, July–August 1990

Chubais, Igor, 'The democratic opposition: an insider's view', Radio Liberty, *Report on the USSR* 3, 18, 3 May 1991

Clark, William A., 'Token representation in the CPSU Central Committee', *Soviet Studies* 43, 5, 1991

Colton, Timothy J., 'The Moscow Election of 1990', *Soviet Economy* 6, 4, 1990

Critchlow, James, '"Corruption", nationalism and the native elites in Soviet Central Asia', *The Journal of Communist Studies* 4, 2, June 1988

Efimova, L., Sobianin, A. & Iur'ev, D., 'K voprosu ob antagonizme', unpublished

Embree, Gregory G., 'RSFSR election results and roll call votes', *Soviet Studies* 43, 6, 1991

Friedgut, Theodore and Siegelbaum, Lewis, 'Perestroika from below: the Soviet miners' strike and its aftermath', *New Left Review* 181, 1990

Gill, Graeme, 'Ideology, Organization and the Patrimonial Regime', *The Journal of Communist Studies* 5, 3, September 1989

Gill, Graeme, *The origins of the Stalinist political system* (Cambridge, CUP, 1990)

Gill, Graeme, *The Rules of the Communist Party of the Soviet Union* (London, Macmillan, 1988)

Gooding, John, 'The XXVIII Congress of the CPSU in Perspective', *Soviet Studies* 43, 2, 1991.

Gorbachev, M. S., *Avgustovskii Putch. Prichiny i sledstviia* (Moscow, 1991)

Gorbachev, M. S., *Dekabr'-91. Moia pozitsiia* (Moscow, 1992)

Gorbachev, M. S., *Izbrannye rechi i stat'i* (Moscow, 1987)

Gorbachev, M. S., *Perestroika i novoe myshlenie dlia nashei strany i dlia vsego mira* (Moscow, 1987)

Gustafson, Thane & Mann, Dawn, 'Gorbachev's first year: building power and authority', *Problems of Communism* 35, 3, May–June 1986

Gustafson, Thane and Mann, Dawn, 'Gorbachev's next gamble', *Problems of Communism* 36, 4, July–August 1987

Hahn, Jeffrey, 'An experiment in competition: the 1987 elections to the local soviets', *Slavic Review* 47, 3, Fall 1988

Hahn, Jeffrey W., 'Local politics and political power in Russia: the case of Yaroslavl'', *Soviet Economy* 7, 4, 1991

Hahn, Jeffrey W., 'The Soviet state system', in Stephen White, Alex Pravda and Zvi Gitelman (eds.), *Developments in Soviet Politics* (London, Macmillan, 1990)

Harasymiw, Bohdan, 'Changes in the Party's Composition: The "Destroyka" of the CPSU', *The Journal of Communist Studies* 7, 2, June 1991

Hill, Ronald J., 'The CPSU: From monolith to pluralist?', *Soviet Studies* 43, 2, 1991

Hill, Ronald J., 'The Twenty-eighth CPSU Congress', *The Journal of Communist Studies* 7, 1, March 1991

Hill, Ronald J. and Frank, Peter, 'Gorbachev's cabinet-building', *The Journal of Communist Studies* 2, 2, June 1986

Kiernan, Brendan and Aistrup, Joseph, 'The 1989 Elections to the Congress of People's Deputies in Moscow', *Soviet Studies* 43, 6, 1991

Lentini, Peter, 'Reforming the electoral system: the 1989 elections to the USSR Congress of People's Deputies', *The Journal of Communist Studies* 7, 1, March 1991

Lowenhardt, John, 'Democratization of party elections in the Soviet Union. Central Committee CPSU Instructions on Elections, 1937–1988', *Acta Politica* 1, January 1989

Mann, Dawn, 'The challenges facing Gorbachev', Radio Liberty, *Report on the USSR* 1, 35, 1 September 1989

Mann, Dawn, 'Leadership of regional communist party committees and soviets', Radio Liberty, *Report on the USSR* 2, 51, 21 December 1990

Mawdsley, Evan, 'The 1990 Central Committee of the CPSU in Perspective', *Soviet Studies* 43, 5, 1991

McAuley, Mary, 'Politics, economics, and elite realignment in Russia: a regional perspective', *Soviet Economy* 8, 1, 1992

McFaul, Michael and Markov, Sergei, *The troubled birth of Russian democracy. Parties, personalities and programs* (Hoover Institution Press, Stanford, 1993)

McNeal, Robert H., 'The beginning of Communist party financial exactions from the Soviet State', D. A. Loeber (ed.), *Ruling communist parties and their status under law* (The Hague, Nijnhoff, 1986)

Medvedev, Zhores, *Gorbachev* (Oxford, Basil Blackwell, 1986)

Miller, J. H., 'How much of a new elite?', in R. F. Miller, J. H. Miller and T. H. Rigby (eds.), *Gorbachev at the helm. A new era in Soviet politics?* (London, Croom Helm, 1987)

Moses, Joel C., 'Soviet provincial politics in an era of transition and revolution, 1989–91', *Soviet Studies* 44, 3, 1992

Mote, Max E., 'Electing the USSR Congress of People's Deputies', *Problems of Communism* 38, 6, November–December 1989

Orttung, Robert W., 'The Russian right and the dilemmas of party organisation', *Soviet Studies* 44, 3, 1992

Rahr, Alexander, 'Who is in charge of the party apparatus?', Radio Liberty, *Report on the USSR* 1, 15, 14 April 1989

Rees, A. E.(ed.), *The Soviet Communist Party in disarray. The XVIII Congress of the Communist Party of the Soviet Union* (London, Macmillan, 1992)

Roxburgh, Angus, *The second Russian revolution* (London, BBC Books, 1991)

Rutland, Peter, 'Labor unrest and movements in 1989 and 1990', *Soviet Economy* 6, 4, 1990

Rutland, Peter, 'The search for stability: ideology, discipline, and the cohesion of the Soviet elite', *Studies in Comparative Communism* 24, 1, March 1991

Ryzhkov, Nikolai, *Perestroika: istoriia predatel'stv* (Moscow, 1992)

Sakwa, Richard, *Gorbachev and his reforms 1985–1990* (New York, Philip Allan, 1990)

Sartori, Giovanni, *Parties and party systems. A framework for analysis* (Cambridge, CUP, 1976)

Schmidt-Hauer, Christian, *Gorbachev. The path to power* (London, Tauris, 1986)

Senn, Alfred Erich, 'Toward Lithuanian independence: Algirdas Brazauskas and the CPL', *Problems of Communism* 39, 2, March–April 1990

Shevardnadze, E.A., *Moi vybor v zashchitu demokratii i svobody* (Moscow, 1991)

Shostakovskii, V.N., 'Oshibki ili zakonomernost'?', *Perspektivy* 3, 1991

Slider, Darrell, 'The CIS: republican leaders confront local opposition', RFE/RL, Research Report 1, 10, 6 March 1992

Sobchak, Anatoly, *For a new Russia* (New York, The Free Press, 1992)

Surovell, Jeffrey, 'Ligachev and Soviet politics', *Soviet Studies* 43, 2, 1991

Tatu, Michel, '19th Party Conference', *Problems of Communism* 3–4, May–August 1988

Teague, Elizabeth, 'Estonian Party publishes draft program', Radio Liberty, *Report on the USSR* 1, 38, 22 September 1989

Teague, Elizabeth, 'Fall of representation of party apparatus in CPSU Central Committee', Radio Liberty, *Report on the USSR* 1, 19, 12 May 1989

Teague, Elizabeth and Mann, Dawn, 'Gorbachev's dual role', *Problems of Communism* 39, 1, January–February 1990

*The second Russian revolution*, BBC Television, 1991

Tolz, Vera, *The USSR's emerging multiparty system* (New York, Praeger, 1990)

Tolz, Vera, Slater, Wendy and Rahr,Alexander, 'Profiles of the main political blocs', RFE/RL Research Report 2, 20, 14 May 1993

Unger, Aryeh L., 'The travails of intra-party democracy in the Soviet Union: the elections to the 19th Conference of the CPSU', *Soviet Studies* 43, 2, 1991

Urban, Michael E., *More power to the soviets* (Aldershot, Edward Elgar, 1990)

Urban, Michael E., 'The Soviet multi-party system. A Moscow roundtable', *Russia and the World* 18, 1990

*Vos'moi s'ezd RKP(b) Mart 1919 goda. Protokoly* (Moscow 1959)

Vsesoiuznoi tsentr izucheniia obshchestvennogo mneniia po sotsial'no-ekonomicheskim voprosam pri VTsSPS i goskomtrude SSSR, 'Obshchestvennoe mnenie v tsifrakh', Vyp. 10(17) (Moscow, April 1990)

White, Stephen, 'The CPSU and its members in late communist Russia', unpublished

White, Stephen, *Gorbachev and after* (Cambridge, CUP, 1991)

White, Stephen, 'Gorbachev, Gorbachevism and the Party Conference', *The Journal of Communist Studies* 4, 4, December 1988

Willerton Jr, John P., 'The political leadership', in Stephen White, Alex Pravda and Zvi Gitelman (eds.), *Developments in Soviet Politics* (London, Macmillan, 1990).

Yakovlev, Alexander, *Muki prochiteniia bytiia. Perestroika: nadezhdy i real'nosti* (Moscow, 1991)

Yakovlev, Alexander, *Predislovie Obval Posleslovie* (Moscow, 1992)

Yel'tsin, Boris, *Ispoved' na zadannuiu temu* (Moscow, 1990)

# Index

258